THE CHRISTIAN GUIDE TO JOBS AND CAREERS

by

Charles Humphreys

'In the midst of economic shaking and "The Great Recession," the Lord is still raising up apostles in the marketplace. Hear practical Biblical wisdom from Charles Humphreys speaking to the current career challenges you may be facing.'

Ché Ahn
Senior Pastor, HROCK Church, Pasadena, California

OUP
Onwards & Upwards
Publishers

Onwards and Upwards Publications
Berkeley House
11 Nightingale Crescent
West Horsley
Surrey
KT24 6PD
England

The Common Sense Series

www.onwardsandupwards.org

ISBN: 978-1-907509-08-7

Cover Design: Leah-Maarit

Printed in the UK

ACKNOWLEDGEMENTS

There are a number of people to whom I am deeply indebted for the completion of this book, and without their contributions it would have remained merely a glint in my spiritual eye.

Firstly, I would like to thank my amazing wife, **Amanda**, for her continual encouragement. I would also like to thank my three young boys for providing me with many sources of inspiration.

A big 'thank you' is owed to my parents-in-law, **Alan and Lesley Bryan**, who spent countless hours proof-reading and correcting my manuscripts. Thank you so much – without your valuable input, the book would have remained a rough diamond.

A 'thank you' also goes to **Norman and Margaret Moss** who initially encouraged me to get going when the book merely consisted of a few incomplete chapters.

I would also like to honour the support and teaching that I have been given by the excellent leadership team of my church – **Oasis** in Colliers Wood, London, especially that of **Pastor Sam Onyenuforo**.

I would like to thank some old friends – **Mike and Trudy Nieto** – who often spoke positive and inspiring words into my life, especially during those times when circumstances were particularly challenging.

Finally, I want to thank you Lord for the grace, love and patience that You have shown me over the years. It has certainly been my experience that You are the most incredible Shepherd – always guiding and providing faithfully. You are indeed an amazing God!

Foreword

I am delighted to have been asked to write the foreword to The Christian Guide to Jobs and Careers by Charles Humphreys.

This book has come through Charles' own personal journey as well as insights gained from many years of working as a Careers adviser. Charles spoke to me some years ago when this book was just a prompting in his heart and I have seen the development of his ideas through a number of careers seminars and drop-in sessions he ran at Oasis Church from which many benefited immensely. I can confidently say that the contents of this book, prior to its publication, have helped people to define their career pathways and has taught them how to seek God when making decisions about their careers. I am excited to see it in print and in a form that will enable many more people to benefit.

It is amazing to see the number of people in our society who are struggling in their jobs. Some are not sure if they are in the right career, some are unfulfilled with their jobs and some, still out of work, are not sure of how and where to begin their searches for new jobs and new careers.

Charles, in The Christian Guide to Jobs and Careers, has achieved what no other book I know of in this field has by approaching this all important subject from the perspective of God being interested in our jobs and wanting to guide us through the process of making decisions about our lives and, especially, our careers. He has combined his years of experience as a careers adviser with the Christian principles of how to seek and receive God's perspective on the issues of delay, career wilderness, waiting on God, timing and so on as well as practical aspects such as researching jobs, seeking careers advice, writing CVs, preparing for interviews and understanding the skills and qualities employers are looking for amongst others.

In this current climate where news of job cuts or planned cuts is widespread, the publication of this book has come at a perfect time for a lot of people. It is my prayer that those who read this book will be encouraged and receive guidance through the tried and tested precepts laid out in its pages. Enjoy!

Sam Onyenuforo
Pastor, Oasis Church, London

CONTENTS

Who Could Find This Book Useful?

This book presents a unique look at a subject that is central to most of our lives — jobs and the development of a livelihood. The reader is offered a Christian perspective on the topic of career guidance. The book takes us on a journey to discover not only the employment that God could have in store for us, but also how He could be using this important area to mould us according to his plan.

Some people view jobs simply as a way of supporting another activity such as bringing up children or running a ministry, whilst for others the development of a career is of the utmost importance. Whatever is our take on jobs, God wants to bless us richly and to enable us to walk according to his plan. Jesus said that His sheep follow Him because they recognise His voice. Today, God is calling us into a deeper relationship with Him so that we are better able to hear His voice when He speaks to us about any area of our lives, including our job situation.

There are three particular groups of people who could benefit from reading this book: pastors and church leaders, people who are out of work, and those people who are in work but are looking for a new job.

People who are in work, but are looking for a new job

You do not need to be out of work to experience pain and discomfort in your job situation. This difficulty could be a consequence of many factors such as a mismatch between your work and your giftings or what you feel God is calling you to do. However, God can sometimes allow difficulties to arise in any of our job situations so as to bring about necessary changes in our lives, such as greater levels of faith, trust and love for Him. When He has determined that we have learnt the lessons from this season, God will lead us as a changed person out from a land of want and into a land of plenty.

People who are out of work

There can be many reasons why you find yourself out of work. However, you can be certain that God wants you to lead a fulfilling life and to use the gifts and abilities that He has placed in you. This book offers an honest look at what God could be saying to you during a difficult period in your life. The Bible tells us that 'in all things God works for the good of those who love Him,' and 'all things' includes periods out of work.

You should be aware that God takes great delight in you and He can use lack of employment to draw you into a closer relationship with Him. An aim of this book is to enable you to discover what He could be saying to you about the changes that He wants to bring about in your life. You will also be taken on a trip of discovery through the different ways that God can choose to reveal His plans regarding your life. He is not merely interested in you reaching a destination by finding you new employment, but He also longs to join you on this journey. When this happens, you will not only arrive at a new job, but you will also be transformed into a changed person.

Church leaders, as a resource

Whether the church you lead is large, small, or somewhere in-between, there will undoubtedly be people in your congregation who are either out of work or have issues relating to employment. This book will give you an indispensable resource to offer spiritual input on an important subject, and also empower you to help members of your church in a practical way to find a job.

Even though there is much career-related material on the market, this book's approach should enable church leaders to tackle this highly relevant subject from a spiritual perspective. A number of important issues are raised including:

- How God can use a period of unemployment to shape character and to deepen a relationship with Him.

- How to seek God's revelation in regard to jobs.

- How to move forward in the employment market in God's strength.

The book also offers practical career-related resources to help the members of your church in finding suitable employment. It covers topics such as: job search techniques, CV construction, job interview performance, and personality and skill reviews.

Introduction

Be Encouraged, God Wants to Amaze Us!

The year was 1977, and I remember sitting at my desk at primary school. It was an old Victorian-style desk with a hinged lid under which I kept all my school books, half-eaten apples and paper aeroplanes. On this particular day our form teacher decided that it would be constructive to remind many in my class of the poor quality of their work. Whilst looking down at my desk, I heard Mr Hughes (not his real name) stop in front of me and start tapping his foot on the floor. I looked up and saw him holding my exercise book containing the homework that he had just marked. Waving it in the air, he said something that would remain with me for a long time:

'Humphreys, what is this? You will never amount to being anything more than just a dustman!'

If Mr Hughes were still around today I would tell him that despite his low expectations for me – no disrespect to those in waste disposal – I have, nevertheless, always benefited from God's guidance in each area of my life, including my career. I may not have reached the ultimate career pinnacle and have been told by Lord Alan Sugar, 'You're hired', and earned a six-figure salary. However, I would be able to tell my primary school teacher that God had higher expectations for 'Humphreys' than he had for me!

Yet despite being aware of God's guidance in my life, my career has frequently been hit by frustration and, for a long period of time, a lack of focus and direction. I would often ask myself, 'Where has it all gone wrong? Why does my career feel like a rudderless ship?' Had I got it wrong somewhere and misunderstood what God was telling me regarding my job situation? Or was it possible that He had made some terrible administrative error and sent the wrong directions concerning my career?

This book is for anyone who has suffered frustration and setbacks in a job situation, and who can relate to any of the following statements:

- **Why doesn't God just give me that career break as soon I ask Him?**

- **What is the value of my spending all those years in a job where I am not using my talents?**

- **What was the point of my being made redundant for the third time in as many years?**

- **If God loves me so much, why does He leave me unemployed and put me through such frustration and sorrow?**

These are very real questions that demand substantial answers. This book is designed to suggest some potential answers and also to take a look at what could be happening spiritually behind the scenes, including what God could be telling us about ourselves through our work situation. Whether we have complete faith in God, are 'trying Him out' for the first time or are somewhere in-between, this book aims to encourage us with the knowledge that He has excellent things planned for our lives. This includes all of us being employed in a job that meets our financial needs and allows us to use our gifts and talents.

For several years I was a careers adviser in South London, where I helped unemployed people find work, many of whom had never before held down a job. The barriers to work in many of my clients' lives were often formidable, and included issues such as lack of skills, few qualifications, low self-confidence and poor finances. Whether we are also experiencing some of these difficulties or just seeking guidance for our next career move, our task is to seek out available information and advice that can help us find a job. During this time, I began to hear clearly from God about His desire to be deeply involved in guiding His people specifically in their job situations. Christians believe that if they take time to listen to God, they will hear Him speak personally to them on all matters. However, there can still be a tendency amongst many to keep their Christian beliefs separate from the most important parts of their lives. Instead of inviting God into their personal circumstances, some can ring-fence specific issues, such as those to do with employment, and consider these to be no-go areas for God. However, the promises of God found in the Bible cover every aspect of our lives: health, relationships, provision, area of ministry and certainly our job situation.

Even though the Bible does not actually mention the word 'career', it nevertheless recalls the jobs that various people did and the important role that these occupations played in their walk with God. Furthermore, despite scripture not mentioning the phrase 'careers advice', the Bible has a great deal to say about people who sought God's direction for their lives in a wide range of circumstances. It was often through jobs that God was able to most clearly demonstrate His amazing ability to transform personal situations, such as David rising up from a shepherd to a king or Joseph ascending from prison to the palace of the Pharaoh.

In fact, the very idea of a 'career' is a fairly modern phenomenon; historically, ordinary people had to take any work just to survive. In this subsistence life-style any thought of developing a career simply did not exist, and the privilege of being able to choose your occupation belonged mainly to the ruling classes. An important point to make at this stage is that our jobs and careers can often be quite separate from what God is calling us to do. Some people can be satisfied in any job because it supports them in more important activities such as raising children or caring for a relative, following a ministry or doing voluntary work for a local charity. Paul, the apostle, who wrote most of the letters in the New Testament, was a tent maker by trade, which he did to support his evangelistic work.

Whether we desire to develop a fulfilling career or whether we are looking to find a job to enable us to perform another activity, God wants to be involved in our employment situation. He would also encourage us to hold every part of our lives open so as to receive His guidance and revelation. If we deny God access to the issues around our jobs, it could result in us not receiving His blessing and provision. On the other hand, if we invite Him into our hopes and the circumstances surrounding our employment, then we will start a journey where we will begin to see God bring breakthrough and favour into our lives.

There are many Christian resources covering different areas of our lives such as health, relationships, role in the church or even our calling. However, even a quick glance on the internet or in high-street bookshops shows that there is a need for resources on the subject of jobs and careers from a Christian perspective. In addition to this, when we consider the on-going economic climate, there appears to be an urgent need for material that provides a clear biblical point of view on today's complicated job market. *The Christian Guide to Jobs and Careers* aims to plug this hole by giving assured scriptural teaching and encouragement to those of us looking to God for answers regarding our job situation. It offers us a pair of 'biblical spectacles' to gain a godly perspective on our past experience and also for our future hopes of the job market. The aim of the guide is to enable us to examine what God could be saying to us not only about His plans for our jobs, but most importantly about the depth of our relationship with Him.

Section One – What's Happening Lord?

The first section of the book covers seven chapters and takes a good look at the changes that God could be introducing into our lives during a season spent in a 'career wilderness'. A career wilderness is any time of hardship surrounding our job situation, such as a period of unemployment. A theologian would call this testing period a time of sanctification – when God brings about refinement to make us more Christ-like. On the other hand, a chef on daytime TV might liken the same process to being blended in a food processor and then put in an oven for twenty-four hours! This section will help us to evaluate the qualities that God wants to develop or even prune away in our lives. For example, is He using our present situation to increase our faith and trust in Him or possibly to create in us a more Godly character? To the world, any time spent in a career wilderness has little value. However, God views these testing times as an opportunity to shape us and to draw us into a closer relationship with Him. The sooner we understand what God wants to achieve during our wilderness season the better, because He will normally only allow us to move on once we have taken on board the changes that He wants to bring about.

Section Two – Receiving God's Revelation

The second section contains nine chapters, and explores how God can reveal His plans concerning our lives and especially our jobs. In particular we discover how God brings revelation through His word and by the power of the Holy Spirit. This section also looks at how He can guide us regarding our jobs specifically through our innate abilities, personality, deeply held desires and also through the advice that we receive from people around us. We will also look at some factors that can prevent us from receiving this revelation for our job situation and what we can do to stay 'in tune' with God's guiding voice.

An important point that must be considered in this section is that if God is calling us to do something specific, such as making a change in career, it is essential to look for confirmation of this through a number of different sources. When God asks us to move in a certain direction, not just one factor but many will align themselves to provide us with a clear indication of His will for us. However, there are people who do not seek such confirmation and drop everything they are doing to start something completely different, only to experience failure and disappointment a short while later. All of us, without exception, carry large L-plates. Even though it is unlikely that we will always hear 100% correctly from God, we can rest assured that if we make a mistake and take a wrong turning, then God will bring us back on track.

Section Three – Appendices: Practical Careers Advice

If we are unemployed or wishing to change our current role, the challenges surrounding employment can provide us with many opportunities to step out and demonstrate our faith in God. If we have faith that He will guide us in our career, then we must show this belief by investing the necessary time in our job search and so allow God to open or close doors according to His will. To help us in this task, the third and final section of the book offers a number of appendices that contain useful careers information and advice resources. Some of the practical topics covered include: constructing a winning CV, developing an effective job search strategy, performing well during a job interview and making an assessment of our skills.

How to Use This Book

A feature of the book are worksheets to encourage the reader to address the topics covered by each chapter. The exercises are designed to discover what God has to say to each of us personally concerning the issues surrounding our employment situation. They provide an opportunity for both self-reflection and prayer, possibly with a partner, and the chance to invite the Holy Spirit to bring healing and release into specific issues which are addressed in the book. Although designed to be read chapter-by-chapter, the book can be dipped into to find out about particular topics.

My hope is that this book will encourage the reader to develop a closer relationship with God and, through this, a greater degree of trust in Him for employment. Of course, it is true to say that even without reading this book God can turn our job situation around in the blink of an eye! The book does not offer a formula to get a new job out of God. Hopefully, what it offers is a refreshing and exciting look at what heaven, and not a primary school teacher, has to say about our jobs and careers.

So, be encouraged – **God wants to amaze us!**

SECTION ONE

What's Happening Lord?

The focus of this section is on how God could be using our employment situation to bring about changes to ourselves and to our relationship with Him. Over the following seven chapters we shall see how God can use a 'career-wilderness' – a period of hardship such as unemployment – to mould us and to draw us deeper into His love.

The Bible explains that God disciplines those He loves, and the way in which He does this is similar to a gardener who prunes away branches – either because they are disease-ridden or to encourage more abundant growth. The one thing that is assured is that the circumstances surrounding our employment can offer God plenty of opportunities to introduce such a period of discipline into our lives. Even though seasons spent in a career wilderness are, by their very nature, difficult to endure, the Bible assures us that if we persevere, we shall emerge more fruitful and walking in closer step with God.

We shall examine the qualities that God wants to develop in each of us including being honest with Him, accepting His timing and increasing our faith and trust in Him. The sooner we understand the changes that He wants us to make and take them on board, the sooner God will lead us out of our wilderness into the land – or job – that He has prepared for us.

Chapter 1

A Trip into the Wilderness

There is no getting around the fact that jobs are very important for many different reasons. Everyone, including the Queen, has taxes to pay and bills to settle. People also look to jobs for self-fulfilment, an opportunity to use their skills and interests. It is when you are a child that the future, including your job situation, appears to be wonderfully simple and straightforward. Ask a child what they plan to do when they grow up and they will invariably choose a job where they will have lots of fun and enjoyment – like my six-year-old son who intends to become the owner of an

Department for Work And Pensions (National)
Can't find your dream job? It could be child's play.

Jobcentre Plus shows how childhood career aspirations may hold the key to job satisfaction.

Children in the UK dream of becoming a teacher, footballer or police officer, according to research released today for Jobcentre Plus, part of the Department for Work and Pensions. Other professions appearing in the top ten of youngsters' aspirations were vet, fireman, hairdresser, nurse, dancer, doctor and driver.

The poll of 397 primary school-aged children, conducted by LVQ Research revealed that boys are most likely to aspire to sporting or 'protection' professions and girls to caring or nurturing professions. One in ten boys (10%) dream of being a footballer and 7% a police officer or fireman, whilst 13% of girls would like to become a teacher and 9% a nurse.

ice-cream van, and sell goodies to all his friends!

The idea of work all started in the Garden of Eden, where God assigned Adam various jobs. So we know that in the beginning work was not a chore but a pleasure. When asked to describe God's work, one child replied:

God's most important job is making people. He makes them to replace the ones that die, so there will be enough people to take care of things on earth. He doesn't make grownups, just babies. I think because they are smaller and easier to make. That way He doesn't have to take up His valuable time teaching them to talk and walk. He can just leave that to mothers and fathers.

God's second most important job is listening to prayers. An awful lot of this goes on, since some people, like preachers and things, pray at times besides bedtime. God doesn't have time to listen to the radio or TV because of this. Because He hears everything, there must be a terrible lot of noise in His ears, unless He has thought of a way to turn it off.

Adam's fall from grace and his expulsion with Eve from the Garden of Eden had incalculable effects upon the rest of mankind. One of the major changes for Adam was now that he was outside God's presence work became a chore – a thing of stress and 'aggro'. Does that sound familiar? You can be assured that it wasn't in God's original plan for His children to suffer frustration and to struggle whilst they worked for a living. However, when many of us reflect over our job situations, this is what we experience.

If anything, despite huge advances in technology, work-life is getting more complicated. Competition from emerging international markets frequently places economic stress on the organisations we work for, often resulting in redundancies or changes in working patterns that are not compatible with family life. Also, the massive rises in housing costs in recent years mean that not only can people no longer afford to live near to their places of work, but that both partners now have to work to pay the mortgage or rent. If a couple has children then this situation can lead to further financial stress caused by associated childcare costs.

The frustration of work doesn't always end there – many people are either out of work or in a job that does not suit their character, skills or personal circumstances. It is hard to imagine how God's plan for our lives can include such things as long-term unemployment and unfulfilled career dreams when His promises in Jeremiah[1] for our lives include our future being full of prosperity and hope. Yet if we look around at society, the effects of poor employment prospects are clearly visible[2]. From many studies[3] conducted in the UK and abroad, it can be seen that there is a clear link between the work situation and levels of physical and mental health and the quality of the family environment.

When I worked as a careers adviser in London, I gave many people advice and guidance on either how to find employment or to develop a career in a direction that better suited their interests and abilities. People view jobs in different ways and consequently many of us will have varying expectations and desires relating to jobs. Some people attach a high degree of importance to the development of a career, seeking progression, promotion and acquisition of a portfolio of skills and qualifications. For others, the development of a career is of less importance and a job is viewed as support for another activity such as bringing up children, caring for a relative or developing a church ministry. Other than for self-fulfilment, financial factors and the drive for social interaction are some other obvious reasons for seeking work.

However, when we take even a brief glimpse at our job situation it may appear that God has simply forgotten to prepare any quality jobs for us. Whether our desire is to develop a career or to find a convenient, local job during school hours, how often does it feel like God has not been listening to our prayers? Over the years I have struggled in many different ways with my career and have equally struggled to understand why God has apparently allowed me to suffer so much frustration. I prayed and even fasted for a breakthrough, but often to no avail. What was going on? For so long it felt like God had left town and was only taking messages on His answer machine, which He would eventually get around to answering. At a more rational level, I knew that this wasn't the case, but it certainly felt like it was!

Many people have cried out to God with questions, such as:

- **What happened to the dreams that you laid on my heart all those years ago and why have they stalled or apparently evaporated?**
- **How come my circumstances dictate differently to what I know you've put on my heart to do?**
- **Why do I still not know the direction you want me to go in?**

On occasions, I have cried out all three of the above to God. During these times one of the rocks that I clung to was the fact that Jesus, on the cross, also cried out in desperation to God[4]. If Jesus could cry out a shout of desperation, then it would mean that there was hope for my situation. Since the cross was part of God's plan for our salvation, then Jesus' crying out was also part of God's plan. This gave me strength because it showed me that despite my painful situation, His plan for giving me a hope and a future included what I was going through.

Are we passing through a career wilderness?

One dictionary[5] defines a wilderness as: *a wild, uninhabited and uncultivated area…any desolate area.* On a number of occasions in my life, this description could have accurately summed up my career prospects. There will be no doubt when do we pass through a career wilderness because job opportunities will be few and far between, and if some work does arise, it will often appear like a cactus – prickly and difficult to handle! When does a career wilderness happen? It could arrive with a redundancy or trying to return to work after many years looking after children. It could be the result of long-term illness or disability, which can present major challenges in returning to work. Perhaps it could happen as a result of scant work history and a lack

'You can use the fan if it gets a bit hot.'

of work skills and qualifications. Also, frustration with current work through lack of purpose or opportunity to use gifts and talents can lead to the feeling of being in a career wilderness.

The wilderness has frequently played a very important role in people's lives in the Bible. The whole nation of Israel spent forty years passing through one on their circuitous route to the 'promised land', and David spent seven years in another fleeing from Saul, before ascending to the throne. Jesus also spent forty days in the wilderness being tempted by Satan before starting His ministry. In each of these times spent in the wilderness, God was tailoring, shaping and equipping His people to be ready for the next stage of His plan for their lives.

Each of these wilderness experiences in the Bible also had an exit. That is, a time and a place where each person was able to emerge from a barren landscape into a land of fulfilled promises and green pastures. However, nobody wants to stay in a wilderness any longer than they have to. It's important to remember that if we are experiencing a wilderness season in our lives it should be viewed as only a *trip* into the wilderness with an exit on the far side – we are *not* setting up camp, but only passing through. It is also vital that we should see this as a time for walking as closely as possible with God so as to ensure that He sets us on the right path to the exit.

Nehemiah 9:19

'Because of your great compassion you did not abandon them in the desert. By day the pillar of cloud did not cease to guide them on their path, nor the pillar of fire by night to shine on the way they were to take.'

A career wilderness is a very personal place and our own experience may or may not fit some of the descriptions above. However, we need to be encouraged to persevere during these periods by considering what the Bible has to say about a difficult period of our lives.

Is God disciplining us?

Some readers may be surprised that in a book that is designed to help people find their God-appointed work, the focus of this chapter is directed towards understanding why God allows us to enter into a seemingly negative season in our lives. The reason for this is very simple: our Christian walk is all about increasing the closeness of our relationship with God. God wants us to worship Him and to love Him for who He is and not for the blessings that we can get from Him, such as release in jobs. God wants His children to be walking so closely with Him that blessings flow naturally from this relationship.

John 15:5

'I am the vine; you are the branches. If a man remains in me and I in Him, he will bear much fruit; apart from me you can do nothing.'

Recently on a television programme there was a story about a professional gardener who was preparing rare orchids for the Chelsea Flower Show. The preparations start many months before the show and the gardener featured in the story displayed many of the qualities that Jesus hinted at in John's Gospel. First of all, to enable the orchids to flower just on time to win the Gold Award, the gardener had to have a huge amount of knowledge about the plants she wanted to display. Secondly, she had to create just the right conditions necessary for the flowers to come into bloom artificially many months before they did so naturally. Thirdly, and most amazingly, over a period of a week, the gardener had to get up several times during the night to brush pollen over the stamens of the flowers. She explained that this was the only way of pollinating this particular variety of orchid because, in the wild, pollination only took place at night by a particular insect. This meant that to artificially pollinate these flowers, she had to replicate the natural conditions.

The level of determination and devotion displayed by this gardener for her prize orchids illustrates in a small way the love and dedication that God has for each one of us. Just like the gardener, Jesus knows exactly what needs to be done in our lives to bring us into a deeper relationship with God. To achieve this, He will sometimes use extreme measures. For the Hebrews it took forty years in the wilderness, but thankfully it will take considerably less time for most of us to take on board the changes God wants to happen in our lives.

Deuteronomy 8:2–5

Remember how the Lord your God led you all the way in the desert these forty years, to humble you and to test you in order to know what was in your heart, whether or not you would keep His commands. He humbled you... Know then in your heart that as a man disciplines his son, so the Lord your God disciplines you.

In this passage, God reminds the nation of Israel how He led them though the wilderness for forty long years. There are two immediate points to consider: firstly, God had not abandoned them because during this time He was leading them; secondly, the length of time was determined not so much by God, but by the

Hebrews themselves. How do we know this? God says that He led them during all of this time in order to humble them and also to test their mettle. God wanted to discover what was in their hearts:

- **How would they react to difficult situations?**
- **Would they turn to Him in their desperation and need?**
- **Would they turn elsewhere for their answers?**

We know how even Moses, despite all the miraculous provision given to his people, showed a lack of faith, which resulted in God denying him entry into the 'promised land'. If the Hebrews had demonstrated a different attitude and been less stiff-necked, then it is possible that they would have entered into their inheritance much earlier than they did. For their own sake, God could not allow them to enter into the 'promised land' with their hearts turned away from Him because He knew that it could only be through His almighty power that they could overcome all the tribes already occupying Canaan. The whole wilderness process was designed to discipline the Jews and increase their intimacy with God. If this took forty years to develop, then that is what God was prepared to do. It could have been worse, it could have taken eighty years!

What is God saying to us today?

The passage in Deuteronomy provides one of the key scriptures in the entire Bible for giving understanding on the purposes of God during hardship and testing circumstances. It recalls not merely an historical event, but also offers prophetic guidance for every Christian seeking to enter into the whole measure of the fullness of Christ[6]. So, what does this passage say to those of us who are currently in a career wilderness? It suggests that the reason why we might find ourselves in this desolate position is that God is choosing to discipline us, just as a father disciplines his son. We are reminded in the Book of Hebrews that discipline, although never pleasant at the time, produces a harvest of righteousness and peace.

| Hebrews 12:11 | **No discipline seems pleasant at the time, but painful. Later on, however, it produces a harvest of righteousness and peace for those who have been trained by it.** |

God can certainly use the job scene to discipline and sharpen us, as well as to increase our faith in Him. He knows the near inevitable consequences of allowing us to remain in a comfortable place for too long – it is a place where our faith can so easily descend into disuse, and eventually corrode and die. God will not 'sit' idly by and allow this to happen. Though it may seem unlikely or incredible, God could be designing a job wilderness experience for the purpose of testing us. The test is not designed to enable God to discover what is in us, because He already knows us inside out[7], but for each of us to discover for ourselves what we are made of and how we will react under pressure.

As with the Hebrews, God may want us to discover, during a wilderness season, what is in of our hearts:

- **How will *we* react to difficult situations?**
- **Will *we* turn to God in our desperation and need?**
- **Will *we* turn elsewhere for our answers?**

We may not share the same characteristic stubbornness of the Hebrews and be in need of receiving a forty-year dose of humble pie. In fact, we may not have done anything wrong at all. In all things, even during a wilderness experience, God works for the good in our lives[8]. This means that He can bring about a period of discipline to ensure that we walk closer with Him and thereby deepen our relationship with, and love for, Jesus. The end product is not merely a job with our name on it but, more importantly, the production of faith in Jesus Christ which we are told is of far greater value than gold and other precious metals.

| Job 23:10 | **But He knows the way that I take; when He has tested me, I shall come forth as gold.** |

In our present season of wilderness we are producing something that will cause the angels to continually praise Jesus: faith in God.

Review of Chapter

Whatever our desire is for a job, it can sometimes appear that God has not prepared anything for us and has failed to hear our prayers. Any lengthy period of difficulty that we experience can be referred to as a career wilderness. This season of testing can arrive in our lives from many different quarters such as redundancy or trying to return to work after many years looking after children.

A wilderness period frequently played an important role in people's lives in the Bible. In each case God used a difficult period to test and to discipline so that change could be brought into their lives. In the same way, God can use our job situation to make us grow as individuals and, most importantly, to bring us into a deeper relationship with Him. The test during this season in our lives is not for God to discover what we are made of, but rather for us to discover this truth. Even though it may feel that God has abandoned us, the Bible tells us that God disciplines those who He loves. Each wilderness period is designed with an exit and, before He allows us to pass through it, God wants us to learn which parts of our lives need changing.

The following worksheet will enable you to address some of the issues that have been raised in this chapter. The exercise can be carried out on your own or alongside a prayer partner. Take time to consider each question as honestly as possible, and record your responses on a separate sheet.

Exercise 1

A Trip into the Wilderness – is God Disciplining You?

The reason why we find ourselves in a wilderness season may have little to do with anything that we have done wrong. Our period of testing can often be explained by the fact that God introduces a time of discipline for our own good, to make sure we walk closer with Him and to deepen our relationship with Jesus. God may want us to use this season to discover more about ourselves and our relationship with Him.

For Prayer & Reflection

The following verses, which were used in the chapter, have been chosen to help you to focus on your own circumstances. Take some time to reflect on your situation through the questions that follow these verses.

Deuteronomy 8:2–5

Remember how the Lord your God led you all the way in the desert these forty years, to humble you and to test you in order to know what was in your heart, whether or not you would keep His commands. He humbled you... Know then in your heart that as a man disciplines his son, so the Lord your God disciplines you.

Hebrews 12:11

No discipline seems pleasant at the time, but painful. Later on, however, it produces a harvest of righteousness and peace for those who have been trained by it.

- **How are you reacting to your present, and possibly difficult, situation?**

- **Have you turned to God to meet your need or have you only looked elsewhere, such as self-help programmes, for your answers?**

- **On your own or with a prayer partner, invite the Holy Spirit to reveal those areas in your life where God is seeking to bring about growth and/or change.**

- **Write down those areas in your life where you believe you are being disciplined and stretched by God.**

Dreams and Plans

_____

_____

_____

_____

_____

_____

_____

_____

_____

_____

_____

_____

_____

_____

_____

Chapter 2

Being Honest with God

In the previous chapter we looked at how God can take us into a wilderness period for the express purpose of disciplining us in order to bring lasting change in our lives. God can use anything, including our job situation, to bring about such a transformation, with the changes designed to bring us into a closer relationship with God. It's important that we take a careful look at the underlying reasons why we find ourselves in a serious job situation, and getting to the bottom of this issue can be a complicated business.

Understanding the experience of a career wilderness

Recently when my three-year-old son returned from nursery we discovered that he had wet himself which, despite his tender age, was a bit surprising since he had been doing very well at being potty trained. When I gently asked him why he had wet himself he replied, 'Because I is a boy', pleased that this explained his little accident! His explanation for what had happened can be put down to his young age, but how often do we adopt a similarly simplistic viewpoint to explain the current situation regarding our careers? How frequently do we take time to consider why we find ourselves in this situation, and how much time do we spend discovering what God is saying to us during this season? In tackling the complex issues surrounding career guidance, gaining a Christian perspective not only offers a way of understanding the underlying reasons behind our job situation but may also offer a unique opportunity to allow the word of God into our careers.

From the world's perspective, a period of time in a wilderness-type situation, such as unemployment, has no or little value. However, from a Christian perspective, the same wilderness situation can yield many positive things – as long as we are seeking God's will for our lives. Although God knows that the job scene is a very real need in all of our lives, He is primarily concerned at producing fruit that lasts not just for a few years or decades, but for eternity.

Matthew 6:31–33

'So do not worry, saying, "What shall we eat?" or "What shall we drink?" or "What shall we wear?" For the pagans run after all these things, and your heavenly Father knows that you need them. But seek first His kingdom and His righteousness, and all these things will be given to you as well.'

When we consider our job situation, is it possible for us to determine if God is using this season to bring about change in our lives, to raise our level of faith and expectation, or to refine our character? Or is God using this season to deepen our trust in Him and help us to increase our perseverance and hope? The one thing that is certain is that whatever God is achieving in our lives during this wilderness season, it is being done to deepen our relationship with Jesus.

In this chapter we begin to examine what God could be saying to each one of us personally, and to consider some possible answers to the question: what changes does God want to introduce into our lives during a wilderness season?

- **Does God want us to be more honest with Him?**
- **Does God want us to walk more closely with Him?**
- **Does God want us to learn to wait for His timing?**
- **Does God want us to deepen our levels of faith and trust?**
- **Does God want to work on our character?**

We consider the first of these questions in this chapter, and the other questions in the following four chapters.

Does God want us to be more honest with Him?

A friend recently told me how he had been complaining to God that his career could be compared to someone who was standing on a wet and windy platform for a train that was never going to arrive. In his spirit, he heard God's reply: 'It's the journey that I take with you that I am interested in, not the arrival at the destination.' How closely are we walking with Jesus and allowing Him to shape us into the individuals He predestined us to be? One of the major factors that determines the closeness of our walk with Jesus is the extent to which we are real and honest with God. Let me explain what this means. Being in any difficult situation is bad enough without having to pretend that everything is going fine and to 'give face' not only to friends and the pastor, but also to God. It might be possible to fool people and convince them that all is rosy and going well, but God knows all our affairs intimately. What's the point of trying to be anything less than honest with Him when He knows each and every word we say even before it leaves our lips?

Psalm 139:3

You discern my going out and my lying down;
you are familiar with all my ways.
Before a word is on my tongue
you know it completely, O Lord.

It is amazing how being 'economical with the truth' can come so naturally to young children. Parents frequently hear 'I didn't touch it!' or 'I don't know' when asked about who spilt the drink or who broke the priceless 13th Century Ming vase! Not telling the truth can be a habit that some adults develop into an art form. The following amusing quotes are taken from insurance claim forms, which allegedly give drivers' honest explanations for their accident:

- **An invisible car came out of nowhere, struck my car and vanished.**
- **The car was all over the road. I had to swerve a number of times before I hit it.**
- **Coming home I drove into the wrong house and collided with a tree I don't have.**

At the base of any good relationship is openness and honesty. God wants us to be real with ourselves, our family and our friends, but especially with Him. British reserve is a cultural characteristic that has helped the army retain a stiff upper lip in many wars. For example, it was this ability that enabled British troops to stand in a defensive square position at the Battle of Waterloo. However, although effective against cavalry attack, this formation left the troops exposed to cannon fire, and it was only their incredible bravery and a stiff upper lip that prevented them retreating from the enemy.

This attribute, on the field of battle, is fine. However, in our everyday encounters with life's 'bullets', the ability to deal honestly and openly with our emotions can, in the end, be a more fruitful attitude to adopt. Other cultures possibly have a more healthy way of expressing their emotions.

Job 2:12

When they (*Job's friends*) saw him from a distance, they could hardly recognise him; they began to weep aloud, and they tore their robes and sprinkled dust on their heads.

It is crucial to be honest with God about how we feel regarding our job situation. Even though He already knows, He wants us to tell Him because we are His children – He desires a relationship with us that is real and runs deep.

A great characteristic of the Bible is that it records the full range of human feelings, and in doing so, this shows that the Bible fully relates to the human condition. It can only be a Holy Spirit-inspired book that permits the writers to moan, groan, complain and accuse, and then for the Holy Spirit to graciously record their repentance.

Jeremiah 20:7

O Lord, you deceived me, and I was deceived; you overpowered me and prevailed. I am ridiculed all day long; everyone mocks me.

Losing Your Job: Don't Despair – And Don't Get Angry

'Redundancy may feel like a 'kick in the teeth', but it can be a blessing in disguise,' says Nick Kochan[9]

When a senior employee at Northamptonshire County Council was called into his manager's office one black Monday morning and told that his position was under review for redundancy, he had one thought in his head: "Why me? Why my department and none other?"

From then on, he felt nothing but anger and despondency for months on end. "The first thing you feel is very, very angry. You do all the things that you can possibly do. You complain, you moan to people, you go to lawyers, and trade unions. You feel very bitter."

The Council's offer of counselling courses to help him deal with the prospect of redundancy at first provoked yet more anger. "You say to yourself, 'I don't want these **** courses. I want to know why these **** have done this at all."

He attended the course nevertheless. It compounded his feelings of confusion, but also dealt with the anger. He recalled that meeting other people in the same position was "humbling and embarrassing, although slightly hopeful at the same time. It is very confused emotionally."

Then came the anger management and release. "The counsellors allowed me to get my anger out, get my feelings out. They didn't try and avoid the issue. They gained the confidence and trust of people sitting round the room, who all had totally different stories."

Releasing anger is the first stage to recovering from the shock, says Rob Nathan, managing director of the London-based Career Counselling Services (CCS). "People go through a series of emotions in response to an unexpected change, which is all about loss. You go through shock then you go through denial."

In the same way, God wants us to be real and honest with Him. In the Bible He gives us fallible men and women who messed up and even accused God of deceitfulness! Even though this was wrong to do, God allowed this to be included in the scriptures because He knew we would relate to it at some point in our lives.

Why is honesty with God important?

The reason why honesty with God is important is that it allows Him to work in our lives. David was a man whose heart was after God; in fact he was completely sold out to Him.

Psalm 51:10,12

Create in me a pure heart, O God,
and renew a steadfast spirit within me.
Restore to me the joy of your salvation
and grant me a willing spirit, to sustain me.

Likewise, the Bible instructs us to have an open heart so God can clean it and mould it according to His purposes. Jesus warns us in Matthew[10] that the things that come out of the heart make us unclean. It is when we open our hearts to God that He can begin the healing and cleansing process. Through a realisation of his many faults, murder and adultery among them, David prayed what we read in Psalm 51. He declared openly the things that were on his heart, but he did not just leave it there; repentance followed and led to a willingness that allowed God to move in and transform his situation.

A real relationship with God allows us to acknowledge our emotions and fears before Him rather than lock them away. He wants us to bring career-related issues such as unfulfilled dreams, redundancy or age discrimination to the foot of the Cross, and to leave them there. God does not want us to languish in a job that is not suited to our needs or remain in a state of long-term unemployment. Jesus said that, 'He came that they may have life, and have it to the full'[11]. However, God has overwhelming respect for our freedom of choice, and He will not intrude or take away this option. It was an open and contrite heart that allowed David to leave the fields and become the anointed leader of Israel.

'Oh, hi pastor. Yes, everything's fine, no problems - thanks for calling!'

Review of Chapter

God wants us to be honest with Him about how we are feeling. The level of honesty we have with God will determine the closeness of our walk with Him. He already knows everything about us including how we feel about our job situation, so trying to fool God by pretending that we feel okay, when we're not, is not going to work!

The reason why it is important for us to be honest with God about every issue is that it will allow Him to work in our lives. It is only when we open our hearts to God that He can begin the healing and cleansing process. He wants us to bring all of our career-related issues to the foot of the Cross, and to leave them there. The reason why David was able to leave the fields and become King over Israel was because he had an open heart that allowed God to work in his life. In the same way God desires us to have a similar heart that will allow Him to transform our lives. Are we ready to leave our fields and enter into our anointed positions?

The following worksheet will enable you to address some of the issues that have been raised in this chapter. The exercise can be carried out on your own or alongside a prayer partner. Take time to consider each question as honestly as possible, and record your responses on a separate sheet.

Exercise 2

Being Honest with God

One factor that determines the closeness of our walk with Jesus is the degree to which we are real and honest with God. The Bible instructs us to have an open heart in order that God can clean it and mould it according to His purpose. Are we ready, like David, to allow God into our lives and transform our situation?

For Prayer & Reflection

The following verses, some of which were used in the chapter, have been chosen to help you to focus on your own circumstances. Take some time to reflect on your situation through the questions that follow these verses.

Romans 8:27

And He who searches our hearts knows the mind of the Spirit...

Psalm 51:10,12

Create in me a pure heart, O God,
and renew a steadfast spirit within me.
Restore to me the joy of your salvation
and grant me a willing spirit, to sustain me.

Jeremiah 20:7

O Lord, you deceived me, and I was deceived; you overpowered me and prevailed. I am ridiculed all day long; everyone mocks me.

Job 6:2–3	If only my anguish could be weighed and all my misery be placed on the scales! It would surely outweigh the sand of the seas –…
Psalm 42:3	My tears have been my food day and night, while men say to me all day long, 'Where is your God?'

• Looking at these scriptures, can you relate to feeling the same in regard to your work situation?

• As honestly as possible write down how you are presently feeling about your work situation. Don't worry, God already knows!

• With a prayer partner, talk about those feelings that you are comfortable to share.

• It is important to have a contrite heart, which may mean asking for God's forgiveness. Pray that God would give you a 'pure heart' – a heart that is open to receive instruction and guidance.

Dreams and Plans

_____

_____

_____

_____

_____

_____

_____

_____

_____

_____

_____

_____

_____

Chapter 3

Walking Closely with God

This is the second of five chapters that look in detail at some areas of our lives and our walk with God where He wants to bring about growth and change. In this chapter, we shall examine how God could be using our present career wilderness to examine how closely we are walking with Him.

God is calling us back to Him

Recent advances in the understanding of the human genome have revealed some amazing facts. In particular, all men and women have something important in common: we are all descended from the same ancestor. By studying DNA from people alive today, it is now possible to say how they are related, who their distant ancestors were, and when and where they lived. What has become clear is that all humans derive from a common ancestor living in Africa about 200,000 years ago – the so-called mitochondrial Eve. It's good to see how accurate the Bible is on these matters!

Another common feature in our lives, descending all the way down the line from Adam and Eve, is sin. The good news is that Jesus dealt with the long-term consequences of this sin by dying on the cross. The not so good news is that the evidence of sin is still all around and within us. The Bible, in both the Old and New Testaments, records the story of humanity's walk with God. There are some shining examples of people such as Moses, David and the apostles, whose walk with God was very close. However, a large part of the Bible describes how the nation of Israel drifted away from God and became disobedient in its ways. The consequences of this were inevitably dire: famine, war, exile and occupation.

In his letter to the Romans[12], Paul describes the struggle that many Christians experience: they know what they ought to be doing, but it doesn't get done.

Romans 7:19   **For what I do is not the good I want to do; no, the evil I do not want to do – this I keep on doing.**

One possible reason why we might be experiencing a wilderness season with our jobs is that we are not presently walking closely with God. In other words, we may have decided to deal with our next job move on our own and keep Him out of the situation. It is possible that we might still be hearing from God regarding our jobs, but that we have decided to ignore what we feel He is telling us[13]. More seriously still, our relationship with God may have cooled off or become frozen altogether, to the point where Jesus is now a far off figure in our lives. Jesus had a warning for the early in church in Ephesus that, having lost their first love, they should come back to Him and repent for their lack of passion[14].

When Moses was in the Wilderness with the task of leading the nation of Israel into the 'promised land', he pleaded that God's presence should never leave them[15]. He went on to say that if God left them now, how would other people know that His favour was with this people or see what would set them apart from other nations? Moses was well aware that it was vitally important for them all to remain close to the presence of God. The consequences of losing God's presence would be that they would also lose His protection, provision and guidance. On the other hand, if they remained in God's presence He would continue to protect, provide, and guide them out of the wilderness and into their inheritance – the 'promised land'.

What is our experience of allowing God into important issues such as our work situation? How much time have we spent getting to know God and placing Him first in our lives? It is possible that we have never approached God for anything, or that our relationship with Him has run out of steam, which has resulted in a loss of enthusiasm and love for Him. The good news is that regardless of our history, experience and knowledge of God, today He is calling us back into His presence and a relationship with Him. In later chapters we shall look in depth at how God speaks to us once this relationship has been resumed. He has much to tell us regarding His plans for us. These might include returning to college to take further qualifications, taking a training course to gain a professional skill or the type of career we should be entering. To move forward, it is not only important for us to listen to God, but also to be obedient and courageous in our walk with Him.

Receiving the love of the Father

In the Gospel of John[16], Jesus gives an amazing revelation about the Father's love for every single person who accepts Him into their lives. Up until this moment, God the Father had been seen as an awesome and remote God. However, Jesus shatters this image by describing the extravagant love that the Father has for each of us. In his letter to the Romans[17], Paul describes this intense love by explaining that God didn't wait for us to be perfect in order to show His love, but showed it when we were still sinners. In other words, God made the first move in revealing His love for us. Furthermore, John says[18] that the only reason why we can love at all is because God first loved us.

The amazing truth about God's love is that He chose us in the first place and *not* the other way around. If we have accepted Jesus into our lives, this is only ever done *in response* to God's call[19]. When we spend time in His presence and allow His love for us to enter our hearts, both ourselves and our situations will be transformed.

John 15:16

You did not choose me, but I chose you and appointed you to go and bear fruit – fruit that will last. Then the Father will give you whatever you ask in my name.

The Father's desire is for us to spend time in His presence and actually experience His love. At times this will mean being still and quiet before Him, but when this is not possible, to hold the fact of His love continually in our minds[20]. However, the trouble is that sometimes we can be resistant to receiving this love. To make this happen the Father may allow a difficult situation to arise in our lives, such as a career wilderness, to force us to cry out in desperation to Him.

Psalm 63:1

O God, you are my God,
earnestly I seek you;
my soul thirsts for you,
my body longs for you,
in a dry and weary land
where there is no water.

When he was fleeing from Saul, David experienced a desperate situation that caused him to cry out to God. The Bible tells us[21] that David was a man whose heart was turned completely to God, and he understood that when he entered God's presence he ceased to rely on his own ability and began to operate in God's power. When we seek God's presence in the same way as David, we will also begin to learn how to act according to His plans. When we do this, two things will happen: our desires will be satisfied[22] and we will experience lasting fruitfulness in our lives[23]. When we respond to the Father's love and begin to search for Him with everything inside us, He will satisfy our hunger and make us fruitful in all we do. This will include many things such as finding a job suited to our needs and desires.

In fact, in the Book of Jeremiah, God appears to be fairly blunt when He gives instructions about how we should seek Him and find His will for our lives.

Jeremiah 29:13–14

'You will seek me and find me when you seek me
with all your heart. I will be found by you,'
declares the Lord, 'and will bring you back from
captivity. I will gather you from all the nations
and places where I have banished you,' declares
the Lord, 'and will bring you back to the place
from which I carried you into exile.'

When we read this passage, the image that comes to mind is that of a father playing hide-and-seek with his children. He doesn't want to make it too difficult for the children to find Him, but just hard enough to make them scramble around. After a while of fruitless searching, the dad calls out to make the children turn in the right direction because, after all, he can't wait for them to discover his hiding place. And there is one sure thing about when children play, they enter into the game with complete passion and excitement.

Whilst this picture doesn't completely represent what God is telling us in Jeremiah, what is certain is that God yearns for us to go after Him and to find Him with our entire hearts. The Bible makes it clear that 'our God is a jealous God'[24] who wants nothing less than our complete devotion to Him. He wants us to be as sold out to Him as He is to us. God's desire is to bring us to a place where we're no longer trying to 'bend His right arm behind His back' by fasting and pounding at Him with our prayers. He still wants us to pray, but longs for us to be in such a close relationship with Him that when the breakthrough eventually comes in our job situation, we'll know with all our hearts that it is because of God and not ourselves.

There are many instances in the Bible of breakthroughs happening when God's people called out to Him in desperation. In each case where His people had the whole of their gaze and focus upon God, He supernaturally brought power, influence and salvation to turn situations around. This happened to the disciples just before Pentecost when they prayed constantly[25] for the release of the Holy Spirit. Similar breakthroughs happened to David in the fields looking after the sheep, to Joseph in prison and to Daniel after being thrown to the lions. Picture David in the following Psalm:

Psalm 63:6–8

On my bed I remember you;
 I think of you through the watches of the night.
Because you are my help,
I sing in the shadow of your wings.
My soul clings to you;
Your right hand upholds me.

In this psalm, David is in the Judean wilderness hiding from a vengeful Saul and it is his turn to keep watch during the night. As he sits on rough stony ground in the dark with his knees drawn up to his chin and a blanket around his shoulders to keep warm, David ponders over how God has consistently been at his side helping him during his struggles with Saul. Does this sound familiar? How many of us have been in a job or a situation that had little to recommend it? Despite the doubt and fear that must have been nipping constantly at David's heels, his reaction wasn't to try to figure out a way of resolving his situation through his own devices. David's present accommodation and job could be summed up as:

Address: 1 Stony Hill, Judean Desert, Palestine.
Occupation: Watchman.

Nevertheless, David gave thanks for the knowledge that he lived continually under the 'shadow of the wings' of the almighty God from whom came his help. God would have us adopt the same trusting attitude as David who didn't rely on his own strength, but sought the love of the Father with all his heart. This allowed God to bring him out of his wilderness. David's open and honest heart enabled him to search for God with everything he had. In the process, this released the supernatural hand of God to open doors and guide him to his anointed position as King over Israel.

God creates a burning hunger in each one of us that can only be satisfied when we draw close to Him. It is when we place ourselves under God's protection and cease to strive in our own efforts, that we allow God to fight our battles for us. In the context of our jobs, this does *not* mean that application forms need not be completed or CVs given out, but that when we draw into His presence, we have the certainty that God is in control of our situation.

Review of chapter

A possible reason why we might be experiencing a wilderness season with our jobs is that God wants to increase our hunger for Him. His desire for us is to be walking so closely with Him that we are able to hear His voice guiding our every step. However, it is sometimes easy to allow our relationship with God to grow cold, and for us to exclude Him from important parts of our lives such as the decisions we make regarding our next career move. Moses understood that to remain in a close relationship with God meant that he would also continue to receive God's favour. Whilst in the wilderness Moses made sure that the Hebrews remained in God's presence and continued to receive His protection, provision, and guidance.

Whatever our experience has been, the good news is that God is calling us back into a relationship with Him. He wants us to adopt the same trusting attitude as David, who didn't rely on his own strength, but sought the love of the Father with all of his heart. This attitude enabled God to bring David out of his wilderness. The question for us is: how hungry are we to receive the love of the Father and experience His provision in our lives?

The following worksheet will enable you to address some of the issues that have been raised in this chapter. The exercise can be carried out on your own or alongside a prayer partner. Take time to consider each question as honestly as possible, and record your responses on a separate sheet.

Exercise 3
Walking Closely with God

Challenging questions for us are: Could God be using this wilderness period in our lives to deepen our hunger for Him? How much do we want God in our lives and to walk according to His plan? The amazing truth about His love for us is that He chose us in the first place and *not* the other way around. When we spend time in His presence and allow His love to enter our hearts, both we and our situations will be transformed.

For Prayer & Reflection

The following verses, some of which were used in the chapter, have been chosen to help you to focus on your own circumstances. Take some time to reflect on your situation through the questions that follow these verses.

Psalm 63:1   **O God, you are my God, earnestly I seek you; my soul thirsts for you, my body longs for you, in a dry and weary land where there is no water.**

Exodus 33:15   **Then Moses said to Him, 'If your Presence does not go with us, do not send us up from here.'**

- **What is your experience of allowing God into important issues such as your work situation?**

- **As honestly as possible ask yourself how important a place God currently has in your life. Is He central to everything you do or has He become a distant figure?**

The Father's desire is for us to spend time in His presence and actually experience His love for us. For this to happen, we sometimes have to slow down and quite literally rest in the presence of His Holy Spirit. Meditate on the following two verses that tell us about the Father's amazing love for us.

John 16:27

No, the Father Himself loves you because you have loved me and have believed that I came from God.

1 John 3:1

How great is the love the Father has lavished on us, that we should be called children of God! And that is what we are!...

- Whilst listening to quiet music, you can invite the Holy Spirit to speak to you about the love that God the Father has for you. Jesus said that the Holy Spirit will guide us in all truth, including the love of the Father.

- On your own or with a prayer partner, write down what you think God is telling you about your love and passion for Him.

Dreams and Plans

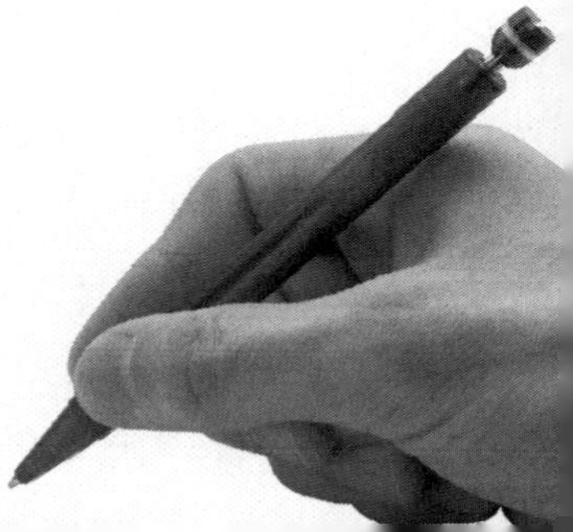

Chapter 4

Learning to wait for God's Timing

This is the third of five chapters that look in detail at areas of our lives where He wants to introduce growth and change. In this chapter, we shall examine how God could be using our present career wilderness to teach us about His timing of events.

Our concept of time

Since becoming a father I have learnt an enormous amount about the concept of time and the ability to wait for things to occur. For example, my three-year-old son refers to any event that has already taken place as having happened *yesterday*. Recently he was getting frustrated with me for not being able to understand what he was trying to say. He wanted me to get out the game with all the balls that he was playing with yesterday. After quizzing him at some length I eventually understood that he wanted to play with his ball-pool that he got for his first birthday, something that had been in the loft for well over a year. To him everything before he got up this morning was bunched together as having happened *yesterday*. Conversely, everything happening in the future will happen on *Tuesday* – a word he liberally uses for an event at nursery the following day or Christmas Day in a few months' time. Likewise, his concept of being able to wait for something to happen is equally bewildering to an adult. The immediate situation is overwhelmingly important for a young child. Part of my son's routine before going to bed is to have a beaker of milk and a plain biscuit with a bedtime story. If something gets in the way of my giving his milk and biscuit, such as putting the kettle on or answering a knock at the door, it can result in him throwing himself on the floor in frustration at having to wait an additional thirty seconds. Now means NOW, and not NOW + time!

My son's reaction to events can be both amusing and exasperating, not merely because of the energy levels required to deal with toddler tantrums, but also because in him I can see a parallel with my own attitude to waiting for God to move in my life. The timing of my own career development has been challenging to say the least. It has been characterised by many false starts and seemingly dead-end decisions. After leaving school feeling wholeheartedly that God was calling me to the Roman Catholic priesthood, I first planned to enter a Benedictine monastery and then later a missionary order. However, after a period of travelling abroad, I dropped these plans. This whole episode led to a later-than-normal entry into university. In the ensuing five years I entered a long wilderness of what I felt were unfulfilling jobs, where I held junior positions in which I could not develop my 'graduate potential'. It is a testimony to the grace of God that my faith survived those years. However, God was performing deep surgery on me during this time. It is said that when you're in the midst of a miracle, it is easy not to see God in action. The actual understanding of what is going on spiritually often comes only once the situation has moved on and the miracle has occurred. It was only after literally years of praying and of tears that I finally received assurance that I was in a career that I knew was for me.

For many people the development of a career is not important, and God can equally call them into any type of work where they can be salt and light to those around them. Others may view employment as a way of enabling them to carry out, what for them, is a more important activity such as performing voluntary work. However, whilst I longed to develop a career, I could not understand why this was taking such a long time and why I had to endure such frustration. I would also ask myself, why did God allow my self-esteem to sink? Didn't He know that I had been waiting since my fifteenth birthday to find out what I was destined to do?

God engineers time to meet His purposes

People frequently dream about changing or correcting past events, and often state something along the lines of, 'if only I could go back in time, I would do things differently'. If only this was possible and we could manipulate time! Science fiction writers have no difficulty doing so: H.G. Wells invented his time machine and Dr Who used a Tardis to travel through time and space. In the film *Back to the Future*, we weave our way through time in an adventure where the heroes attempt to influence past and future events. In the real world of science, a prediction of Einstein's theory of relativity is that a form of time travel could indeed be possible. For example, if one twin remained on earth and the other journeyed in a space rocket at nearly the speed of light to the closest star and then returned to earth, the twin who remained on earth would now be older than the one who travelled.

Even though the laws of physics states the impossibility of manipulating time, the Bible tells us that in all events, whether it is Israel waiting for the Messiah or ourselves waiting for a career break, God is fully in control of the timing. In the previous chapter we looked at the prophetic message for us today in the story of the nation of Israel being led through the wilderness for forty years. Just as this historical event has prophetic significance for Christians today, so also does the long period of waiting for a Messiah to come and deliver the Jews from the tyranny of their enemies.

It is now worth spending some time looking at how God engineered the perfect time and circumstances in which Jesus the Messiah arrived in Palestine. The reason why this is relevant for those of us enduring a long season of waiting for a job breakthrough is straightforward: God is as much in control of our job situation as He was in control of the timing of the arrival of Jesus in Bethlehem. Whether our desire is to develop a career or to find a convenient job in order to perform another activity, God's timing is everything. If we are serious about entering into God's will regarding our career, and we are obedient to His word, it will never be a question of *if* but *when* we will receive His blessings. Is it possible that God has introduced this wilderness season into our lives to bring us to an understanding of this truth?

God sent His Son at the right time

In his letter to the Galatians, Paul assures us that the arrival of Jesus was an event that God had planned carefully from the beginning of time.

Galatians 4:4

But when the time had fully come, God sent His Son...

In God's promise to Abraham – to produce descendants as innumerable as the stars – we now have the benefit of hindsight to see how His timing played a critical role in the salvation of both the Jewish and Gentile world. However, if we were to step back 2000 years to the time of Jesus, it may well have appeared to us that God's timing and His plans were not succeeding. The hope of the coming Messiah became the lifeblood that sustained Israel through many traumatic years such as the exile to Babylon and the Roman occupation 400 years later. This desperate hope is expressed in the book of Micah where the Messiah will shepherd His people to safe pastures. However, there is a strong 'not yet' message attached.

Micah 5:3
Therefore Israel will be abandoned until the time when she who is in labour gives birth...

God is telling His people that the time is not yet ready and compares Israel to a woman in labour. The pregnancy must go the full term if the baby is to be born healthy and alive. Despite contemporary beliefs in Israel such as, 'If all the people of Israel for just one single day kept the Law of Moses to the exact word then the Messiah would come', God's timing of events was clearly at odds with their way of thinking. The time was not yet right!

It is not merely God's timing that can be difficult to grasp, but also the way in which He makes things happen. When the time was right and Jesus did appear, He was a profound disappointment to many people. Instead of being born into an affluent and influential family, He was born in a stable to parents of low social standing. Years later, instead of entering Jerusalem on a war-horse, Jesus rode in on a donkey. To most people, the greatest disappointment of all was that He suffered the most demeaning of deaths, by crucifixion – a death that is normally reserved for criminals. At face value, this was not how humankind would have ushered in the long-awaited promise of God for Israel. The beginnings of Christianity appeared to promise no future for the spread of the new faith.

The spreading flame of Christianity

Given the seemingly weak start to the Christian faith, how were Jesus' followers going to bring about making Abraham's descendants out of the nations? Because the time was right, God had plans to prepare the world to receive the 'good news'. One of the Jewish leaders called Gamaliel pointed out[26] to the Sanhedrin that there had been other messianic pretenders, such as Theodas and Judas the Galilean, who had all come to nothing. He warned that if this new faith did indeed come from God then the Jews would be unable to put a stop to it. Despite this stern warning, certain Jews took it upon themselves to try to quench this new flame. Starting with the martyrdom of Stephen, the followers of Christ became a persecuted people on the run from the authorities. Paradoxically, God was using extremist Jews, such as Saul, to help bring the gospel to the nations. Instead of resting comfortably in Jerusalem, the followers of the 'New Way' were in effect being forced out to spread God's New Covenant.

There were other factors now in place that also facilitated the rapid spread of Christianity. The Diaspora of the Jews to other parts of the world, including Egypt, Greece, Rome and parts of Asia Minor, had been happening for centuries as a result of foreign domination. Also the poor economic conditions in Palestine encouraged the business-minded Jews to migrate to richer lands. In Rome, for example, there were at least eleven synagogues, and in Alexandria in Egypt there were over one million Jews. These Jews kept themselves separate from local social life and maintained a strict moral code to which many Gentiles were attracted. Judaism was synonymous with stable life and charitable activities, and many devout Gentiles became converts to this faith. It was amongst these Jews and especially amongst these Gentiles that the Christian missionaries found their first converts – they were very much dry tinder through which the flame of Christianity could spread. They held high moral values, were well versed in the scriptures, and the messianic story would have been well known to such people. These communities helped the missionaries to fix a strategy of where to aim for converts.

Again, paradoxically, the Roman Empire, which oppressed both Jews and

Christians for many years, helped enormously with the fast and efficient spread of the Gospel. Since all roads led to Rome, this meant that inexorably the Good news made its way either by the well-established shipping lanes in the Mediterranean or on the excellent system of roads. These roads were well maintained to facilitate trade and the rapid deployment of troops throughout the Empire. Along these highways Roman colonies were maintained to safeguard trade and communications, and to ensure that the power of the Roman state was enforced locally. If the Good news could be planted in these settlements then it would spread to the surrounding areas, and Paul targeted these colonies seeing them as strategic advances in converting Gentile lands. The fact that both Paul and Silas possessed Roman citizenship qualified them to travel unhindered throughout the Empire, establishing and strengthening Christian communities.

Until about 60 AD, Christianity enjoyed protection under the Romano Religio Licita, and was seen as part of Judaism rather than a cult. Even though Judaism was often held in contempt by the Gentiles, nevertheless, it was a recognised religion with a firm base in Palestine. As long as Christianity could be regarded as part of Judaism then it too could enjoy this protection. This prevented the early Christians suffering the same fate as the followers of the self-proclaimed Messiah called Judas of Galilee who, after he was crucified, were also executed. Under the protection of the Religio Licita, Christian missionaries could preach in the open without fear of incurring the wrath of Rome. During this period the common language was Greek, and it became increasingly necessary for the Jews outside Israel to have the scriptures written in this language. The Septuagint, which was commissioned by Ptolemy, was considered to be a God-inspired translation of the Hebrew scriptures. With the Jewish scriptures now in an understandable language, the early church had liturgical material that would otherwise have been denied them. God's timing was enabling His people to take on an international aspect.

Until the Christian persecutions under Emperor Nero in 64 A.D., the early Church enjoyed over thirty years of peace and was able to spread all around the then known world. The Pax Romana was responsible for a melting pot of cultures to gather in many cities across the Empire such as Rome, Athens, Corinth and Antioch. It was in Antioch that 'The Way' took hold and was first given the label, *Christianity*. The stability of the whole region engendered an environment in which people could think of things other than the insecurities of war. People could pass their time on weightier matters such as searching for the meaning of life and maybe even go as far as examining the latest cult from the Middle East proclaiming forgiveness of sins and offering everlasting life! It was into such a peaceful setting that Paul found himself when he came to Athens. Religiously, the world had never been as ready as it was then to receive a new, meaningful and vibrant religion. The old religions had become stagnant and empty, and people were looking for something new and fresh. Paul arrived at just the right time to proclaim the Good news to many nations, and the flame of Christianity continued to spread. With the accession of Constantine in 312 A.D., Christianity became the established belief system of the new Christian Romano Empire.

Seeking understanding of God's timing

If we have gone into some detail about the spread of Christianity, it is for an important reason. Two thousand years on, it is very easy to take for granted that Christianity not only took hold and survived but also, in a relatively short time, became the religion of the Empire itself. There were similar messianic figures in and around the time of Jesus, but all of them came to nothing. On this evidence we can see that if man alone is behind a faith movement it will not survive. What made the difference with Christianity? Quite simply, God's chosen time acted as a conduit for His government to be established on earth. If Jesus had arrived before He did, the conditions would not have been right to enable the fledgling religion to spread across the Roman Empire in the way that it did. God waited until just the right moment to send His Son.

Despite our present circumstances with unfulfilled career expectations, the test of our faith is to learn patience and to acknowledge that God is as much in control of the timing of our jobs as He was in the timing of the arrival of Jesus. When the time is right, God will engineer a miracle in our job scene; until the time is right, we must be patient. The lesson for us is a profound one: God's timing is crucial. When astronauts re-enter the Earth's atmosphere, it is essential that the angle of approach is correct. The 're-entry window' is extremely narrow and if missed it can result in a catastrophic burn-up or in the space capsule bouncing off the earth's atmosphere back into space. God's timing hits the re-entry window every time and if we follow His lead in our lives it will never end in disaster.

Furthermore, the Bible tells us that we have to be humble in the way we seek God for understanding about His timing.

1 Peter 5:6–7   **Humble yourselves, therefore, under God's mighty hand, that He may lift you up* in due time. Cast all your anxiety on Him because He cares for you. (****promote you – The Message****)**

When we experience, for example, repeated redundancies or discrimination in the workplace, it is not always possible to understand why such things happen. Like many people, I have had experiences at work that have led me to being angry and frustrated rather than being humble. On the occasions when my emotions dominated I also lost sight of God's plan and the sense of His presence. In difficult situations where understanding is not possible, the Bible tells us to avoid becoming angry and instead allow God to develop a humble character in us. Such humility will not only give us a sense of peace but also an assurance that God is working behind the scenes to engineer a way out of the situation in due time.

Review of chapter

Though it may not always appear to be so, God's control of the timing surrounding our job situation is as sure as it was in the coming of the Messiah. If our walk with God is close and we are listening for His voice, it will only ever be a question of timing for His purposes to arrive in our lives. Whether our desire is to develop a career or to find a convenient job in order to perform another activity, God's timing is everything.

The lesson for us from the history of the early church is not to become discouraged. The news of a local event – the death and resurrection of Jesus – spread far and wide as a result of the stability and excellent means of communication in the Roman Empire. In the same way that God engineered the favourable circumstances for the spread of Christianity, we must believe that He can also do the same for our careers. The test of our faith is to learn patience and to adopt a humble attitude that will give us the assurance that God is working behind the scenes. When the time is right, God will engineer a miracle in our job scene.

The following worksheet will enable you to address some of the issues that have been raised in this chapter. The exercise can be carried out on your own or alongside a prayer partner. Take time to consider each question as honestly as possible, and record your responses on a separate sheet.

Exercise 4
Learning to Wait for God's Timing

Whether our desire is to develop a career or to find a convenient job in order to perform another activity, God's timing is everything. The Bible tells us to develop a humble character so that we can wait patiently for His timing of events in our lives. This will give us a sense of peace that God is working behind the scenes.

For Prayer & Reflection

The following verses, some of which were used in the chapter, have been chosen to help you to focus on your own circumstances. Take some time to reflect on your situation through the questions that follow these verses.

1 Peter 5:6–7   **Humble yourselves, therefore, under God's mighty hand, that He may lift you up in due time. Cast all your anxiety on Him because He cares for you. (*promote you – The Message*)**

Galatians 4:4   **But when the time had fully come, God sent His Son,…**

Psalm 31:15   **My times are in your hands; deliver me from my enemies and from those who pursue me.**

Romans 5:6   **You see, at just the right time, when we were still powerless, Christ died for the ungodly.**

- Think of occasions in your life when God eventually allowed you to move on. Can you now understand, retrospectively, why God might have delayed you?

- What do your circumstances 'say' about how ready you are to move into a certain career or out of your present one?

- Sometimes when we think God is saying 'no' to our prayer request, He is actually saying 'not yet'. Pray that God would bring you clarity on which of these two He is saying to you today.

- Have you sought prophetic guidance from your church regarding God's timing for your life?

Dreams and Plans

_____

_____

_____

_____

_____

_____

_____

_____

_____

_____

_____

_____

_____

_____

_____

Chapter 5

Deepening our Faith and Trust in God

This is the fourth of five chapters in which we look in detail at some of the areas in our lives where God wants to bring about growth and change. In this chapter, we shall examine how He could be using our present career wilderness to deepen our levels of faith and trust in Him.

The Bible places huge importance on our level of faith in God, saying[27] that without faith it is impossible to please God. The reason why God places such importance on our faith and trust is profound. It is based on our faith in Jesus that our future through eternity is determined[28] and, therefore, faith is something that God wants us to be well practised in. The Book of Hebrews devotes an entire chapter to this subject. In Chapter 11 many biblical heroes are named who through faith were justified and entered into the promises of God. Each of their circumstances was designed beforehand by God to ensure that their faith was tested over time and, as a result they were all commended. This book gives us a fantastic definition of faith:

Hebrews 11:1   **Now faith is being sure of what we hope for and certain of what we do not see.**

Such were the levels of faith in God of these people that, despite a complete lack of tangible evidence, they adamantly believed that He would eventually bring about an answer to their prayers.

Similar to faith, trust in God is something that is deepened by our experience of seeing Him operate in our lives. A team-building exercise at work demonstrated effectively how much trust and faith one had in a colleague. The test involved one person standing in front of another. The person in front was instructed to look forward and then to slowly fall back into the arms of the person behind whose job it was to catch. Needless to say, not everyone succeeded in demonstrating the trust needed to let themselves fall! In our walk with God, He wants us to get to know Him to the point where we have absolutely no hesitation about letting ourselves fall into His arms. Paul, in his letter to the Romans[29], prayed that the God of hope would fill his friends with joy and peace as they placed their complete trust in God. The Psalmists wrote a great deal about trusting the Lord, mentioning 'trust' thirty-seven times in all. Jesus comforted His disciples[30] by saying that they should not let their hearts be troubled, but should place their trust in God and also in Him. Jesus also portrayed Himself as the Good Shepherd guiding a flock of sheep that follow His voice with trust.

'It's good to know that you're a reliable pers......!'

However, the simple fact is that it can be difficult to place our complete faith and trust in God, especially with important areas such as employment. Some of us may have greater levels of faith and trust in one area of our lives than in another, whilst others find it impossible to trust God at any level. Whatever the levels of our faith and trust, the Bible is a record of people who have also had great difficulty in this same area. Habakkuk lived at a time of great turmoil in Israel. The people lived under an oppressive regime that had fallen away from God, and the world around them was at war. The Book of Habakkuk records a spiritual journey from terrible doubt to renewed hope and trust in God. At the beginning, Habakkuk is overwhelmed by the negative circumstances engulfing him. His trust in God has taken a massive battering and he believes that God has withdrawn from Israel. But by the end of the book, his tone has completely changed. He is no longer controlled or even anxious about his circumstances, and his eyes have been lifted upwards to a new found faith and trust in God. At the centre of this change in attitude stands a clear message:

Habakkuk 2:4   **...but the righteous will live by his faith...**

The apostle Paul took this statement and made it the heart of the Gospel: that the righteousness of God cannot be gained by what we do, but only by faith in Jesus[31]. The Gospel message regarding why we should place our faith and trust in Jesus is because He is the answer to all our needs and our hope for the future. The reason why Habakkuk is relevant today is because he reminds us that it is okay to ask the question, 'Why?' Through his book, the Bible invites us to present our difficult questions to God and to look to Him for an explanation for what is happening in our lives. Despite the strife that was going on around him, Habakkuk was able to find answers to his questions, and his faith and trust in God was renewed.

Habakkuk 3:19   **The Sovereign Lord is my strength; He makes my feet like the feet of a deer, He enables me to go on the heights.**

To obtain answers to their life situations, Habakkuk along with others in the Bible, asked searching questions of God. Many of these were centred on their need to receive assurance that He was up to the task of rescuing them and turning their crisis around. Habakkuk's closing words demonstrate that he did indeed receive reassurance from God.

Reasons to place our faith and trust in God

The world of the twenty-first century is an increasingly unstable place and beset by one crisis after another. To know where we are pinning our hopes, it is important to understand some key aspects of God's character. In his second letter[32], Peter encouraged the early church to grow in the grace and knowledge of Jesus Christ, and the call for us to do the same today is as important as it ever was.

Hebrews 12:2 **Let us fix our eyes on Jesus, the author and perfecter of our faith...**

The remaining parts of this chapter examine some important characteristics of God and offer reasons for why we, like Habakkuk, should place our faith and trust in God for all of our needs, including our jobs.

1) Increasing our knowledge of God: He is unchangeable

At first glance the fact that God is unchangeable may not seem that important. However, if we consider the alternative that He could change, the importance of this becomes clear. If He could improve then it would mean that God could become better than He was, and was not the best possible God when we first placed our trust in Him. On the other hand, if He could change for the worse then what sort of God would He become? If He could become a little bit evil, then why not mostly evil? How could we place our faith and trust in a God who could change in even the smallest way? Furthermore, if God's character could change, what about His promises? How could we trust Him for eternal life and our life's needs such as providing jobs?

This untenable situation could never arise as the Bible categorically states[33] that everything about God is unchangeable, and without this assurance the foundations of our faith begin to fall apart. This is because our faith and hope in God depend on a person who is completely worthy of trust; and He, His purposes and His promises are absolutely and eternally unchangeable. These are the firm foundations that Jesus spoke about in His parable of the wise and foolish builders[34]. The fact that God cannot change provides a solid platform upon which we can build our faith and trust in Him.

2) *Increasing our knowledge of God: He is omniscient (all-knowing)*

God will never be in the position of buying a flat-pack piece of furniture and resorting to the familiar formula: 'when all else fails follow the instructions'! The Bible says that God knows everything[35] and is also perfect in knowledge[36]. In his letter to the Romans, Paul writes eloquently about God's amazing wisdom and knowledge.

Romans 11:33 **Oh, the depth of the riches of the wisdom and knowledge of God!...**

In the Book of Isaiah[37], God asks if there is anyone like Him, and the answer is a resounding 'No'. God existed before creation and nothing at all is hidden from Him; He is fully aware of everything. If He wanted to let us know the number of grains of sand on every beach or the astonishing number of stars and galaxies, then He would be able to tell us instantly. He does not need time to ponder an answer because He has it fully present in his consciousness; what He knows He never forgets. Paul in his first letter to the Corinthians[38] says that the Spirit of God searches everything, even the depths of God Himself. Not only does He know Himself completely, but He also knows and understands each one of us inside out. Jesus said[39] that God knows everything we need even before we ask, as well as the smallest details of our lives.

Part of the problem that I experienced with my own career was confusion over what I wanted to do. God always knew what this was and, after many years walking with Him, He was able to share the knowledge of His plan for my life. In God we have a person who has complete knowledge not only of His plans for us, but also of ourselves, including our needs and desires.

3) *Increasing our knowledge of God: He has infinite wisdom*

Wisdom refers to what God does with the knowledge He has – the strategies He uses to achieve His goals. Whatever He does, it will always be wise. In Romans[40] He is called by Paul 'the only wise God', Isaiah says[41] that God is 'wonderful in counsel and magnificent in wisdom', and the Psalmist[42] praises God for His wisdom in making all creatures. The wisdom of God is also demonstrated in His great plan of salvation. In his first letter to the Corinthians[43], Paul says that Christ is 'the wisdom of God' to those who are called, but for those who reject the cross God's plan appears as 'foolishness'. God's wisdom is also demonstrated in our own lives where He will use anything, even our own mistakes and disobedience, to bring about good.

Romans 8:28

And we know that in all things God works for the good of those who love Him, who have been called according to His purpose.

In this verse Paul is assuring us that God exercises wisdom in every part of our lives, and through all of these things He is transforming us into the image of Christ. During the time spent in the wilderness, this should give us confidence and peace that God allows all things, including unemployment or past mistakes, to move us on to His ultimate goal to be more like Christ.

The Bible tells us[44] that we can also ask God to give us His wisdom for when we need it, and this is gained mainly through reading the word of God. Wisdom is a valuable commodity when making career decisions. For example, many of us will be faced by complex issues such as: a decision to return to college to gain a new qualification, the correct time to return to work after an illness or raising children, or the right time to make a career move in a new direction. Jesus promised[45] that the Holy Spirit would bring instruction for our lives in such situations. Even when we do not understand what God is doing, it pleases Him when we display faith and trust in His infinite wisdom.

4) *Increasing our knowledge of God: He is entirely truthful and trustworthy*

Another reason why it is good to place our trust in God is because the Bible tells us that everything about Him is based on absolute truth. His truthfulness means that everything about Him, including His knowledge and words, is true. It is reassuring to know that the God we hope in is completely reliable and true to His word. We are also told that God is the true God, as opposed to other 'gods' which are just idols that will not last. We might ask who sets the definition of truth, and who decides what is meant by a true God? The Bible states clearly that since we have been created by Him there is no way we ourselves can define who God is; only He can say what the true God is like. But because He has built us in His own image[46], He has given us the ability to recognise Him as the one true God.

Because He is the one true God it also follows that all His words are true, which means that the Word of God found in the Bible is entirely trustworthy. In terms of His promises, this means that God always does what He promises to do and we can depend on Him to never fail or be unfaithful[47]. In fact the Bible tells us that not only are God's words true, but that they are *truth* themselves – the ultimate definition of truth itself. This enabled Jesus to say to His Father[48], 'Your word is truth.' Because of this, God's word will always be founded on perfect knowledge.

In a world where truth is an ever-changing concept, it may come with some relief to know that we can utterly depend on the reliability of the promises found in His word. In fact the essence of trust and faith in God is the ability to take God at His word without any physical evidence, and to rely on Him to do what He has promised. This idea readily translates to our job situations. Despite rejections of applications or the weakness of our employment history, our hope for improved prospects for work is founded on the trustworthiness and reliability of God's word.

5) *Increasing our knowledge of God: He is entirely loving and good*

One of God's most amazing attributes is the incredible love that He has shown to humanity; His desire is to bring goodness into our lives. God is the ultimate standard of goodness and the one most worthy of approval. Jesus tells us[49] that no one is good apart from God. In one of his psalms[50], David encourages us to 'Taste and see that the Lord is good'! Similar to the word of God actually *being* truth, John says[51] that God actually *is* love – a perfect love that existed even before the earth was formed. This self-giving love characterises God's relationship to us. In his letter to the church in Rome[52], Paul describes how it is always God who makes the first move in restoring the relationship between Him and us. It was God's exuberant love that caused Him to give His only son, Jesus, to die on a cross so that believers would have eternal life. It should bring us great joy to know that it is the purpose of God to bring us true happiness not just for now but for all eternity. It is this kind of love that Christians are expected to show to those around them[53].

In the Book of Hosea we read of a people who needed to hear about the love of God. The problem with the nation of Israel at this point in their history was that they were deaf to God's word. To get around this, God used a novel method to force His people to understand the extent of His love for them. Hosea was chosen to be a living sermon to God's people, and the way he did this was to marry a woman who would later be unfaithful to him. The woman's unfaithfulness in her marriage to Hosea reflected the state of affairs that existed between Israel and God – the people of Israel had become unfaithful and begun to worship other gods. They had also begun to think of love as something that could be purchased for self-gratification. They had lost sight of the fact that good things flowed out of a right relationship with God, and had begun to concentrate solely on the pursuit of gain. Despite all of this, God's deep love for His people persisted with a longing to draw them back to Him.

Hosea 11:8   **'How can I give you up Ephraim? How can I hand you over, Israel?…all my compassion is aroused.'**

Because of His great love for us and the fact that He is the source of all good, God becomes the ultimate good that we seek. The Bible tells us that we should always seek His goodness first. God knows about the things we need, such as a new job, and these will be given to us once we have placed God first in our lives. The Psalmist[54] tells us that God does not hold back on giving good things to those who are in close relationship with Him. On a number of occasions[55], Jesus tells His disciples that if they ask God for anything in His name then it will be given. However, this invitation to His followers was always given in the context of their being in a close relationship with God. Out of the love of God in our hearts, we will naturally seek after the good things of God for our lives.

Romans 8:28

And we know that in all things God works for the good of those who love Him, who have been called according to His purpose.

Paul assures us that when we love God, goodness can come out of the most unlikely periods in our lives. It is good to know that despite the many different reasons that have caused us to be in our current wilderness God is, nevertheless, using it for our good. Whether God has introduced this lean season or we are here as a result of our own mistakes, He wants to remind us today that in *all* things He works for the good of those who love Him. Not all of us are called to high powered or high salaried jobs. However, all of us are called to receive God's joy, which will come when we fix His love in our lives. It may surprise us to discover how many good things God has in store regarding our job situation.

6) *Increasing our knowledge of God: He is an awesome God*

Someone once said that our expectation of what God can deliver in our lives is controlled by our *perception* of who He is. If our idea of God is limited to a cartoon character wearing a beard and sitting on a cloud, then it follows that our expectation of what He can do through His word will be similarly small and limited. However, if our perception of God is immeasurably massive and powerful, as described in Isaiah[56], then it will follow that our expectation of what God can do in our lives, including our job situation, will also be immeasurable.

| Isaiah 40:25 | **'To whom will you compare me? Or who is my equal?' says the Holy One.** |

We read in Hebrews[57] that scripture is not merely a collection of pleasant-sounding words that give comfort in times of trouble, like a collection of poems, but is actually a living thing that is able to turn our lives around. Scripture, the word of God, is without doubt the most powerful force in the universe and it is responsible for the creation of everything that we see, and don't see, around us.

Current thinking in the field of astrophysics is that visible matter – that which can be seen such as stars and planets, makes up as little as 4% of the universe. The remainder consists of a mysterious substance called dark matter together with dark energy. The Word of God created everything from dark matter and sub-atomic particles to you and me. The Word of God also created the countless stars and galaxies that are so distant from the Earth that their light has yet to reach us. We can experience a measure of the awesome power and majesty of God by viewing some breathtaking pictures of the universe on the Hubble Telescope website[58].

Yet, even more amazing, than creation itself, is the knowledge that this same God, the Creator, became a tiny unborn child to an unwedded, teenage mother. This baby would eventually die a shameful death to bring us back into a relationship with God.

| Matthew 19:26 | **Jesus looked at them and said, 'With man this is impossible, but with God all things are possible.'** |

God, the God of the impossible, is saying to our job situation today: allow me to come in – nothing is too difficult for me to transform!

Review of chapter

The world today is an unstable place and in this environment our faith and trust in God can take a real battering. However, God wants us to be well-practised in faith and trust, and the Bible tells us that it is upon these that our future through eternity will be determined. God wants us to get to know Him to the point where we have absolutely no hesitation about trusting Him completely, not only for eternity, but for all our needs. However, the simple fact is that it can be difficult to place our complete faith and trust in God, especially with important areas in our lives such as employment. At the time that Habakkuk lived, Israel was lurching from one disaster to another. The reason why this book is relevant today is because it encourages us to ask why we should place our faith in God and trust in His salvation.

Peter encouraged the early church to grow in the grace and the knowledge of Jesus Christ. It is equally important for us living in the twenty-first century to increase our knowledge of who Jesus is in God, because it will help us to understand exactly who it is we are pinning our hopes on. The reasons why we should place our faith and trust in God include: He is unchangeable; He is omniscient; He has infinite wisdom; He is entirely truthful and trustworthy; He is entirely loving and good; and He is an awesome God.

The following worksheet will enable you to address some of the issues that have been raised in this chapter. The exercise can be carried out on your own or alongside a prayer partner. Take time to consider each question as honestly as possible, and record your responses on a separate sheet.

Exercise 5

Deepening Our Faith and Trust in God

Our present world is an increasingly unstable place, and in this climate it can be difficult to place our faith and trust completely in God. However, God wants us to get to know Him to the point where we have absolutely no hesitation about trusting Him completely for all our needs. So that we know who exactly we are placing our faith in, the Bible encourages us to grow in the grace and knowledge of Jesus Christ.

For Prayer & Reflection

The following verses, some of which were used in the chapter, have been chosen to help you to focus on your own circumstances. Take some time to reflect on your situation through the questions that follow these verses.

Hebrews 11:1	**Now faith is being sure of what we hope for and certain of what we do not see.**
Hebrews 12:2	**Let us fix our eyes on Jesus, the author and perfecter of our faith...**
Psalm 57:10	**For great is your love, reaching to the heavens; your faithfulness reaches to the skies.**
Hebrews 10:23	**Let us hold unswervingly to the hope we profess, for He who promised is faithful.**

If you find it difficult to place your trust in God, it can be constructive to 'dig around' and try to get to the bottom of this issue. Is your difficulty based on:

- **A bad experience where you felt you were let down by God?**

- **A bad experience where you felt you were let down by a parent or a close friend?**

- **Your feeling that God is not sufficiently interested in your life?**

- **Your preference to be in complete control of your life?**

On your own or with a prayer partner, write down what you think God is telling you about your levels of faith and trust in Him. What is He teaching you during this season?

Reflect prayerfully on your own or with a prayer partner, on the following truths about God that were looked at in the chapter. In particular, consider whether any of these facts about God alter the way you are able to place your trust in Him:

- **God is unchangeable**

- **God is omniscient / all knowing**

- **God has infinite wisdom**

- **God is entirely truthful and trustworthy**

- **God is entirely loving and good**

- **God is an awesome God. Further amazing facts about God's creation:**

☞ **A single glass of water contains more atoms than there are cups of water in all the oceans.**

☞ **Light travels at 186,000 miles per second or, put another way, 670 million miles per hour. Our own galaxy, the Milky Way, is an average-sized spiral galaxy, but light still takes 200,000 years to travel from one side to the other.**

Dreams and Plans

_____

_____

_____

_____

_____

_____

_____

_____

_____

_____

_____

_____

_____

Chapter 6

Developing a Godly Character

This is the last of the five chapters that look in detail at some of the areas in our lives where God wants to bring about growth and change. In this final part, we shall examine how He could be using our present career wilderness to develop in us a more God-like character.

Every Christmas, a company I once worked for gave its employees a £25 supermarket voucher, which I always used to buy a fine bottle of Scottish Malt Whisky. There is something very satisfying about sitting in front of a fire at home sipping a fine malt out of a crystal tumbler. Though I'm not a whisky expert, I made the mistake recently of accepting a wee dram of a very expensive vintage. It was as smooth as velvet and had a delicious smoky taste that left me feeling that my old Christmas treat was like vinegar by comparison. Over a period of thirty years, this classic whisky had matured and slowly acquired the subtle tastes of its oak cask, and the reason why such value is placed on vintage malts is that it is not possible to rush this process. If the maturing process could have been speeded up, someone would already have found a way to do it. All that the distilleries can do is place the casks in a cool place and wait for time to create the character that sets a vintage apart from younger and inferior malts.

Why are we talking about whisky and what has this got to do with what may be happening to us during our career wilderness? Just as the vintage malt was left to mature and acquire great quality, God can use time and circumstances (though hopefully not thirty years) to mature and develop our character to be more Christ-like. Even though God uses our entire lifetime to mould us, He can use specific seasons to speed up this process. Could God be using our present career wilderness to create in us a more Godlike character?

A Christ-like character helps us to walk in step with the Holy Spirit

What is character? One dictionary[59] defines character as follows: a description of a person's attributes, traits or abilities. Another way of putting this is: how you behave when nobody is looking! God is overwhelmingly interested in our individual character, and Paul[60] urged the early church in Corinth to be as Christ-like as possible in all they did.

1 Corinthians 11:1   **Follow my example, as I follow the example of Christ.**

One of the clear messages from the New Testament is that a Christian should continually try to imitate Christ in all that they do. Paul, in his letters, frequently lifts Jesus up as the role model we should base our character upon. He gives specific examples where we should follow Jesus in the way we conduct ourselves: how we should welcome people[61], how husbands should treat their wives[62] and how we should forgive everyone[63] at all times.

The church in Galatia had a serious problem with destructive relationships. In his letter to that church, Paul warned that if they continued to hold on to sinful practices such as sexual promiscuity and drunkenness, it would prevent them from moving in the power of the Holy Spirit.[64] Paul went on to list[65] the fruit of the Holy Spirit which, if embraced, would enable them to be guided by God. His warning to the Galatians was clear: if they wanted to keep in step with the Holy Spirit, they would have to lead more Christ-like lives.

It follows that if we are praying for the Holy Spirit to guide us in our job situation, then it is important that we allow this to happen by continually reviewing our own character. Where necessary, we should seek God and ask Him what part of us needs changing.

A Christ-like character increases our hope of salvation

The Bible also tells us that we can become more Christ-like during periods of suffering. Peter told the early church[66] to endure suffering with patience because 'Christ suffered for you', leaving us all an example to follow. Today, this is not a popular way of thinking because many people interpret any type of discomfort as evidence that something has gone wrong or that God has abandoned them. However, Paul reminds us that God can use suffering greatly to our benefit.

Romans 5:3–4   **...because we know that suffering produces perseverance; perseverance, character; and character, hope. And hope does not disappoint us...**

The world in which Paul wrote his letter to the Romans was, in many ways, similar to our own. Although technology has advanced considerably over the last two thousand years, the Christian walk is still confronted by struggles and difficulties today. Far from threatening our faith, Paul assures us that these sufferings, which could include persecution or even long-term unemployment, should actually reinforce in us our great hope of salvation.

The order of the words in this scripture is important; each word is a consequence of the one before. Suffering, we are told, is used by God to produce perseverance – the ability to endure; this in turn produces character – the inner strength developed by testing; this, finally, leads to hope. A Christian persevering during a testing ordeal could be likened to a sword that is heated in a furnace. During this process the sword is tempered and becomes a weapon of strength with all of its impurities and weaknesses removed. Replace 'sword' with 'Christian' and we have Paul's message.

James' letter in the New Testament also explains the important role that perseverance has to play in the development of our character[67]. The people who he was writing to knew their scripture well. They would be fully aware of the story of Abraham, who was rewarded after his time of testing, and also of Job, who provides an outstanding example of endurance. James says that when the believer perseveres during a period of testing they become 'mature and complete, not lacking anything', similar to a tempered sword. The Greek word for 'mature' is often translated as 'perfect'. This is what Jesus was referring to when He called for His followers to be perfect (in character) as their heavenly Father[68]. It is by persevering through our difficult situations that God makes us more mature in Christ.

'I feel that the Bishop still has a few rough edges left to him.'

Although trials in our lives are by their nature unpleasant, James encourages believers to rejoice. This is not because we should actually enjoy the experience of the trial itself, but because we should have a perspective that looks beyond the present trial to the hope that lies ahead. This enabled Paul to say that perseverance leads to character that is able to contain hope. The hope that Paul was referring to is the unchangeable foundation of God's love for His people in Christ. Peter refers[69] to a living hope achieved through faith in the resurrected Jesus – a hope and an inheritance that can never fade or be destroyed.

Our God-like character can be compared to a container for holding liquid, the larger the container, the more it is able to hold. Similarly, the more Christ-like our character, the more hope it will contain for the guarantee of our salvation. How can this be applied to our current career wilderness? We can perhaps begin to recognise that God may be using our present testing situation to increase our perseverance in order to build character that not only pleases God, but also deepens our conviction of our own salvation.

A Christ-like character helps us to be fruitful in all we do

Another consequence of our character becoming more Christ-like is that we become more fruitful in what we do. In his second letter, Peter tells us that we have everything we need to live Godly lives, and that this means that believers in Jesus have at their fingertips the indispensable power of God to carry out whatever He asks them to do[70]. Peter suggests that the way we operate in this power is for us to make every effort to become more like Christ Himself.

2 Peter 1:5–8	**For this very reason, make every effort to add to your faith goodness; and to goodness, knowledge; and to knowledge, self-control; and to self-control, perseverance; and to perseverance, godliness; and to godliness, brotherly kindness; and to brotherly kindness, love.**
	For if you possess these qualities in increasing measure, they will keep you from being ineffective and unproductive, in your knowledge of our Lord Jesus Christ.

Peter provides steps in the process of our developing more Christ-like character, as follows:

- **Faith –** we must be able to express our faith by acting on it.
- **Goodness –** this emerges when we express our faith in action.
- **Knowledge –** when we do good things that arise from our faith, the outcome will be a deepened understanding of God.
- **Self-Control –** from our knowledge of God we will gain a better understanding of ourselves and how to practise self-control.
- **Perseverance –** self-control leads to perseverance.
- **Godliness –** we are better able to persevere when we motivate ourselves with the thought that we shall 'participate in the divine nature'.
- **Brotherly kindness –** this new attitude will lead us to be kinder and more loving to those around us.
- **Love –** all this leads to us loving God more.

This scripture offers two completely different choices. On the one hand, we can shape our character with these qualities and become not just more fruitful in what we do, but also become drawn into a deepening relationship with God. On the other hand, we can resist any change towards letting ourselves become more Christ-like. Peter calls such people short-sighted and blind; short-sighted because they have forgotten the lives that they have been delivered from, and blind because they fail to see the awesome promises that await them in Jesus Christ.

The fact that Peter uses the phrase 'make every effort' in the process of acquiring these qualities, highlights the fact that a great deal of effort can be required. Could God be using our present wilderness as a time for us to develop these Christ-like qualities so that we become more fruitful in our walk with Him? Is God using this season for us to review our character so that we are able to take on the tasks that He has set us? Is God using this season to develop the gifts and talents that He has placed within us? Our character can either prevent or enable us to walk according to God's plan.

Review of Chapter

Even though God uses our whole lifetime to change us, He can use specific seasons to speed up this process. He can use time and circumstances to develop our character to be more Christ-like. Paul tells us that if we allow the fruit of the Holy Spirit into our lives, we will find it easier to be guided by God. If we are praying for the Holy Spirit to guide us in our job situation then it is important that we allow this to happen by continually reviewing our own character.

The Bible also tells us that we can become more Christ-like during periods of suffering. Far from threatening our faith, Paul assures us that these sufferings should actually reinforce in us our hope of salvation. James explains the important role that perseverance, during a time of hardship, has to play in the development of our character. He explains that when a believer perseveres during a period of testing, they become 'mature and complete, not lacking anything'. Paul says that the more our character is Christ-like, the more hope it will contain for the guarantee of our salvation.

Lastly, another effect of our character becoming more Christ-like is that we also become more fruitful in what we do. Peter suggests that the way we operate in God's promises and in His divine power is by making every effort to become more like Christ Himself. What is God saying to us today regarding our character, and how we can allow Him to move more easily in our lives?

The following worksheet will enable you to address some of the issues that have been raised in this chapter. The exercise can be carried out on your own or alongside a prayer partner. Take time to consider each question as honestly as possible, and record your responses on a separate sheet.

Exercise 6
Developing a Godly Character

God is intensely interested in our character because it will determine how much we are able to move according to His will. The more Christ-like our character, the more in tune we will be with the Holy Spirit, and the more He will speak to us about different areas in our lives such as our jobs and careers.

For Prayer & Reflection

The following verses, which were used in the chapter, have been chosen to help you to focus on your own circumstances. Take some time to reflect on your situation through the questions that follow these verses.

1 Corinthians 11:1

Follow my example, as I follow the example of Christ.

Romans 5:3–4

...because we know that suffering produces perseverance; perseverance, character; and character, hope. And hope does not disappoint us...

2 Peter 1:5–8

For this very reason, make every effort to add to your faith goodness; and to goodness, knowledge; and to knowledge, self-control; and to self-control, perseverance; and to perseverance, godliness; and to godliness, brotherly kindness; and to brotherly kindness, love. For if you possess these qualities, in increasing measure, they will keep you from being ineffective and unproductive in your knowledge of our Lord Jesus Christ.

- Are there parts of your character which you feel you could change that would allow you to hear more clearly from God about your job situation?

- Could God be using your present situation to increase your perseverance in your walk with God?

- Could God be using your present wilderness as a time to develop in you more Christ-like qualities so that you become more fruitful and able to take on the tasks that He has set for you?

- Can you think of someone that you know whose character inspires you? Can you identify what it is about that person that makes you stop and take note?

- On your own or with a prayer partner, ask God's forgiveness for any part of your character that falls short. Invite the Holy Spirit to help you to become more Christ-like in this area of your life.

Dreams and Plans

_____

_____

_____

_____

_____

_____

_____

_____

_____

_____

_____

_____

_____

_____

Chapter 7
Exiting the Wilderness and Planning Ahead

When I was five years old our family went on holiday to Switzerland with some friends. It was in the mid 1970s and my parents were being fairly adventurous in attempting a non-stop car journey of many hundreds of miles across unfamiliar, foreign territory. Why we didn't stop for the night along the way in one of the many picturesque French towns is unclear, but the adults in charge clearly felt that a twenty-six hour trip in the car with young children was the thing to do. To pass away the time I remember counting every line in the corduroy-textured car seat and the number of cigarettes my father managed to smoke. The journey for a five-year old seemed to take a lifetime, and when we eventually arrived in Switzerland I was shocked to see how close it looked to our home in Wales on the map. Surely, I thought, we should have been at least in Africa for all the time it took us! I wonder if that is how the Israelites felt after wandering around in the wilderness for forty years!

Taking a mature look at where we are

How do we feel at the moment after spending time in our wilderness? Do we feel that we should be further along in our career than where we are now, or that certain frustrations about our job situation have yet to be resolved? During my time working as a careers adviser, I found that such feelings were shared by many people, so these experiences are not, in any way, unusual. However, as we have seen, God is in the business of not only bringing us to our destination but also transforming us along the way. In a similar way to my friend who complained to God that his career felt like a long wait on a station platform, we can often be tempted to look at where we are on the 'map'. The map I am referring to is the one which shows the distance we have yet to travel to reach our career goal. My own experience of doing this has frequently led to disappointment. I not only carried out regular map-reviewing exercises, but I also fell into the common trap of comparing my progress against a sibling – my older and very successful brother. I eventually learnt that a more mature way to look at my own career progression was to ask the question: what sort of person am I now for having been through this wilderness experience?

If Paul could forget his past, which included leading an early reign of persecution against the church, and completely embrace the salvation of Jesus in his life, then there is no reason why we cannot do something similar ourselves. Whatever changes God has been introducing into our lives during our wilderness season, Paul's advice is to adopt a mature attitude and to press on wholeheartedly in our relationship with God and the pursuit of all that He has prepared for us.

Philippians 3:15   **All of us who are mature should take such a view of things. And if on some point you think differently, that too God will make clear to you.**

God will move us on when He is satisfied that we have learnt the lessons that He has lined up for us during this season. The amount of joy and relief that we feel upon arriving at a destination will be determined by how much we want to be there in the first place, and also the difficulty of the journey itself. A quick trip to the dentist rarely leads to shouts of jubilation, whilst the arrival at the Swiss campsite made a five year-old boy go wild with excitement and relief! The Hebrews must have felt similar levels of joy when God spoke to Moses about leading His people out of the wilderness.

Deuteronomy 2:1–3   **...For a long time we made our way around the hill country of Seir. Then the Lord said to me, 'You have made your way around this hill country long enough; now turn north.'**

When we are ready, God will lead us out of our wilderness

How much would we like the Lord to say to us in our job wilderness, 'Come, you've spent long enough where you are, it's time to move on.' If we think that God doesn't say that kind of thing, well, He certainly said it to the children of Israel. Knowing Jesus as our Saviour means that we are children of God, and if we allow ourselves to be led by the Holy Spirit then, at the right moment, He will tell us when to leave our wilderness.

God was careful to remind Moses that both he and His people should be careful to follow everything that He had revealed. In fact, the choice facing Israel was clear-cut. On the one hand they could be obedient and follow God's ways, and the 'promised land' with all of God's promises would be theirs. On the other hand, they could continue to be disobedient and refuse to be disciplined, and so remain outside the land flowing with milk and honey.

'My people say that they would prefer a Sat' Nav', thank you.'

These words are still relevant to us today, even if we do not operate under the law of the Old Testament. The writer of the letter to the Hebrews reminds us not to be discouraged[71] when God rebukes and disciplines us, since God does this for our own good. However, He also warns us to let go of everything sinful in our lives and to run with perseverance the race marked out for us. Later in the same scripture we are further warned not to refuse God when He speaks to us. This is similar to the caution given to the Israelites that sets out the conditions for them to be led out of the wilderness.

Deuteronomy 8:6–7

Observe the commands of the Lord your God, walking in His ways and revering Him. For the Lord your God is bringing you into a good land – a land with streams and pools of water, with springs flowing in the valleys and hills…

When God led His people out of Egypt there is no doubt that He knew that the shortest distance between two points is a straight line. However, had God used this route between Egypt and the 'promised land', it would have taken His people through the land of the Philistines, where they would inevitably have encountered hostility. God knew that His people were not ready for this, so instead of leading them along the more direct but dangerous route, God chose the longer, safer way through the Wilderness. Even though many of the Israelites complained about the lack of sense in these directions, it made perfect sense to God because He was using the longer journey to prepare His people.

Having complete confidence in God's leading

If we begin to question the path God has chosen for us, just keep in mind that He protects His people as they follow His guidance. In the same way that God gave His constant presence in the wilderness, we can continually experience the Father's presence by inviting the Holy Spirit into our lives. Just as a cloud led the Hebrews in the wilderness during the day and a light during the night, God will speak and guide us through the Holy Spirit. He will direct our career search and tell us when to 'turn north' out of our wilderness.

John 10:27 — **My sheep listen to My voice; I know them, and they follow me.**

Recently I was made redundant from a company where I had been employed for many years. As I walked to my local Jobcentre Plus office to sign on, it dawned on me that God is not without a sense of humour. The office where I was signing on was the same one in which I had worked as a Careers Adviser for three years. Now here I was myself experiencing life from the other side! At the first interview I was handed a job diary which I would have to complete and present to the Jobcentre every fortnight. The diary would allow them to see the plans that I was making to get me back to work, and there were a number of columns to record actions that I had completed, such as sending off CVs and job application forms.

As I looked at the job diary it occurred to me that there should be an additional column simply entitled: God's lead. It's important, of course, for us to have our own plans, but the Bible says that, despite these plans, it is the Lord who determines our steps[72]. It is far better to find out directly from God what His plans are for our life or our next job. Could God have been using our last wilderness experience for the express purpose of developing our levels of faith in order to encourage us to find out His plans? This has certainly my experience. When faced with having to make plans for our next job, there is no better place to start than going to God, and if we do this as genuinely and honestly as possible, He will always respond.

God's track record in guiding His people

Before we take a look at how we should approach God, let us take a quick look at His track record (not a definitive list) in guiding His people:

Abraham – God led him from his homeland to the land of Canaan with the promise that He would make him into a great nation, as numerous as the stars. Even though this seemed improbable due to his and his wife Sarah's ages (both aged around one hundred), we can clearly see today that God's promise to Abraham has been kept. We are told[73] that Abraham obeyed God and went, even though he didn't understand all the details. He trusted God's guidance and was rewarded for his faithfulness.

David – One of the most inspiring men in the Bible, not because he was perfect, but because of the huge zeal and love that he had for God. David constantly sought God's guidance for all parts of his life, and many of his Psalms encourage us to do the same.

Psalm 25:4–5

Show me your ways O Lord,
teach me your paths;
guide me in your truth and teach me,
for you are God my Saviour,
and my hope is in you all day long.

David's start in life wasn't highly favoured: he was a shepherd, which was a very low status job, and the youngest of seven sons. Despite this, God not only raised David up to become King of Israel but also the start of a lineage out of which Jesus would be born.

Nehemiah – Whilst the Jews were still in exile in Babylon, Nehemiah repented of his sins and prayed that God would return the nation of Israel to Jerusalem once again. He trusted in God's ability to lead Israel out of exile and back to their 'promised land'. God rewarded this trust by granting him the royal favour of Artaxerxes, King of Persia, and also by providing him with the resources to rebuild the walls of Jerusalem. Despite hostility and repeated attacks, Nehemiah successfully completed rebuilding the walls in only fifty-two days. God's guidance had not only brought His people back into their land, but also back into a close relationship with Him, something that had been lost when they had been taken into exile seventy years earlier.

Paul – He provides one of the most vivid illustrations of someone who continually received guidance from God. His life was dramatically derailed in the famous incident on the Road to Damascus, when Jesus Himself appeared to Paul in a blinding light. From that moment on, his life would never be the same. In his extensive travels to the Gentile world, he was consistently sustained by God, which included Paul receiving divine warnings of attempts on his life and dreams about where he should preach the good news[74]. Paul's mature attitude enabled him to ignore his past and look ahead to everything that God had planned for him.

Have we invited God into our career planning?

What are our plans regarding our own work situation? There are many factors that may have to be taken into consideration when planning our next job:

- **Where will it be based and what are the transport links like?**

- **What is the pay like and is there a company pension?**

- **What are the chances of progression and promotion?**

- **Is it in a stable industry?**

- **Are our skills and qualifications up to the job?**

- **Will there be a crèche?**

- **Are we too young or too old?**

- **What about our disability?**

Attempting to make a realistic career plan that takes into consideration some or all of the above factors can be a confusing and overwhelming process. In my work in the careers service, I used to advise people who were planning a career move to see themselves as being at a crossroads. Instead of there just being the normal average number of three or four choices of direction to choose from, I challenged them to see the potential number of 'turnings' to be many times more. By a process of elimination based on interest, ability, circumstance, personal character and qualifications, we could then realistically examine in which direction they could turn.

The whole process of receiving guidance for our jobs through one-to-one interviews and using careers information resources on topics such as job search techniques can play an important role in finding a new career. However, for those of us who are looking to God for our needs, the question that arises is this: are our career plans also founded on prayer or have we made them without God? The Bible assures us that His guidance is certainly not restricted to people in the Bible, but is equally available for us today.

Proverbs 16:9   **In his heart a man plans his course, but the Lord determines his steps.**

How do we gain this guidance, and how can we be certain that our plans for every aspect of our lives, including our jobs, are being directed by God? The answer to this question is found in the depth of our relationship with God, and this topic will be looked at in detail in the next chapter.

Review of chapter

After spending a period of time in the wilderness we can often feel that we should have made more progress in our careers than we have actually made. From his own experience, Paul tells us that the mature way to view our present position is to ask: what sort of person am I now for having been through this wilderness experience? God will move us on when He determines that we have learnt the lessons that He has for us in this season. The letter to the Hebrews reminds us not to be discouraged when God rebukes and disciplines us for He does this for our own good. However, God also warns us that we should let go of everything sinful in our lives and persevere in what He has given us to do.

The Bible assures us that God's guidance is not restricted to the great heroes of the Bible. In the same way that a cloud led the Hebrews in the wilderness during the day and a light during the night, Jesus will speak to us through the Holy Spirit about the issues in our lives. He will give instruction on our career search and tell us when to 'turn north' to lead us out of our wilderness. However complicated our situation may appear concerning our jobs, there is no better way to start than by going to God. If we do this, He will always respond.

The following worksheet will enable you to address some of the issues that have been raised in this chapter. The exercise can be carried out on your own or alongside a prayer partner. Take time to consider each question as honestly as possible, and record your responses on a separate sheet.

Exercise 7

Exiting the Wilderness and Planning Ahead

Whatever changes God has been introducing into our lives during our wilderness season, Paul's advice to us is to adopt a mature attitude and to press on wholeheartedly in our relationship with God and the pursuit of all that He has prepared for us. God will move us on when He determines that we have learnt the lessons that He has for us in this season.

For Prayer & Reflection

The following verses, some of which were used in the chapter, have been chosen to help you to focus on your own circumstances. Take some time to reflect on your situation through the questions that follow these verses.

Philippians 3:15

All of us who are mature should take such a view of things. And if on some point you think differently, that too God will make clear to you.

Deuteronomy 2:1–3

...For a long time we made our way around the hill country of Seir. Then the Lord said to me, 'You have made your way around this hill country long enough; now turn north.'

Proverbs 16:9

In his heart a man plans his course, but the Lord determines his steps.

John 10:27

My sheep listen to My voice; I know them, and they follow Me.

- Are there areas in your life where, having been able to adopt a mature attitude and forget what is behind you, you have made a change and pressed ahead into the things of God?

- Equally, have there been areas in your life where adopting a mature attitude to change has been difficult to do?

- Are your career plans about your job situation founded on prayer or have you made them without God? Have you invited God into your situation to guide you through some of the complex issues that may stand between you and your return to work?

- How confident do you feel about God's ability to guide you into what He has prepared for your next job?

- On your own or with a prayer partner, invite the Holy Spirit to speak to you about your attitude and your willingness to accept change in your life.

Dreams and Plans

_____

_____

_____

_____

_____

_____

_____

_____

_____

_____

_____

_____

_____

_____

_____

SECTION TWO

Receiving God's Revelation

This section contains nine chapters and examines different ways that God can reveal His will for our lives – in particular for our jobs. We shall discover that He not only communicates with us through the Bible and the Holy Spirit, but equally through the more day-to-day parts of our lives such as our abilities and personality, our deeply held desires and the advice that we receive from other people. So that we remain open to receive this revelation, we shall also look at factors that can prevent us from walking fully according to His will.

Because we all carry L-plates when it comes to hearing from God, there is an important rule that we must all observe. Before we take any action on what we believe we are hearing, it is essential for us to receive confirmation from a number of different sources. When God asks us to do something, He will confirm this by giving us more than just one source to affirm His will. For example, if we feel that He is asking us to move into a specific job, this could be confirmed by a keen desire that is backed up by a natural ability, favourable circumstances facilitating a decision, and then possibly reinforced by prophetic insight. All of these factors will be looked at in this section.

When we are seeking God to receive His instruction, the Bible tells us that we must show discernment.

1 John 4:1 **Dear friends, do not believe every spirit, but test the spirits to see whether they are from God, because many false prophets have gone out into the world.**

There are, unfortunately, people who do not display such wisdom and do not wait to seek confirmation that God is indeed asking them to do something. I recall one such case where someone left his established job to start up life in another part of the world, but only for him to return one year later with his plans in tatters. When asked about how sure he had been that he had heard from God in the first place, it transpired that he had made this big decision solely on the basis of receiving a single prophecy. Instead of seeking confirmation from other sources to make sure that he was really hearing from God, he ended up making a wrong move.

If we do mishear from God, then He promises to bring us back on track. However, if we are serious about receiving His revelation, then we should always make sure that we have obtained confirmation from as many sources as possible before we make any big decision.

This section concludes with a worksheet that draws on the material covered in the following chapters. The exercise is designed to help us review the sources of confirmation that we have received from God concerning our choice of job.

Chapter 8
Seeking God's Face and His will for our Lives

The previous chapter left us with the question of how we can gain guidance and revelation from God concerning our lives and jobs. I am convinced that the answer to this question is to be found in the depth of our relationship with God. In his letter to the Roman colony at Philippi, Paul explained[75] the value that he placed on having Jesus in His life, saying that he considered everything else was like rubbish compared to the 'surpassing greatness' of knowing Him. Jesus tells us[76] that one of the works of the Holy Spirit is to bring glory to Him. The Holy Spirit does this is by bringing people into a new relationship with Jesus and also by encouraging believers to deepen their relationship with Him. Today, the Holy Spirit continues to call us all to pursue God and into a place of increased intimacy with Him. Out of this deepening relationship with God will flow many blessings that will impact our lives, including guidance in our careers. Carol Arnott, who co-pastors the Toronto Airport Church, said:

'God is raising up a people today who hunger and thirst for Him, a generation raised up by the Holy Spirit to reveal the glory of the Lord in these end times. These are the ones who know the times and seasons of God and sense the urgency of the hour.'[77]

Most of us who are experiencing or have experienced a wilderness period in our job situation would do anything to know the times and seasons that God has set for our lives. The good news is that God would like nothing better than to have a nonstop discourse about what He has planned. However, there is also our side of the bargain: we have to draw close to Him and turn towards His face. In Exodus[78] we are told that the Lord spoke to Moses face to face 'as a man speaks with his friend'. At this time Moses had a unique relationship with God that allowed him to speak directly with God and then to pass on His instructions to the children of Israel. In Jesus, we have even closer access to the Lord through the Holy Spirit who lives inside every believer.

| Romans 8:11 | **And if the Spirit of Him who raised Jesus from the dead is living in you, He who raised Christ from the dead will also give life to your mortal bodies through His Spirit, who lives in you.** |

In Moses' day the Spirit of God could only be found in the Holy Sanctuary and could only be approached by anointed priests. Today, all those who have accepted Jesus into their lives have the same Spirit living in them. Jesus said[79] that the Holy Spirit would guide us into all truth, and God's promise is that He will speak to us with instruction for our lives. Whatever experience we have had of turning to God, He invites us to turn to Him now to hear what He has to say about every aspect of our lives including our jobs.

| Ephesians 1:11 | **It's in Christ that we find out who we are and what we are living for. (*The Message*)** |

It used to be said that the Sun would never set on the British Empire. Those days may be long gone, but in 2004 NASA spacecraft Smart-1 discovered a place where the Sun shines all the time, and it's on the Moon[80]. The Peak of Eternal Light is a mountain at the lunar South Pole that is always in view of the Sun. Its year-round temperature is, by lunar standards, a comparatively mild $-20C$, making it a possible base for future exploration. It is possible that God created the Peak of Eternal Light on the surface of the Moon for the express purpose of giving us a wonderful image of how God's people should be living their lives – with their faces turned continually towards God.

As believers in Jesus Christ, it is good to practise the discipline of finding out what God has to say regarding the issues in our lives. He can communicate in whatever way He chooses, but His word says that He blesses those who are seeking His face and walking close to Him.

Psalm 24:5–6

He will receive blessing from the Lord
and vindication from God His Saviour.
Such is the generation of those who seek Him,
who seek your face, O God of Jacob.

Seek God's face and He'll show you who you are; get into His word and He'll reveal your identity and calling!

What does it mean to seek God's face?

In the Hebrew language, the words for 'favour' and 'face' are from the same root. This can be seen in Psalm 119 where some translations read, 'I have sought your face' and others, 'I have sought your favour.'

Psalm 119:58

I have sought your face with all my heart;
be gracious to me according to your promise.

In many parts of the world during Old Testament times, if you wanted to make a petition to your king there was a formal and ritualised process that you would have to go through. When you reached the king's throne, you would have to literally seek the face of the king. If the king never looked at you it meant that he did *not* agree to your request, and you would be turned away to face your unresolved problems. However, if the king looked at you, even before you spoke, you would have known that you had gained His favour and that your request would be granted.

Picture yourself three thousand years ago as a petitioner wishing to gain favour from your king. As you enter the palace grounds, a pompous and arrogant official tells you to join a long line of petitioners who are shuffling slowly forward towards a desk at the far end of a room. A whole day goes by whilst you wait in line; then, without apology, you are told that the king won't be seeing any more petitioners that day. He has gone hunting, and you should return in two days' time. You return as requested and start queuing before the sun rises. The court officials eventually enter the hall and the queue slowly shuffles forward again. The heat in the hall is stifling and you kick yourself for not having brought sufficient water or food to keep you going. At last, just before evening, you reach the front of the queue and an officious clerk demands to know the nature of your petition to the king. Your request might have related to a dispute over land with a neighbour or maybe to gain a licence to sell and export something from his kingdom. The clerk scribbles away on a parchment and looks up at you with a blank expression as if waiting for something. You suddenly understand the clerk's unspoken request: he is waiting for a bribe. Unless you pay him a sum of money, your request will never make it past this point. You look in your purse and reluctantly hand over the last of the money that you had set aside to pay for your family's return journey home. To gain the favour of the king, what choice do you have but to pay the bribe?

The next day at the palace gate you show the parchment given to you by the clerk, and you are directed to a waiting room with dozens of other people all wanting to petition the king. Hours go by as you wait in the queue. Again, you wait all day in the oppressive heat, but at last your name is called and you are ushered into the king's audience chamber. As you approach the king's throne you are aware that he would

'I hear the price of Chaldean pears has gone up again.'

103

already have been advised on the nature of your request. You are surprised at the large number of well-dressed people standing around in the hall, all looking towards the king and laughing and clapping sycophantically whenever he makes a comment. You are led by a court official towards the king's dais, where you are halted by a low, golden barrier encrusted in gemstones. You kneel before the king, as instructed, and then you look up at his face, which is turned to an official standing to one side. Dread fills your heart, perspiration dampens your brow and your hands cannot help trembling. Suddenly, you feel a court official pulling on your elbow, directing you to leave. You retreat from the throne, walking backwards and bowing as you go. You want to shout and protest that you haven't been given enough time, but you know that would be futile. Disconsolate, you are led out of the hall – the king hadn't even noticed you were there, and you know that your request has been denied.

C.S. Lewis once arrived late to a university debate on Christianity, and when he entered the room it was clear that a heated argument had taken place. The local vicar beckoned him over to the table and informed him that they had been trying to decide what made Christianity unique amongst all religions. Factors such as charitable works, prayer, fasting and tithing were proposed as being unique to Christianity, but each one was disproved with an explanation that another religion also possessed these characteristics. When asked for his input C.S. Lewis slowly puffed on his pipe and declared that the answer was obvious. Quickly gaining everyone's attention, he said that the *only* thing that distinguishes Christianity from all other religions is the grace of God given to us through Jesus Christ.

It is this amazing grace that enables us to approach the throne, not of some long-forgotten ancient king, but of God Himself – the King of Kings. And we can do this at any time, day or night. It is a palace that allows us instant access to the King, without danger of encountering corrupt officials or long, exhausting queues. As God's children, the Bible reassures us that when we come to seek His face there will only ever be a positive and loving response from God.

Hebrews 4:16   **Let us then approach the throne of grace with confidence, so that we may receive mercy and find grace to help us in our time of need.**

God wants us to seek His face today because that is where His favour and blessings are to be found.

Numbers 6:22–27

The Lord said to Moses. 'Tell Aaron and his sons. This is how you are to bless the Israelites. Say to them: "The Lord bless you and keep you; the Lord make His face shine upon you and be gracious to you; the Lord turn His face towards you and give you peace." So they will put My name on the Israelites and I will bless them.'

Seeking God's face is not about seeking His blessing such as a new job only for the sake of getting hold of the blessing. It is not a prosperity message, which focuses in an unbalanced way on trying to wring things out of Him. Seeking God's face is about drawing into His awesome presence; it is about loving God more fully, seeking Him with a passion and placing Him first. It is also about having a fuller revelation of who God is and His plans for our lives. Seeking God's face draws us into the very wonder of who He is: an awesome God, but also our Father. The word that Jesus used for Father in the Lord's Prayer[81] is the Aramaic word for daddy – 'Abba' – and Jesus invites us to use the same intimate word to address God. This has profound importance because it shows how closely God wants our relationship with Him to be: like that of a child and his daddy.

The revelation of God is all about uncovering what has already been prepared for us in heaven, and it is revealed to us by the Holy Spirit. The 'what has already been prepared' includes everything in our lives: our 'daily bread', our relationships, our health and also our jobs and careers. God's provision for our needs already exists in heaven. Let's find out how God can reveal this and how we can call it down into our job situation. In the following eight chapters, we shall look at ways in which we can seek God's face and receive His revelation, especially in regards to our job situation. Once we place ourselves before His throne, the Father's blessings will begin to be released into our lives, bringing answers to many of the issues that we face.

Psalm 27:8

My heart says of you, 'Seek His face!'
Your face, Lord, I will seek.

Review of chapter

If we are experiencing a career wilderness, there is good news: God wants nothing more than to share with us what He has planned for our lives. However, there is also our side of the bargain – to hear God, we have to draw close to Him and turn towards His face. He can communicate in whatever fashion He chooses, but His word says that He blesses those who are seeking His face and walking close to Him. When we do this, the Bible assures us that there will only ever be a positive and loving response from God.

Seeking God's face is about drawing into His presence and placing Him first. It is also about having a fuller revelation of who God is and His plans for our lives, including our jobs. God wants us to seek His face today so we can experience His favour and blessing. The many things needed in our lives already exist in heaven, and are waiting to be revealed and called down into our lives.

The following worksheet will enable you to address some of the issues that have been raised in this chapter. The exercise can be carried out on your own or alongside a prayer partner. Take time to consider each question as honestly as possible, and record your responses on a separate sheet.

Exercise 8

Seeking God's Face and His Will for our Lives

Most of us who are experiencing a wilderness period in our job situation would do anything to know the times and seasons that God has set for our lives. The good news is that God wants to have a nonstop discourse with what He has planned for us. However, there is our side of the bargain, we have to draw close to Him and turn ourselves towards His face.

God wants us to seek His face for every part of our lives. When we do this, our knowledge and love for Him will increase and, as a consequence, we will begin to experience blessings flowing in all parts of our lives including our jobs.

For Prayer & Reflection

The following verses, which were used in the chapter, have been chosen to help you to focus on your own circumstances. Take some time to reflect on your situation through the questions that follow these verses.

Psalm 24:5–6

**He will receive blessing from the Lord
and vindication from God His Saviour.
Such is the generation of those who seek Him,
who seek your face, O God of Jacob.**

Psalm 119:58

**I have sought your face with all my heart;
be gracious to me according to your promise.**

Hebrews 4:16

Let us then approach the throne of grace with confidence, so that we may receive mercy and find grace to help us in our time of need.

• How confident are you about your ability to approach God's throne for all your needs?

• If you are reluctant to approach God, is it possible to examine the reasons for this? Could it be due to a lack of confidence in God's ability? Could it be due to a fear that He will condemn you?

• The Bible tells us that we should pray to God about our needs. However, how much of your relationship with Him is just about getting what you want from Him as opposed to deepening your relationship and increasing your understanding of who He is?

• On your own or with a prayer partner, invite the Holy Spirit to help you to gain a deeper understanding of your position before God as a cherished son or daughter.

Dreams and Plans

_____

_____

_____

_____

_____

_____

_____

_____

_____

_____

_____

_____

_____

Chapter 9

The Word of God in our lives

A common way that God can speak to us is though reading His word in the Bible. The Bible says that God's word is like a sword that can be used by us in all of life's battles. In this chapter we shall see how the word of God can not only bring instruction for our lives, but also how it can overcome the many barriers that can hold us back from entering into His plans.

Allowing the word of God to fill our minds

An important way of seeking God's instruction is to read the Bible, and Paul teaches[82] that this is something we should be doing on a regular basis. In his second letter to Timothy[83], Paul says that not only is all scripture inspired by God, but it is also able to give clear guidance for all areas of our lives. When we seek God's face by reading the Bible, we are promised that the Holy Spirit will help us to understand the teachings contained in scripture[84]. We read of this happening after the resurrection on the road to Emmaus[85], when Jesus appeared to two followers.

Luke 24:32

They asked each other, 'Were not our hearts burning within us while He talked with us on the road and opened the scriptures to us?'

In a similar way, when we read the Bible, the Holy Spirit will use scripture to speak to us concerning our own lives. How many of us have read a familiar part of scripture, one that we have previously read a thousand times, only for it to jump out of the page as we suddenly gain a new insight or revelation into its meaning? This is the work of the Holy Spirit operating within us. God's promise regarding our job situations is that as we seek His face by getting into His word, the Holy Spirit will speak to us and give direction. God will give us understanding about what scripture has to say to each one of us personally regarding our careers.

Recent studies in the USA have shown some worrying trends in the amount of television that people watch. These have shown[86] that the average American watches over four and a half hours of television every day. If we add that up it comes to over thirty hours per week or almost six days per month or more than two months per year. One study showed[87] that children aged eight and older spent nearly seven hours each day watching television, surfing the internet or playing video games. The study also revealed that children who consistently spent more than four hours each day doing these sorts of activities were more likely to be overweight. Furthermore, when they watched violence, they were more likely to show aggressive behaviour and also to view the world as a scary place where bad things could happen to them.

There is no doubt that what we allow into our minds has a big affect on the way we think and act. A pastor once spoke about a 'sewer' running down the centre of everyone's living room – referring to the easy access of violence and pornography on our televisions and computers. Jesus said[88] that it is out of our hearts (or minds) that all sorts of evil thoughts and other sins emerge, and if we allow evil things to enter our minds through what we watch on television or the computer, then little good can come out of us. If we are serious about approaching God and finding out what He wants for our job situation, then we have to ensure that we get the right balance of what we allow into our minds. The Bible tells us in a direct way what this balance should be: we should allow as much scripture into our minds as possible[89] - everything else is unimportant. Many people think that far eastern religions discovered meditation, but this is not the case. Nearly three thousand years ago, the psalmists wrote about the good things that come from meditating on God's word.

Psalm 119:15   **I meditate on your precepts and consider your ways.**

To meditate means to engage in thought or to contemplate and reflect. However, there is another meaning attached to the word, which is to accompany this reflection with action. When the Psalmists used the word 'meditation', they meant it not only in the sense of musing over scripture, but also with the intention of acting upon God's word. Consequently, the word meditate is used in a proactive sense as well as in a passive sense.

Accepting God's word into our lives

It is not sufficient to merely read God's word; we must also take an active step and accept the truth contained in scripture. Reading scripture but not accepting its truth is a bit like holding a gun in our hand and not understanding that in order to make it fire we have to pull the trigger. There is a further amazing fact about scripture. All of the promises to God's people in the Bible, including those made to Abraham, David and Peter, apply equally to us. Paul tells us that if we have accepted Jesus into our lives, then *all* of God's promises and revelation are for us today.

2 Corinthians 1:20 **For no matter how many promises God has made, they are 'Yes' in Christ. And so through Him the 'Amen' is spoken by us to the glory of God.**

For the promises found in scripture to become *personal*, we have to accept and receive the following truth: it is through Jesus that we have full and equal access to all of the promises found in the Bible. When we have accepted this truth, the promises will turn into personal revelation. For example, those made to Jeremiah[90] to give him a hope and a future, to prosper him and not to harm him, also speak to our lives. The promise of blessings made to Israel in Deuteronomy[91] and the one made in Malachi[92] to throw open the floodgates of heaven, also speak directly concerning each of our lives. It is because of Jesus that we can take each promise contained in the Bible and make it our own.

Once we have accepted the personal relevance of scripture, the Bible says that we have to then confess these truths over our lives. The word 'confession' comes from the Greek 'homolagia', meaning to say the same. As soon as we agree and say 'yes' to the promises of God, even if we have no idea how we are to achieve it, God will give us the ability to perform His will. Paul explains the power and the significance of the part played by confessing God's truth in our lives: it is at the point when we speak out our need and desire to have Jesus as Lord that we become saved[93]. When we actually confess out loud that Jesus is our Saviour, this is the action that causes us to be saved. Similarly, it was following Peter's confession of faith[94], where he declared that Jesus was the Christ that Jesus revealed to him his true identity: a rock, which means Peter, upon which He would build His church.

As soon as Peter spoke out God's truth, he received personal revelation concerning his life. In a similar way, when we start to confess His word and the promises it contains, then we too shall begin to receive revelation. As a consequence of speaking the word of God over our lives, we come into agreement with His promises for our future. If we do this, then God guarantees that His word will achieve His purposes:

when He hears His word being spoken by ourselves, He 'rushes' to make sure that it happens.

Isaiah 55:11

'...so is my word that goes out from My mouth: It will not return to me empty, but will accomplish what I desire and achieve the purpose for which I sent it.'

The words we confess release angels

The Psalmist tells[95] us that when we confess the word of God, angels are released to ensure that what we say from scripture actually comes into being. It is extraordinary that faith-filled words from the Bible spoken by ordinary people release angelic activity. In many respects it shows what an unequal battle we are engaged in – as Paul put it, 'If God is for us, who can be against us?'[96]. We should keep this in mind when we next declare the word of God over our job situation, and remember that not everyone has the advantage of quite literally being able to call down angelic assistance!

Many of us will have tried to change ourselves, perhaps through self-help programmes involving positive thought processes or even hypnosis. However, if we speak in agreement with God's word concerning issues, such as our jobs, then he will act. The very act of agreeing with God brings release into our lives, and in this process our minds will also be renewed. When we agree with God, he enables us to live according to His plan from the beginning of time.

Hebrews 13:20–21

May the God of peace, who through the blood of the eternal covenant brought back from the dead our Lord Jesus, that great Shepherd of the sheep, equip you with everything good for doing His will, and may He work in us what is pleasing to Him...

Someone once said: don't talk to God about your mountain, talk to the mountain about God! It is time that we spoke to the circumstances surrounding our jobs about the power of God for those who believe in Christ[97]. As believers in Jesus, we should declare to whatever is affecting our job prospects that God knows His plans for our lives. We need to assert this truth to our own personal mountain, which could include a disability, a lack of skills and qualifications, a difficult family situation or even a lack of career focus. Whether we have been a Christian for many years or only a few minutes, the challenge is to have a go at declaring these biblical promises, and then to persevere until our situations move. Faith-filled scripture spoken over our life, is an infinitely powerful force.

Job 6:25   **How forcible are right words** (NKJV)

God's word – the sword of the Spirit

Earlier in the chapter, we pointed out that merely reading the word of God but not acting on it is a bit like holding a gun without having the key information about how to make it work – pull the trigger. The writer to the Hebrews provides us with instructions on how to activate the word of God in our lives. We are told[98] that we should avoid being 'lazy' and inactive but should instead imitate those people in the Bible who were able to claim the promises of God. How did they activate the word of God and obtain these promises? The book of Hebrews tells us that they did this through faith and patience. What this means for us is that we should show persistence by continually declaring God's word over our job situation, and then look for opportunities to step out in faith into whatever God has planned.

Paul calls the word of God: the sword of the Spirit'[99]; and it is something that we should be wielding against the enemy all of the time. In his letter to the Ephesians, he encourages us to view the declaration of God's word as a sword in the hand of a Roman soldier. One of the reasons why Roman infantry were feared was because their swords were made of high quality steel. This meant that the blades made short work of enemy swords, which were usually made from lesser metals such as bronze and iron. When we declare scripture over our lives it should encourage us to know that no weapon forged by the enemy can withstand the high quality metal found in the word of God[100]. It is also important to realise that we should wield the word of God with as much energy and as many times as a Roman solider engaged in a fierce battle. Whether we like it or not, we are involved in a battle[101], a battle for our lives; and the word of God is the only weapon at our disposal that can defeat the enemy. Whatever God has planned for us, we should constantly declare His word over our situation. Whether we are called to have a high powered career or to do voluntary work to enable us to perform some other task, we must persist in declaring the word of God over our lives.

Psalm 119:133   **Direct my footsteps according to your word**...

The danger of negative words

If the act of confessing the positive word of God releases life, then the opposite is also true. Negative words spoken by ourselves or other people over our lives can have a serious impact on us. Experts estimate that for every single negative word spoken, ten positive words are needed to counter the effect. At the beginning of this book, I recalled how my primary school teacher declared to the whole class that I would not achieve anything beyond becoming a refuse collector. Even though there is nothing wrong with this occupation, the words directed at me were designed to hurt and to damage a young mind.

David was also on the receiving end of negative words spoken by his family. In the first book of Samuel[102], we read the account of when David's brother Eliab was deeply critical of him leaving his sheep and turning up at the camp of the Israeli army. It was not just his negative tone of voice that was so potentially damaging, but it was also his choice of words. In front of the soldiers, Eliab spitefully reminded David of his low status job as a shepherd. David's reaction showed that his brother's words did indeed hit home as intended: 'Now what have I done…Can't I even speak?'.

It is not just other people who can speak negative words about our lives, we can also be guilty of doing this to ourselves. It is something that can become a habit and the normal way that we view life. Even grumbling about the weather can develop into a mindset where we view the whole of life from a negative standpoint. This way of thinking can be infectious, and its source may be traced to the depressing story lines of soap operas or even the gladiatorial-like debates of MPs in parliament. We should remember that Jesus made it clear that we will all be called to account for every careless word that we use[103].

Proverbs 21:23   **He who guards his mouth and his tongue keeps himself from calamity.**

The problem with becoming infected with negativity is that we cease to confess the promises found in God's word. As soon as this happens, we deny ourselves the chance to experience the effect of His word in our lives, which we are told[104] is 'living and active' with the power to change situations.

Beware of a bitter root

The Bible warns us to be on guard to ensure that no bitter root grows in our lives to cause us trouble[105]; negative comments can be both the source *and* the fruit of a bitter root. I recall the occasion when a number of college friends managed to secure lucrative graduate training positions, whilst I languished in a low-paid, low-status job. I also recall feeling jealous and bitter at their success. If we find ourselves in this kind of situation, it is important that we root out this bitterness as soon as possible by confessing and apologising to God.

Apart from the fact that a negative mindset feels unpleasant, there is also another reason why we should not allow a bitter root to become established in our lives. In his letter[106] to the church in Ephesus, Paul warns how anger, once it takes root, can allow the devil to gain a foothold. What we are talking about here is how something psychologically negative in our character can lead to a deeply negative spiritual effect in our lives. In the same way as wasps appear from nowhere in the summer as soon as food is eaten outside, the devil has the ability to 'home in' on our negative words. He has only one aim in mind: to use our words in order to bring us down. Satan will try to convince us with lies and make us feel like a complete mess, which is why Paul tells us[107] to put on the full armour of God and to 'take your stand against the devil's schemes'.

Somebody once prayed, 'Lord, why does the enemy keep reminding me of my past failings and negative comments?' God replied, "Because he's running short of material!'

It is important to understand two facts about the devil's tactics. Firstly, he knows full well that he has already been defeated by Jesus' death and resurrection. All the troubles that we see around us are his last struggles before he is finally thrown into the fiery pit[108]. Secondly, the devil's schemes concerning each one of us are designed to destroy what God has planned for our lives. The negative words that have injured us in the past will often be directed by the devil at the area of our life that has been prepared for us by God. This was the case with David when Eliab criticised him in a mocking way by suggesting that he should leave the company of soldiers and return to the fields to look after the sheep.

Is it possible to review our own lives and detect a consistent pattern to any negative words that have so far prevented us from moving towards a certain type of work?

These words can arrive from many directions: from family, teachers, school friends or work colleagues. Negative words can also emerge from ourselves as a result of low self-esteem or a lack of self-confidence. For example, whilst watching a news report on television we might say excitedly to ourselves, 'I could do that', but instantly a sly, critical voice enters our thoughts and poisons our minds saying: 'What you? You must be having a laugh! Don't you remember your last failure and your poor education etc, etc?' If any of us have been injured by negative words or been able to identify a consistent pattern to such words in the past, there is an exercise at the end of this chapter to help with praying through some of these issues.

Not all negative words are…negative

It is important to give a note of caution at this point. When we are seeking God's guidance in regard to any issue in our lives, particularly for our job situation, it is critical that we are real about our expectations. It is vital that we don't try to be something that we're not designed to be and end up living in a fantasy world. Sometimes we can receive even well-judged advice on our ability or ourselves in a negative way when, in fact, we should receive it maturely. It is also possible that we can be given advice that is difficult to listen to, simply because it is not what we would choose to hear. Such advice doesn't necessarily contain negative words, but is, instead, designed to shed some reality and clarity on our situation. However, because receiving criticism can be difficult to take, even when given in a loving way, it is easy to become defensive and view everything as being negative.

In Chapter 13, we will look at how important it is to take advice from people that we trust; the Bible tells[109] us that this is the wise course to take. If we receive advice, we have to be mature enough, if necessary, to take criticism 'on the chin' and accept that there may be room for improvement in the way we do things. A measure of our maturity is the ability to accept that such advice isn't negative, but rather a timely word to save us from making a wrong move.

Experience victory with God's word

If we have been able to identify moments when others or even ourselves have spoken negative words to discourage us, it is vital that we take steps to turn these words around. What brought David out of his situation? It could have been easy for him to have remained devastated by his elder brother's criticism, and have retreated in shame back to his flocks of sheep. However, rather than dwelling on his brother's scathing words, he made the decision to receive and accept God's promises. As a consequence, David's words were reported to the king, and he was quickly led into Saul's tent where he convinced him that he could defeat Goliath.

Over the many years of being a shepherd, David had stored in his heart the promises of God – promises that had built up like a high interest savings account. When he was faced with a 'heavy bill', which came in the shape of family criticism and the challenge from Goliath, he was able to 'cash in' on all the godly 'interest' that had been accruing for so long in his heart. The result was that he was able to draw on his close relationship with God and produce faith-filled words that spoke of God's might and strength. The Bible tells us that as soon as we pronounce the word of God over our situations, it actually gets to work changing our lives.

1 Thessalonians 2:13　　　**…the word of God, which is at work in you who believe.**

It is easy to allow our situations rather than God's promises to dominate our thoughts and words. I recall an occasion when I had got through to the last three candidates for a particular job. To get this far, I had had to endure a long application form, three interviews and also a gruelling battery of psychometric tests. One afternoon following the final interview, I received a phone call from the employer to say that I had not been successful. My disappointment was further reinforced when I discovered that the winning candidate was a nephew of the Director of the company. It would be untrue to say that at that moment my words were filled with praise for God, expressing my trust in His ability to guide me to my chosen job! However, a week later I found out that the company had been taken into administration, and the nephew had immediately been made redundant.

This whole experience taught me a big lesson at a number of levels. Firstly, I repented for allowing circumstances and not God's promises to dictate my thoughts and words. Secondly, I apologised to God for showing a distinct lack of trust in His ability to know everything concerning my future. My Father in heaven knew precisely that this job would quickly disappear, and so prevented me from leaving a secure job and becoming unemployed.

Psalm 139:16　　　**…All the days ordained for me were written in your book before one of them came to be.**

Review of chapter

An important way of seeking God's instruction for our lives is to read the Bible. When we seek His face by reading His word, the Holy Spirit will use scripture to speak to us. Paul tells us that we should meditate on the Bible as much as possible and, importantly, accept the truth contained in scripture. He tells us the amazing fact that if we have accepted Jesus into our lives, then *all* of God's promises and revelation made in the Bible apply equally to us. Once we have accepted this certainty, the Bible says that we also have to confess these truths continually over every situation that we face. When we say 'yes' to the promises of God, He will give us the ability to do His will.

However, we have to be on our guard against any negative words that have been spoken over our lives either by ourselves or by others. Negative comments can be both the source as well as the fruit of a bitter root, and they can allow Satan to frustrate God's plans for us. But we must be careful not to view all advice that doesn't immediately please us as being negative. Receiving criticism, even when given in a genuine and loving way, requires a great deal of humility and maturity.

It is important that we don't accept negative words that are designed to discourage us or to bring us down. David's decision to accept God's word, and not that of his brother, allowed him to leave the fields and enter into his inheritance. When the pressure was on, David was able to declare faith-filled words that transformed his situation.

The following worksheet will enable you to address some of the issues that have been raised in this chapter. The exercise can be carried out on your own or alongside a prayer partner. Take time to consider each question as honestly as possible, and record your responses on a separate sheet.

Exercise 9

Part 1. The Word of God in Our Lives – God's Promises

An important way of seeking God's instruction for our lives is to read the Bible, God's word, on a regular basis. However, it is not sufficient to merely read God's word. We must also accept the truth, that if we have received Jesus into our lives then all of God's promises in the Bible are also for us.

For Prayer & Reflection

The following verses, which were used in the chapter, have been chosen to help you to focus on your own circumstances. Take some time to reflect on your situation through the questions that follow these verses.

Psalm 119:15

I meditate on your precepts and consider your ways.

2 Corinthians 1:20

For no matter how many promises God has made, they are 'Yes' in Christ. And so through Him the 'Amen' is spoken by us to the glory of God.

Isaiah 55:11

'...so is My word that goes out from My mouth: It will not return to me empty, but will accomplish what I desire and achieve the purpose for which I sent it.'

• **How much time do you spend reading the Bible and allowing God's word to enter your mind?**

• **When you read the Bible, do you invite the Holy Spirit to speak to you through the scriptures?**

The following are meant to give information and to offer encouragement on the way that you read the Bible:

- **There are many ways of reading the Bible. You can read it in traditional print, have it emailed to you, or download it to your desktop or handheld computer. You can also read it cover to cover or just selected parts, such as the Gospels.**
- **Develop a system where you will remember to declare God's promises over yourself. A good idea is to make verses from the Bible as visible as possible wherever you are. For instance:**
- **Make sure your screen saver at home or at work contains a relevant promise**
- **Print off some scriptures and stick them to your fridge door.**
- **Make a bookmark.**
- **Try learning some scripture off-by-heart.**

Whichever way you choose to do it, make a conscious effort to surround yourself with God's word so that you can be reminded to declare these promises wherever you are.

Part 2. The Word of God in our Lives – Negative Words

We have to be on our guard against any negative words that have been spoken over our lives. Negative comments can be both the source and the fruit of a bitter root, and they can allow Satan to frustrate God's plans for us. If we are able to identify moments when others, or even ourselves, have spoken negative words over us, it is vital that we turn these words around. The Bible tells us that as soon as we declare the word of God over our situations it begins to change our lives.

For Prayer & Reflection

The following verses, which were used in the chapter, have been chosen to help you to focus on your own circumstances. Take some time to reflect on your situation through the questions that follow these verses.

Proverbs 21:23
He who guards his mouth and his tongue, guards his soul from troubles.

1 Thessalonians 2:13
…the word of God, which is at work in you who believe.

- **Can you recall any negative words spoken either by yourself or by others regarding your life?**
- **With a prayer partner, invite the Holy Spirit to heal those areas that have suffered as a result of these negative words.**
- **If you have spoken such words about yourself, then it is important to ask God for His forgiveness.**
- **It is also important that you forgive those who have hurt you with negative words, however long ago they were said.**
- **Is it possible to detect in your life a consistent pattern to any negative words that have so far prevented you from moving towards a certain type of work? For example, has someone scorned an ability or interest that you have shown?**
- **Sometimes we can receive even well-judged advice on our ability and ourselves in a negative way, when we should receive it maturely. Can you think of any occasions when, instead of accepting advice, you rejected it because it was too difficult?**
- **Invite God into your present situation so that you end up walking with Him and relying on Him more. David's close relationship with God was developed during the hardships that he went through, and from this he was able to speak out in confidence about God's promises for his life.**

Dreams and Plans

_____

_____

_____

_____

_____

_____

_____

_____

_____

_____

_____

_____

_____

_____

Chapter 10

The Leading of the Holy Spirit

Another way that we can seek God's face and receive His instruction is by actually listening out for His voice. When we become a Christian, the Spirit of God makes His home inside us[110] and begins to communicate with us directly. When God speaks it can be heard like a small voice in our minds or received through an image in our imagination or even through having a strong impression about something. In the book of Acts[111], we are told that God spoke to Paul by sending him a dream of a man telling him to go to Macedonia. Jesus said[112] His sheep follow Him because they know His voice. Just as we instantly recognise the voice of a close friend over the phone, the more time we spend listening for Jesus' voice the easier it will be for us to recognise when God speaks.

Listening for God's voice

God wants to speak to each one of us regarding every part of our lives, and the more time we spend listening for His voice the more we will be able to respond to Him. When God spoke to Elijah in the cave[113], He spoke as a gentle whisper; and this is how He will generally speak with us. One of the big challenges in our busy, western-style lives is that we can often find it difficult to slow down and take time out to listen for God's voice. However, unless we slow down, we could be missing out on what He has to say. Because of this, there is no substitute for waiting quietly for Him, and when we do this God promises to speak with us.

Psalm 46:10   **'Be still, and know that I am God...'**

In the midst of any crisis in our career, the immediate and natural response is either to fly into some sort of action and activity, or to freeze and do nothing. We may rush to locate suitable job vacancies, write off for application forms, or look at college prospectuses in the hope of finding a training course. On the other hand, a job crisis can lead to inactivity as a consequence of despair and disillusionment about our situation. Depression can set in and it can become difficult to see the way forward past the many 'giants in the land'. Both reactions, either over- or under-activity, are understandable and very human ways to behave when under great strain.

During a time of crisis such as redundancy, God's approach to resolving the situation can be very different from our own. Before instructing us to do anything else, God will first tell us to quieten ourselves and get into His presence so that we can hear His voice. Yes, the application forms will still need to be completed and the CVs sent off, but our approach as Christians must be to seek the presence of our Father, and first hear what He has to say to us. Jesus' whole life was a demonstration of someone who constantly sought God's face, and there are many instances where He went off on His own to a secluded place to spend time with His Father.

Mark 6:46
After leaving them, He went up on a mountainside to pray.

In this scripture Jesus had just performed the miracle of feeding the five thousand. Later in Mark's gospel we read how Jesus again took Himself aside to be alone with God, this time in the garden of Gethsemane. These scriptures reveal that whatever he was experiencing, whether good or bad, Jesus was consistent in the way that He sought His Father's presence. Even following the 'mountain top' experience of the miracle of the bread and fishes, He did not start to rely on a feeling of self-success. Instead, He immediately spent time alone with His Father, knowing that unless He sought His presence, He would be unable to continue His ministry.

John 5:30
'By myself I can do nothing; I judge only as I hear, and My judgment is just, for I seek not to please Myself but Him who sent me.'

Communication flowing from a relationship with God

Everything in Jesus' life and ministry flowed from the relationship He had with His Father. All the miracles that He performed and all the teaching given to His disciples had their source in the time that Jesus spent with Him. If we have accepted Jesus into our lives, then we too can enjoy the same closeness that Jesus had with the Father. In one of the most incredible passages in the Bible, Paul tells us[114] that we are now co-heirs with Jesus. In a similar way, Jesus called[115] His disciples 'friends', and said that everything that He had learned from the Father, He in turn had made known to them. Jesus said that through the Holy Spirit, He would continue to make known the Father's will to us today. The Bible encourages us to make it our second nature to seek God's face and, just as Jesus did, to spend time in His presence. We are reassured in the book of Hebrews[116] that we are welcome 24/7 to come before God's presence where we can receive His instruction through the Holy Spirit.

John 14:26	**'But the Counsellor, the Holy Spirit, whom the Father will send in My name, will teach you all things and will remind you of everything I have said to you.'**

Jesus placed Himself in a nonstop communication loop to the extent that He said that He could do nothing without hearing from His Father in heaven[117]. Jesus was so used to getting into and staying in the presence of the Father that He heard clearly every word that was spoken by the Spirit of God. There are a number of times in the New Testament when we are told that the voice of God became audible to people who were around Jesus. We read of one such occasion in John's Gospel.

John 12:28–30	**'Father glorify your name!' Then a voice came from heaven, 'I have glorified it, and will glorify it again.' The crowd that was there and heard it said it had thundered; others said an angel had spoken to Him. Jesus said, 'This voice was for your benefit, not mine.'**

The only person who appears not to have been amazed by this event was Jesus Himself, and He makes it clear that this miracle occurred not for His benefit but for those around Him. In the preceding verses, Jesus gives us the privilege of listening in on an intimate and heart-felt discourse with His Father, something that would normally have taken place in a private and quiet place. However on this occasion, not only does Jesus decide to share His prayer dialogue with the Father openly, but

'Okay, so lets try that again...'

amazingly the Father also chooses to share His response openly. God's audible voice is described by some as sounding like thunder, whilst others thought it was an angel speaking. Clearly, those standing around Jesus were witnessing something supernatural.

However, what was a supernatural occurrence for Jesus' followers was merely a natural one for Jesus – for Him there was nothing more natural and automatic than to speak with the Father and to receive a loving and instructive reply. But what did Jesus mean when He said that His audible voice was not done for His benefit but for others? It seems to indicate that both Jesus and the Father wanted to demonstrate the intimate ties that held them together. From this account we can learn something amazing: if we accept Jesus into our lives, then we can also have a relationship with God similar to the one that existed between Him and His Father. As sons and joint heirs with Jesus Christ[118], we too can have a nonstop discourse with the Father – though we cannot normally expect to hear God's voice in an audible way.

Some years ago, an American friend explained in simple terms how large an area the USA covers. She recalled how once, when travelling by car from Texas to California, she had to rely on her collection of CDs. She explained that signals from radio stations gradually disappeared in the vast open spaces between towns and cities, and only started again when in range of a station in the next big town. For this reason, in the tracts of arid land between towns, in-car entertainment is the only way to listen to music.

The difference in strength between radio signals and the 'signal' of the Holy Spirit is beyond measure. Although we will probably not hear His audible voice, God promises that if we seek His presence and listen then we will never be out of range of the frequency of the Holy Spirit. The only question that remains for us is whether our spiritual ears will be attuned to God when He speaks to us. Is our experience of hearing from God similar to that of Jesus, or are we sometimes like those in Isaiah who had to be reminded to listen and to pay attention to God's word?

Isaiah 34:1   **Come near, you nations, and listen; pay
                     attention, you peoples!
                     Let the earth hear, and all that is in it,
                     the world, and all that comes out of it!**

Aligning our prayers to the will of God

When our spiritual ears are tuned into the Holy Spirit, God will also tell us what we should be praying for. The more we allow our prayers to match what God wants us to pray about, the more revelation and breakthrough we will experience in our lives.

Philippians 2:13   **...for it is God who works in you to will and to act according to His good purpose.**

One result of the close relationship that existed between Jesus and His Father was that everything He prayed for was in complete alignment with the will of God. In other words, He only prayed what He knew to be His Father's will – Jesus said[119] that He did only what He saw the Father doing. He told us that when our minds are tuned in a similar way to the Father, then we can ask for anything in His name and it will be given to us.

John 16:23   **'...I tell you the truth, My Father will give you whatever you ask in My name.'**

This incredible promise shows us the power that can be attached to our prayers. However, the problem that many of us have is that we can often allow our experience and failures to guide the way in which we pray. It is very easy to allow the devil to tell us that what we're praying for is unrealistic and a complete fantasy. The Bible tells us that our prayers should not be focussed on our prior experience (possibly of the job market) but rather on our close, loving relationship with the Father, who knows our needs better than we know them ourselves.

The accuracy of our prayers

There are two factors at work when we pray: the accuracy of our prayers and the persistence of our prayers. Now considering the first of these, prayers that emerge from time spent in God's presence ensure that we continually pray for the right things. For the Christian who is praying for a job with many complicated issues, we have assurance that the Spirit of God will somehow influence the way we pray so that our prayers become the ones God wants us to pray. This will always lead to release and revelation.

At a personal level, I have discovered that as a result of the time that I spend in God's word and in His presence, my prayers are becoming increasingly based on what I believe I am hearing from God. I cannot claim that all my prayer life exhibits such confidence. However, I have found that when I produce prayers that are directed by what I hear from God, then these prayers are more likely to receive answers. As someone said: don't ask God to bless your plans – ask Him to show you how to run with His plans for they are already blessed! In the book of Romans[120], Paul urges that our minds may be transformed to that of Christ so that we will be able to discern the will of God. When we have the mind of Christ, it will be easy to know what to pray in every situation; and it is these prayers, which are in line with the will of God, that bring release, revelation and answers into our lives.

If we want to receive revelation and instruction regarding our employment situation, we should ensure that we spend as much time as possible in God's word and presence. This is the way that we'll hear Him speak to us about what we should be praying. It is interesting that God desires to include us in this equation as undoubtedly He could bring anything into being by commanding it. However, by giving us the chance to exercise our faith and pray Spirit-filled prayers, God hands us an amazing opportunity to participate in His great plan of salvation for the world. Somehow, He enables our faith-filled prayers to actually release His power not only into our own lives but also into the world around us. Time spent in God's presence automatically leads us to having a spirit that cries 'Abba, Father'[121], and one that knows instinctively what to pray because it knows the Father's will for our lives and our jobs.

The persistence of our prayers

The second factor that affects our prayers is persistence. We know from scripture[122] that the need for persistence in our prayer life is linked to an intense spiritual battle going on in the heavenly realms. In the gospel of Luke, Jesus gave the parable of the persistent widow to show how we should never give up in our praying.

Luke 18:1   **Then Jesus told His disciples a parable to show them that they should always pray and not give up.**

In addition to this, in the book of Daniel we are given an incredible insight into what goes on behind the scenes when we pray Spirit-filled prayers. Daniel had a vision where an angel eventually made it through to him with instructions on what he should do next.

Daniel 10:12

'...Since the first day that you set your mind to gain understanding and to humble yourself before your God, your words were heard, and I have come in response to them.'

The angel was sent by God as soon as Daniel began to produce Spirit-filled prayers that placed God's kingdom first. However, this is where the persistence part is relevant. Even though the angel was sent to Daniel as soon as he started praying, we are told that the angel was delayed and attacked for twenty-one days by a demonic spirit. It would seem that the angel only managed to get through to Daniel due to the persistence of his prayers, which brought the timely intervention of the archangel Michael. The Bible doesn't give a huge amount of detail about the spiritual battle that goes on in the heavenly realms, but it is clear that angels are dispatched to bring us revelation when we pray Spirit-filled prayers that reflect the will of God.

Psalm 103:20

**Praise the Lord, you His angels,
you mighty ones who do His bidding,
who obey His word.**

It is important to note that Daniel not only received instructions on how to proceed, but he was also strengthened by the hand of God. The arrival of the angel banished Daniel's fears and also brought him physical and spiritual rejuvenation, which enabled him to carry out God's purposes. In a similar way, God promises that He will strengthen us when, for example, we tire in a job search, and enable us to enter into what He has prepared.

The Spirit of God versus the spirit of the world

The challenge that all Christians face, especially those living in a society which scorns the very existence of God, is to keep their spiritual senses fine-tuned to God's voice. In the western world, we are surrounded by the influence of a spirit that is totally opposed to God – the spirit of the world. Unlike the Holy Spirit, the spirit of the world never leads us to true revelation, but instead tries to persuade us through the use of our five senses. For example, by leading our eyes to adverts on the sides of buses[123], the spirit of the world will tempt us to believe the claim that God does not exist. One of the principal aims of this spirit is to make us abandon our relationship with Jesus and to close down the lines of communication between heaven and us. In the context of finding work, the spirit of the world will try to deafen our spiritual ears so that we no longer hear God speak to us concerning our jobs. It will attempt to persuade us that the credit crunch and the recession will make it impossible for us to find work. It will also seek to discourage by constantly reminding us that our circumstances or lack of qualifications will make us unemployable.

On the other hand, the aim of the Holy Spirit is to glorify Jesus and to bring many people into a right relationship with God. Unlike the spirit of the world, which communicates with us through our senses, the Holy Spirit will communicate to us mainly through our spirit – encouraging and instructing us how to walk according to God's plan. In the first letter to the Corinthians, Paul tells us[124] that 'no eye has seen, no ear has heard, no mind has conceived what God has prepared for those who love Him'; it is only God's Spirit, and nothing else, that brings revelation into our lives. If we allow ourselves to stay in God's presence and practise tuning our spiritual senses to His voice, then a single word from God can turn our situation around.

Isaiah 30:21   **…your ears will hear a voice behind you, saying, 'This is the way; walk in it.'**

If we spend time in His presence and tune our senses to His voice, then God's promise regarding our jobs is that He will give a word that will send us in the right direction – to what He has prepared for us. Just imagine Moses' relief and joy when he finally heard God giving him instructions on how to leave the wilderness and strike out towards the 'promised land'!

Review of chapter

When we become Christians, the Spirit of God makes His home inside us and begins to communicate with us directly. God wants to speak to each one of us regarding every part of our lives, including our job situation, and the more time we spend listening for His voice the more we will be able to respond to Him. When we quieten ourselves and make space for Him, God promises that He will speak with us personally. All the miracles and teaching of Jesus had their source in the time that He spent with His Father. The Bible tells us that we are co-heirs with Jesus. Consequently, we too can enjoy the same closeness of relationship that existed between Jesus and His Father, and also receive the same guidance through the Holy Spirit.

When our spiritual ears are tuned to the Holy Spirit, God will also tell us what we should be praying for, and we can ask for anything in Jesus' name. The more we allow our prayers to match what God wants us to pray about, the more revelation and breakthrough we will experience. A Christian praying for a job has assurance that the Spirit of God will influence the way he or she prays. Within God's time, this will always lead to release and revelation.

Scripture tells us that we also need to persist in our prayer life. This is connected to an intense spiritual battle that goes on, unseen, in the heavenly realms. When we allow ourselves to listen to the spirit of the world, we can become discouraged and cease to pray. However, when we remain focussed on God, He will send angelic assistance to strengthen us and to increase our resolve to pray. When we stay in His presence, the Holy Spirit will encourage, instruct and guide us in our walk with God.

The following worksheet will enable you to address some of the issues that have been raised in this chapter. The exercise can be carried out on your own or alongside a prayer partner. Take time to consider each question as honestly as possible, and record your responses on a separate sheet.

Exercise 10

Part 1. The Leading of the Holy Spirit – Hearing God's Voice

One of the big challenges in our busy, western-style lives is that we can often find it difficult to slow down and take time to listen for God's voice. However, unless we do so, we could miss out on what He wants to tell us; and because of this, there is no substitute for literally waiting quietly for Him to speak. When we do quieten ourselves and make space for Him, God promises that He will speak and instruct us on what we should be praying for.

For Prayer & Reflection

The following verses, which were used in the chapter, have been chosen to help you to focus on your own circumstances. Take some time to reflect on your situation through the suggestions that follow these verses.

Psalm 46:10	**'Be still and know* that I am God...' (*To know in a deep way)**
John 5:30	**'By Myself I can do nothing; I judge only as I hear, and My judgment is just, for I seek not to please Myself but Him who sent me.'**
John 14:26	**'But the Counsellor, the Holy Spirit, whom the Father will send in My name, will teach you all things and will remind you of everything I have**
Philippians 2:13	**...for it is God who works in you to will and to act according to His good purpose.**

Learning to tune our ears to hear the voice of God takes practice. Here are some simple tips to help you to hear His voice.

- Meditate on a passage of scripture.

- Listen to a quiet piece of music and invite the Holy Spirit to 'soak' you with His presence.

- Go for a walk without an agenda other than spending time with God.

- If you listen out for God, He will talk with you concerning all parts of your life. Try it and see what happens.

- Try to make prayer and allowing God into all your thinking as the way you do things. It's like having the traffic report alert switched on all the time on your car radio: you might be washing the dishes or doing the shopping when suddenly out-of-the-blue God's voice enters into your mind.

- How often have you tried to communicate with God in such a fashion?

Part 2. The Leading of the Holy Spirit – Persistence in Prayer

The Bible tells us that our prayers should be focussed on our loving relationship with the Father, who knows our needs better than we know them ourselves, and not on our prior experience, for example, of the job market. It is very easy to let ourselves listen to the spirit of the world and then become discouraged. However, if we place ourselves in God's presence and persist in our prayers, we will see our situations transformed.

For Prayer & Reflection

The following verses, which were used in the chapter, have been chosen to help you to focus on your own circumstances. Take some time to reflect on your situation through the suggestions that follow these verses.

John 16:23   '...I tell you the truth, My Father will give you whatever you ask in My name.'

Luke 18:1   Then Jesus told His disciples a parable to show them that they should always pray and not give up.

- We should try to make sure that our prayers are only based on scriptural promises and what we think God is asking us to pray about. Also, we should avoid allowing our past failures or negative experiences to shape what we're praying for.

- We know from scripture that the need for persistence in our prayer life is linked to an intense spiritual battle going on in the heavenly realms. In Luke's gospel, the parable of the persistent widow shows how we should never give up in our praying.

- If you are confident of what to pray for, it is good to commit yourself to a disciplined programme of prayer. Some people like to get up early in the morning to pray whilst others prefer to go for an evening prayer walk. Whatever your preference, the Bible tells us that we should persist in what we're praying for.

If you find that your prayers are not being answered, here are a number of possible explanations.

- You could be getting the prayer request wrong. It could be time for you to get back into God's presence or to gain prophetic insight from a trusted friend, and then seek God's revelation regarding your job search.

- As we read in Luke and Daniel, you need to persist in your prayer life. You should do this in the knowledge that behind the scenes there is a titanic spiritual battle going on. The Bible doesn't explain how or why persistent prayer helps in this battle; however, Jesus tells us to show persistence when we pray.

- If your prayers for a new job are not being answered, this could mean that God's will is awaiting an appointed time. You could be praying for something that He is not ready to release into your life. That is, God may be saying to you 'not yet' rather than 'no'

- How easily do you give up praying when the pressure is on and nothing seems to be happening?

Dreams and Plans

_____

_____

_____

_____

_____

_____

_____

_____

_____

_____

_____

_____

_____

_____

Chapter 11

Seeking God with our whole Heart

The degree of love that we have for God plays an important role in our ability to receive His revelation and guidance for our lives. If we seek God's face and respond to His gentle whisper with an undivided heart, then His promise is that He will be found by us and that He will lead us out from captivity[125].

I grew up in south Wales during the 1980's, and unsurprisingly the main sport at school was rugby. In fact there were only two options: netball for girls and rugby for boys. Football was positively frowned upon, possibly for the reason that it didn't allow enough physical contact. However, during this same decade supporting the national team was a miserable experience. It was an era of Welsh rugby that was characterised by lack of flare, poor discipline and countless defeats on the field. This was made even worse by the fact that only during the previous decade, our squad had experienced a golden age of 'grand slams' and famous victories.

But the one thing that no one could accuse the Welsh rugby team of lacking during that time was passion for the game. We might have lost most of our matches during these years, but at least we did it with a great deal of emotion, if little else! I have a feeling that if God were a Welsh rugby supporter, He would have granted Wales back-to-back championships for the sole reason that He places a great deal of importance upon having passion. In Exodus[126], God reveals the degree of His passion for Israel and demands that they should not worship anything apart from Him. He declares that He is a jealous God, who is ready to punish His people to ensure that they take His desire for them seriously. The image here is not a lofty and distant figure that you might see in a piece of renaissance art, but rather a red-hot, passionate God who ensures that His will prevails.

The zeal of the Lord is described many times in the Bible, and there can be no doubt that God is a very passionate person.

Isaiah 42:13
> **The Lord will march out like a mighty man, like a warrior He will stir up His zeal; with a shout He will raise the battle cry and will triumph over His enemies.**

In this scripture we don't see God sending out a diplomatic mission to His enemy's camp to avert a conflict, nor do we see God taking any prisoners either. Instead, we see a God who is set on annihilating His enemies and crushing them into the dust. If we aren't convinced about Him being a passionate person then let us consider Jesus' conduct in the temple courts, when He overturned the money lenders' tables and drove them out of the temple using a whip.

John 2:16   ...'Get these out of here! How dare you turn My Father's house into a market!'

Just imagine being there to witness Jesus' anger at the way that people were treating the holiness of the temple with such disrespect. John recalls[127] that the disciples later remembered that David had prophesied that Jesus would be filled with a fierce passion for God's kingdom.

Psalm 69:9   ...for zeal for your house consumes me...

The scene of Jesus using violence in the temple to demonstrate His feelings is at one level shocking because we can so often over-simplify Him as someone who simply healed the sick and was eventually arrested and crucified. However, at a more accurate level we can clearly see that Jesus was a wildly passionate figure. The passion of Christ most clearly demonstrated the full nature of His feelings for us: He experienced a horrendous death and suffered the rejection of the Father[128], all for people who were still His enemies[129].

Being sold out to God

Yet here is the serious bit: God expects anyone who has given their life to Jesus to have a similar level of passion and desire for Him. Jesus said that you are either for Him or against Him[130]. In other words there can be no sitting on the fence in the kingdom of God – no half measures and no Sunday-only Christianity, where our belief doesn't make it beyond the rear-most pew.

In the early nineteenth-century, within Napoleon's army was a legendary core called the Imperial Guard. The guard consisted of veterans who had displayed outstanding levels of valour in many battles. They were paid more than the regular French army, were given splendid uniforms, and were allowed to wear earrings, powdered pigtails and moustaches as signs of their elite status. However, in return, more was expected of them. The regulars within the army might have begrudged the Imperial Guard their privileges but, whenever they went into battle, victory was assured – that is, apart from at Waterloo! The Imperial Guard were Napoleon's 'Immortals' – passionate in their loyalty and fearsome in battle. This is how God wants us to live our everyday lives: to be sold out to Him and to be totally committed to His kingdom. If we are in any doubt about this, just look at the strongly-worded warning in the book of Revelation.

Revelation 3:15–16

'I know your deeds, that you are neither cold nor hot. I wish you were either one or the other! So, because you are lukewarm – neither hot nor cold – I am about to spit you out of My mouth.'

Passion for God leads to revelation and release

God desires that His followers should not be *merely* interested in Him, but rather be *fully* committed to His name. He makes it plain that those who are successful in receiving His revelation and guidance regarding their lives are those who have completely sold out to Him. He is looking for people who do not hold anything back, but instead offer Him every part of their hearts.

Jeremiah 29:12–14	'Then you will call upon me and come and pray to me, and I will listen to you. You will seek me and find me when you seek me with all your heart. I will be found by you' declares the Lord, 'and will bring you back from captivity...'

Jacob is a great example of someone who was fully committed in his pursuit of God and God's plans for his life. In Genesis we have the amazing story of how he wrestled with a mysterious character[131]. We are told that it was because of Jacob's stubborn determination to win God's blessing that his true name and identity – Israel – was revealed to Him.

Genesis 32:27–28	The man asked him, 'What is your name?' 'Jacob', he answered. Then the man said, 'Your name will no longer be Jacob, but Israel, because you have struggled with God and with men and have overcome.'

Placing God's kingdom first

A few years ago, for a significant birthday, my family clubbed together to buy me a special present: a large reflector telescope. There are many different kinds of telescope on the market, but for a complete amateur, like me, the best sort has a small computer attached. Once correctly aligned, it is possible to find up to forty thousand objects in the sky including planets, stars and faraway galaxies.

The first time that I set up the telescope I began by looking at easily found objects such as the moon and Saturn with its incredible rings. Full of confidence, I pressed on to do some 'deep space' viewing and tapped in the co-ordinates of the 'Andromeda Galaxy', the closest to our own 'Milky Way'. I was expecting to see an image comparable to something on the NASA website. Instead, I saw nothing but dark sky. I checked the tracking of the telescope and then began to try to find other galaxies, which, according to my manual, should have been easily observable – again nothing. After a further two hours, I gave up and went to bed.

What is the connection between using a telescope properly and seeking God's face and guidance? After all, not even the most powerful telescopes have been able to gaze beyond the 'pearly gates' to see God's face! The point is that there is a similarity between using a telescope correctly and keeping our 'spiritual eyes' fixed firmly on

God. In both cases, there are important rules that we need to follow.

After seeking advice, I learned some interesting facts about the ability of the human eye that would help me detect the very faint amounts of light given off by distant galaxies. The retina has two types of cells: rods, which detect faint light, and cones, which detect bright light and colours. Both types of cell contain dyes that undergo a chemical change when hit by light. When there are high levels of light, the dyes in the rods become bleached and lose their ability to detect faint light. Once the lights are turned off, the rods eventually return to life. By using a torch to read my telescope manual, I had been inadvertently preventing the rods in my eye from detecting faint light. This was why I wasn't seeing any galaxies. Similarly, how many of us when trying to seek God's face inadvertently disable our 'spiritual eyes', and draw the wrong conclusion that it is impossible to receive His guidance for our lives and jobs.

I'm sure that one thing that has prevented me from receiving God's revelation has been the condition of my heart and how it has influenced the way that I have prayed. Instead of making the coming of His kingdom my top priority, my prayers have often just focussed on my own immediate issues. Sometimes I placed my problem in pole position in my prayer time and demoted God and His kingdom to second place. In the Lord's Prayer[132], Jesus shows us the way in which we should seek God for our needs. Jesus' prayer begins:

- **Our Father / Abba (Daddy) – showing our relationship to the awesome God of Israel.**
- **Hallowed be your name – showing that we are to approach Him with reverence and worship.**
- **Your kingdom come, your will be done – showing that this should be the goal of our lives.**
- **Give us today day our daily bread – showing that we may ask for guidance on specific issues.**

The message given by Jesus is clear: the way that we seek God for our needs should be in a definite order. Jesus instructs us to pray for our daily bread, the matter in hand being guidance in our careers, only *after* we have prayed for the coming His kingdom. So, how should we pray for our job situation? We should begin our prayers by laying aside our requests for employment or for a release of finance for essential retraining, and make the coming of God's kingdom a priority in our lives. Once we have placed Him first, He invites us to bring to Him requests for our daily bread – any genuine need.

After my own redundancy, I knew that God wanted certain changes in my character and priorities. From spending time in His presence, I came to understand that an important way for me to place His kingdom first was to endeavour to become more accepting of my own circumstances. I also realised that I had a tendency to complain and to be dissatisfied about things out of my control; and I knew that God wanted me to pray not so much for a new job, but more for change in my character. In looking back at how I have reacted at times to disappointments and setbacks in my career, my immediate approach has not always been to make a priority of seeking God's kingdom before praying for my own needs. Sometimes, following a job rejection letter, my reaction has been to lay my urgent needs on the 'table' and beg God for an answer. However, I cannot ignore that Jesus teaches us to first of all seek His kingdom in our lives.

Matthew 6:33 **But seek first His kingdom and His righteousness, and all these things will be given to you as well.**

The agony of Jesus at Gethsemane clearly shows how He, despite His initial struggle to accept that He should suffer on the cross, laid aside His own will. It was through accepting God's will and placing God's kingdom first, that Jesus had victory on the cross.

Mark 14:36 **'Abba, Father' He said, 'everything is possible for you. Take this cup from me. Yet not what I will, but what you will.'**

One of the reasons why many of us find this particular teaching so difficult is that it requires us to trust God in a big way. This prayer of Jesus can make us feel vulnerable because it places us and all our needs directly in His hands. Whenever we pray 'Your kingdom come' or 'Not My will, but your will be done', the temptation is to resist and say, 'Hold on, how about me first and what I need for a change?'. I suspect that many of us would find this sort of prayer less difficult if we had a deeper passion for God and a better understanding about who He is. In a previous chapter we looked at some of the characteristics of God as reasons why we can trust Him. Could it be possible that He is telling us that He wants us to review our commitment to Him before He can reveal the next stage in His plan for our career? The passage in Jeremiah 29 tells us that God is on the look out for hearts that are set on His kingdom. It is with people who have such hearts that God chooses to reveal His plans and purposes.

Review of chapter

The Bible tells us that God chooses to reveal Himself to those who seek Him passionately. Furthermore, we are told that if we pursue God wholeheartedly, then He promises that we will find Him and He will lead us out of our wilderness season. He makes it clear that the people who receive His revelation and guidance for their lives are those who have fully committed themselves to Him. God expects anyone who has given their life to Jesus to have a similar level of passion for Him as He does for them, and to live their everyday lives as people who are sold out to God and His kingdom.

In the Lord's Prayer, Jesus teaches that there should be a definite order in our prayers. We should begin by worshipping God and placing His kingdom first. Jesus continues by saying that our request for our present needs, such as a new job, should *follow* seeking God, and not the other way around. When we make His kingdom our top priority, Jesus assures us that our needs will be met.

The following worksheet will enable you to address some of the issues that have been raised in this chapter. The exercise can be carried out on your own or alongside a prayer partner. Take time to consider each question as honestly as possible and record your responses on a separate sheet.

Exercise 11
Seeking God with our Whole Heart

Could it be possible that God is telling us today that He wants us to review our commitment to Him before He can reveal the next stage in His plan for our career? The Imperial Guard were Napoleon's 'Immortals', passionate in their loyalty to Him and fearsome in battle. This is how God wants us to live our lives: to be totally devoted to Him and His kingdom. God makes it clear that those who are successful in receiving His revelation and guidance regarding their lives are those who have fully committed themselves to Him. He is looking for people who hold nothing back, but instead offer every part of their hearts.

For Prayer & Reflection

The following verses, which were used in the chapter, have been chosen to help you to focus on your own circumstances. Take some time to reflect on your situation through the questions that follow these verses.

Isaiah 42:13

The Lord will march out like a mighty man, like a warrior He will stir up His zeal; with a shout He will raise the battle cry and will triumph over His enemies.

Jeremiah 29:12–14

'Then you will call upon me and come and pray to me and I will listen to you. You will seek me and find me when you seek me with all your heart. I will be found by you,' declares the Lord, 'and will bring you back from captivity.'

Matthew 6:9–11	'This, then, is how you should pray: "Our Father in heaven,
	hallowed be your name, your kingdom come, your will be done
	on earth as it is in heaven. Give us today our daily bread."'

Matthew 6:33	But seek first His kingdom and His righteousness, and all these things will be given to you as well.

- As honestly as possible, assess how much love, energy and zeal you have for the things of God.

- On your own or with a prayer partner, ask God for His forgiveness if you feel that your love for Him has grown lukewarm.

- Take another look at the part of Chapter 3 that talks about how we can receive the Father's love.

The actions and decisions that we take can often display the level of our zeal for God. It is easy to talk, but much more difficult to step out into something we feel that God is asking us to do.

- Can you recall any occasions when you have been able to place God's Kingdom first in your life and demonstrated your passion for Him? If so, what was the outcome?

- Can you think of any times when, once you had recommitted yourself to Him, God revealed things to you about His plans for your life? If so, what was the outcome?

Dreams and Plans

Chapter 12

Revelation awaits an Appointed Time

God's revelation concerning all things, including guidance for our jobs, awaits an appointed time. God's 'hand' cannot be forced nor His timing be rushed. The difficulty that many people in the Bible experienced was the temptation to 'jump the gun' and seek an alternative to waiting for God's revelation to arrive. This chapter will look at the important role that time has to play in receiving this revelation and instruction. We shall also examine the significant part we ourselves play when the time is right and God's revelation enters our lives.

Many years ago, a friend told me about prophetic picture that she had received for me. A prophetic picture is an image that comes into our minds from the Holy Spirit for the encouragement or correction of others or of ourselves. The picture showed that I was attempting to find a solution to a problem, and the serious part of the message lay in the actual way that I was trying to resolve the issue. Instead of allowing God to guide me through the dilemma, the picture showed that I was attempting to lead God by the hand, and not the other way around. Needless to say, I was coming off second best in this impossible task! At this particular time, I was praying for revelation on my future career direction. However, after many months of fruitless search, I was becoming impatient and had begun to exhaust myself by applying out of desperation for any job that could get me out of my current role. To be honest, I had given up on God's ability to answer my prayers, and had decided that He needed a little bit of help from me to make things start to happen. When my friend gave me the prophetic picture, I promptlay repented and, not long afterwards, found a satisfying new job

The subject of God's timing and the critical part it plays in the fulfilment of His plans, including those for our next job, was dealt with earlier in Chapter 4. However, because timing has such a significant part to play in receiving God's revelation, it is now worth revisiting this important subject. If we are seeking God for revelation and instruction, the Bible tells us that sometimes we just have to wait for the right moment for it to arrive.

Habakkuk 2:3

'For the revelation awaits an appointed time…Though it linger, wait for it; it will certainly come and will not delay.'

God's timing will certainly come

There really is no easy way to put this. Sometimes, we just have to be patient and wait for God to give the green light. However, scripture is definite about one thing: even though we may have to wait, God's revelation will 'certainly come'. In the book of Ecclesiastes, we read that there is a right time for everything to happen.

Ecclesiastes 3:1–8

There is a time for everything,
and a season for every activity under heaven:
a time to be born and a time to die,
a time to plant and a time to uproot,
a time to kill and a time to heal,
a time to tear down and a time to build,
a time to weep and a time to laugh,
a time to mourn and a time to dance,
a time to scatter stones and a time to gather them,
a time to embrace and a time to refrain,
a time to search and a time to give up,
a time to keep and a time to throw away,
a time to tear and a time to mend,

' You pray and pray, and suddenly three arrive at the same time!'

> a time to be silent and a time to speak,
>
> a time to love and a time to hate,
>
> a time for war and a time for peace.

Many of these verses can be applied directly to our job situation. If we are walking with God there is still the chance that we will encounter some or all of the above at some stage in our lives. However, when the appointed time arrives, God will lead us into a new season. The important truth for us to hold on to is that if we wait with humility and patience then our breakthrough will come in God's time[133].

Warning – don't press on without God!

It is reassuring to know that even many of the great heroes of the Bible tried to take short cuts because they became impatient about God's timing. A fine example of this was Moses' own attempts at liberating God's people from the Egyptians. In this familiar story, Moses encountered an Egyptian doling out injustice to a fellow Hebrew, and he intervened by killing the Egyptian.

Moses was right to see the suffering of his people, but his solution was not God's. As a result, instead of receiving an answer to the captivity of the Israelites, Moses had to flee and ended up living in the wilderness for forty long years. Another example of people who gave up on waiting for God's timing to arrive were Abraham and Sarai. Because of their old age, both of them had serious doubts about God's ability to fulfil His covenant to make Abraham's descendants as numerous as the stars. To 'help' God meet His promise, Abraham fathered an illegitimate son – Ishmael. For both Moses and Abraham, God's promises and revelation had to await divine timing. When the time was right, God appeared to Moses in a burning bush, and following this experience he walked in the power and revelation of the 'Most High God'. Also, despite Abraham and Sarai's initial lack of faith, God's promise was eventually fulfilled through the birth of their son Isaac.

I can recall many occasions when I became worn out waiting for God to move in my own job situation. I used to dread the arrival of New Year as that would signal yet another year of waiting in the same old job. In a similar way to Abraham and Moses, I often felt the temptation to take over from God and take a short cut to make things happen. The way that I would do this would be to forget about praying and exercising faith in God, and instead try to bulldoze my way into a new job by sheer force of effort. Looking back, this approach never did work! What is more, I am convinced that God graciously blocked many of these moves until I eventually learnt to submit to His plans for my life.

Waiting is rarely an easy thing to do. Once Samuel had anointed David, he had to wait seven years whilst on the run from Saul. However, whilst he was still in the wilderness, David was given a prime opportunity to take a short cut to his throne. One night after leading his men into Saul's camp, he was asked if they should take this chance to kill the king. Many people would have counselled that this was a smart move because it would have removed the only barrier between David and the throne of Israel.

1 Samuel 26:8

Abishai said to David, 'Today God has given your enemy into your hands. Now let me pin him to the ground with…my spear…'

However tempting this option was to David, he knew that killing Saul was not part of God's plan. He understood that to become king of Israel, he must do it in God's way and according to His timetable, otherwise there would be no blessing.

Even Jesus spent many years as an unknown person and, apart from a few chapters in the gospels concerning His childhood, the Bible concentrates solely upon the last few years of His life. The question that arises is: what was Jesus doing before His ministry started? The answer is that He was waiting quietly for His Father to tell Him when the time was right. Jesus could have become impatient, just like Abraham and Moses before Him, and have made an unsuccessful and premature start to His mission. However, because Jesus knew His Father so well, He understood exactly when to begin His ministry. He understood God's timing and only did what He saw

'His Father doing'. As a result, God's Spirit of revelation was continually upon Him.

John 5:19

Jesus gave them this answer: 'I tell you the truth, the Son can do nothing by Himself; He can do only what He sees His Father doing, because whatever the Father does the Son also does.'

Is it possible that the revelation that we are seeking from God for our next job awaits an appointed time? To help us wait for His timing, we should ask Him to give us an increased measure of wisdom and patience.

God's call – our action – God's revelation

When the time is right God will bring us His revelation, and once this happens, we have a significant role to play. The first part of His revelation in any given situation is His initial call. To begin with, God will often only reveal part of what we should do, with the full picture of His plans only following once we have responded to this call. That is, He will not reveal His full will first, and *then* call us – it will be the other way around. God will call us *first*, and, as we move forward in faith and obedience, He will *then,* step by step, reveal His complete will. As He does this, He will also release the resources and the right strategies to enable us to advance.

The gospel of Matthew includes an episode in the life of Peter that demonstrates how the miraculous can happen when we respond to the call of God, and illustrates how once we step out in faith and expectation, God will give us further instruction and revelation. He will then enable us to achieve what He has asked us to do. The story is the well-known account of Peter stepping out of the fishing boat and walking on the water towards Jesus.

Matt 14:26–29

When the disciples saw Him (Jesus) walking on the lake, they were terrified. 'It's a ghost,' they said, and cried out in fear. But Jesus immediately said to them: 'Take courage! It is I. Don't be

afraid.' 'Lord, if it's you,' Peter replied, 'tell me to come to you on the water.' 'Come,' He said. Then Peter got down out of the boat, walked on the water and came toward Jesus.

In this story, Peter's first task was to listen out for Jesus' call to step out of the boat and onto the water. His second task was to be obedient to this call and take the risky exercise of quite literally stepping out in faith. His obedience had to take place before the miracle of walking on the water took place – it had to be in that order. As soon as Peter responded obediently to His call, Jesus revealed His plan: for Peter to miraculously walk on water. From then on, the rest of it was God's work. In a similar way, the miracle of the bread and fishes was performed when Jesus instructed His disciples to distribute the food among the many thousands of people. The important thing to note is that the miracle actually took place, not in the hands of Jesus, but in the hands of the disciples. Just as with Peter on the water, as soon as they responded to Jesus' instructions the food began to multiply miraculously.

In both miracles the disciples' knowledge or understanding of how God would actually achieve what He called them to do was of no importance. All God expected of them was an obedient demonstration of their faith. It is almost certain that the disciples did not have any idea about how the small amount of food would stretch to feeding such a large number of people. Furthermore, when called to step out of the boat, it is also certain that Peter did not have a clue about how the surface of the lake would take his weight. However, because the disciples were able to show a sufficient level of faith and obedience, both miracles took place – one in the hands of the disciples and the other under the feet of Peter. Discerning the call and being obedient are our responsibility – making it work is God's.

The call of God to do the impossible

Apart from Jesus, Peter is the only person known to have achieved the feat of walking on water. However, finding a job that is suited to our needs can often feel like a similarly impossible task! What each one of us needs at moments when faced with the impossible is the call from God. The Bible tells us that He is always prepared to reveal His will to those who are ready to listen. However, we have to do something with what we hear from Him – we must give a response. Let us now look carefully at this miracle to see how Peter walked on the water.

- **Firstly, Peter had a relationship with Jesus – he recognised that the figure walking on the water was not a ghost, but was indeed his Lord.**
- **Secondly, Peter spoke to Jesus and asked if he could join Him on the water.**
- **Thirdly, Jesus gave Peter instructions – His call to step out of the boat and walk to Him across the water.**
- **Fourthly, Peter heard God's call.**
- **Fifthly, Peter then took a risk and climbed out of the boat without understanding the next step.**
- **Lastly, through God's power, Peter walked on the water.**

Peter achieved the miracle because he stepped into God's plan and provision for his life. In a similar way, if we are eagerly seeking God's face and His revelation for our jobs, we must respond when God gives us the call.

I can recall sitting in my pastor's office expressing frustration at how God didn't appear to want to share the next stage of His plans about a project of mine. I had begun this project with a very clear sense of God's purpose but, after two years, it was as though I was driving along at night without the headlights switched on. Quite simply, I felt lost. My pastor asked me the direct question: 'Have you completed what God has asked you to do?' The answer to that was simple: 'No'. He then replied along the lines that God was likely to give me my next set of instructions *only* after I had begun to complete what He had already given me to do. It can be humbling to be given such obvious advice! The reason why I had yet to receive further guidance was because I had failed to do my bit of 'stepping out of the boat'. I had received a certain amount of revelation from God, but because I had yet to act upon the little that I had been given, my instructions had dried up.

There appears to be an important heavenly dynamic at work when we are obedient and respond, as best we can, to what we believe to be God's call. The good news is that God, unlike the devil, is *not* a legalist. If we get things wrong when we are doing our best to respond to His call, then God will ensure that we will hear from Him to help us get back on track. The important thing for us to do is to step out in obedience with the small amount of revelation that we have at the time. Today, God would encourage us to try this approach in our job situation. In my experience, asking God for guidance in the search for jobs has always been productive, even if it has sometimes led to 'closed doors'.

My pastor's advice turned out to be sound because once I had recommitted myself to the project I began to receive further instructions from God. This came through prophetic confirmation from people at church, an inner feeling of 'rightness', and also resources that arrived out-of-the-blue – making the project possible. In our walk with the Lord, it is good to remember that He is constantly observing our actions and responding to our acts of faith.

Jeremiah 17:10   **'I the Lord search the heart and examine the mind, to reward a man according to his conduct, according to what his deeds deserve.'**

Can we think of something that God has called us to do but haven't yet got around to doing? This could be a call to take a new qualification or training course, or to apply for a promotion, or possibly break out into an entirely new direction in our career. When God calls us to do something, it is important to remember that He is also a practical God who will offer practical solutions to enable us to arrive at our goal. Just as with the disciples, it is easy to be in a situation where we might hear God's call, for example to start training towards a new profession, but have no idea as to how we are going to achieve it. However, if we are able to show Peter's initial level of trust, then we will not allow worry to get in the way of stepping out into God's call on our lives.

Review of chapter

There can be no doubt that at some time or another, most of us will have wished for a short cut to take us closer to achieving God's plans. However, the Bible tells us that His 'hand' can never be forced nor His timing of events for our lives ever be rushed. The hard fact is that sometimes we just have to be patient and wait for Him to give us the green light. The Bible gives us the promise that if we wait patiently, our breakthrough will come in God's timing.

It can be a relief to realise that even many of the great biblical heroes grew impatient of waiting for God to release His blessings. In contrast, Jesus understood the timing of God perfectly and because He knew His Father so well, He recognised exactly when He should start His ministry. When the time is right, God will call us into action. However, He will often *only* reveal the full picture *after* we have responded and stepped out in faith to His call. As we make our tentative steps in response to this call, God will reveal more of His will until we find ourselves completely out of our 'boat' and walking where He has called us.

Dealing with the issues that surround our career can be as challenging as walking on water, and what all of us require when the impossible is needed is the call from God. Our first task, like Peter's, is to listen out for God's revelation, and our second is to be obedient when we receive this call. Peter's miracle only happened once he had obediently responded to Jesus' call to step out of the boat – the rest of it was God's work. Just as with Peter, all God expects of us is a demonstration of our faith in Him – God Himself will make sure the miracle will happen. The important thing for us to do in our job situation is to step out in obedience and faith with the little amount of revelation that we have been given.

The following worksheet will enable you to address some of the issues that have been raised in this chapter. The exercise can be carried out on your own or alongside a prayer partner. Take time to consider each question as honestly as possible, and record your responses on a separate sheet.

Exercise 12
Part 1. Revelation Awaits an Appointed Time – God's Call

God's revelation concerning all things, including guidance about our jobs, awaits an appointed time. God's 'hand' cannot be forced nor His timing of things be rushed. The difficulty that many people in the Bible had was the temptation to 'jump the gun' and seek an alternative to waiting for God's revelation to arrive. Is it possible that the revelation that we are seeking from God, regarding our next job move, waits an appointed time?

For Prayer & Reflection

The following verses, which were used in the chapter, have been chosen to help you to focus on your own circumstances. Take some time to reflect on your situation through the questions that follow these verses.

Habakkuk 2:3   **'For the revelation awaits an appointed time...Though it linger, wait for it; it will certainly come and will not delay.'**

Ecclesiastes 3:1   **There is a time for everything, and a season for every activity under heaven:...**

- **With hindsight, can you think of occasions when God's timing was instrumental in making something happen in your life or job situation?**
- **Have there been occasions when you have become impatient waiting for God and have 'jumped the gun' to get things going?**
- **If you have remembered instances when you have tried to lead God by the 'hand', it is important to ask for His forgiveness.**

- On your own or with a prayer partner, ask God to give you insight and wisdom in regard to the timing for the job or opportunity that you are praying for.

Part 2. Revelation Awaits an Appointed Time – Our Action

God will not always reveal the full picture of His plans to us all at once. He will often wait for us to make a response to His call, and as we take our first tentative steps, God will reveal more of His will. As God reveals His will, step by step, He will also release the necessary resources to enable us to move forward.

For Prayer & Reflection

The following verses, which were used in the chapter, have been chosen to help you to focus on your own circumstances. Take some time to reflect on your situation through the questions that follow these verses.

Matt 14:28–29

'Lord, if it's you' Peter replied, 'tell me to come to you on the water.' 'Come,' He said. Then Peter got down out of the boat, walked on the water and came towards Jesus.

When any one of us is faced with the impossible, what we need is the call from God. When we hear this call, we must give a response.

- **Can you think of something that God has called you to do, but haven't yet got around to doing?**
- **If you can think of something that God has asked you to do and haven't yet responded, it is important to seek His forgiveness. Try asking Him again because He loves to give second, third, fourth, fifth...chances.**

Let us now look at how Peter achieved the miracle of walking on water, and see if we can replicate its principles for our own job situation:

1) **Peter had a relationship with Jesus.**

   How well do you know Jesus and what is your level of intimacy with Him?

2) **Peter spoke to Jesus.**

   Prayer and communication: how often do you bring your requests for your job to God in prayer?

3) **Jesus gave Peter His instructions.**

   How much do you believe that God will give you revelation regarding your next job move?

4) **Peter heard God's call.**

   How much time do you take to listen for God's voice / call?

5) **Peter took a risk.**

   How much do you trust God?

6) **Peter, through God's power, achieved the miracle.**

   How much do you believe that God can achieve a 'miracle' in your job situation?

Dreams and Plans

_____

_____

_____

_____

_____

_____

_____

_____

_____

_____

_____

_____

_____

_____

Chapter 13

Taking a Good Look at Who we are

In this chapter we shall continue to look at how God can choose to bring revelation and instruction into our lives regarding our future jobs and career. We can gain a fairly accurate picture of what God is calling us to do by taking a good look at who we are, what kind of personality we have and what we're good at doing.

God's leading – our skills and abilities

We are all made by God to be unique individuals and designed to do different things. Some are born with a natural ability to create things with their hands, such as an artist or a chef, whilst others are more suited to academia or the pursuit of scientific knowledge. The point is that we are all different and are equipped with distinct and varying abilities. In the construction of the tabernacle God told Moses how He had raised up Bezalel with the necessary skills to make magnificent temple ornaments.

Exodus 31:3–5

> ... and I have filled him with the Spirit of God, with skill, ability and knowledge in all kinds of crafts – to make artistic designs for work in gold, silver and bronze, to cut and set stones, to work in wood, and to engage in all kinds of craftsmanship.

The Bible is full of examples of people having different sorts of occupations according to their abilities:

- **Joseph** (Old Testament) – shepherd and later governor of Egypt
- **David** - shepherd and later king of Israel

- **Herod** - king of Judea
- **Joseph** (New Testament) – carpenter
- **Peter** - fisherman and later leader of the church
- **Luke** - physician and evangelist
- **Matthew** - tax collector and evangelist
- **Paul** - tent maker and evangelist
- **Ethiopian eunuch** - queen's treasurer
- **Caiaphas** - High Priest
- **Lydia** - trader in purple dye

The Bible makes it clear[134] that God has given us everything we need to perform His will. If we're able to discover where our abilities lie, then this will give us some idea about what God wants us to do for a living. In Appendix 6, we shall look at different methods we can use to help us identify what we're good and not so good at doing. God's calling will always be consistent with our skills and abilities. For example, if we don't like the idea of imparting knowledge to people, then God is probably not calling us to become a teacher. If we weren't 'hot' at science at school then we would be wasting our time applying for a job at NASA. If we're aware that figures and finance are not our strength, why should we think that God might be asking us to get trained up in book-keeping? On the other hand, if we know that we have ability in leading people then a career in management could be the way forward. If we are creative and artistic and also highly competent with computers, then a career in graphic design could be right up our street. It sounds like obvious advice, but it is easy to overlook the fact that God's instructions about what we should do for a job can simply be found in the areas where our natural abilities lie.

However, just because we don't consider ourselves to have expertise in something, we should not *immediately* disregard a certain job or profession. A lack of ability in an area, such as doing accounts and figures, might also be an area in which God is asking us to gain a qualification. If we have a desire to do a certain type of job but lack the necessary skills and experience, voluntary work is an excellent way to gain some experience of a profession. Once we have sampled aspects of the job, we will be in a better position to decide if we have what it takes to do it, before committing ourselves to getting trained up in that area. How to go about finding voluntary work and other practical help will be given in the appendices.

God's leading – our personality

We only need to look at the world in all its huge variety to know that God delights in diversity. Not only do our abilities differ radically but so do our personalities. Each of us possesses different personality traits. Some of us are outgoing and spontaneous and like to live high energy, fast-paced lives, whilst at the other end of the spectrum are people who are more reserved and prefer to live more structured, slower-paced lives. People can also be task-orientated, where outcomes and results are important or, at the opposite end, people-orientated, and are warm, relaxed and live by their feelings. Most of us are a mixture of all four of the above. Useful information to help us understand our personality type is given in Appendix 7.

1 Corinthians 12:11

All kinds of things are handed out by the Spirit, and to all kinds of people! (*The Message*)

When we find a job that suits our abilities and personality we will have a sense of peace or šālôm. The reason for this is that when we work according to our ability and personality we are also working according to the design that God set for our lives. Paul is a great example of someone whose calling matched his abilities and personality. God's plan for Paul always involved his conversion on the road to Damascus, and He ensured that Paul came equipped with the necessary personality, skill set and experience to take the 'gospel' to the Gentile world. If we allow God to mould us, similar to Paul, He will also prepare us so that we have what it takes to perform His will. Here is a list of some of Paul's attributes that enabled him to be so effective in his ministry:

- *Assertive* – able to tell those in charge when they were in the wrong (Galatians 2:11).
- *Adaptable* – content in both times of plenty and want (Philippians 4:12).
- *Observant and creative* – use of the unknown god (Acts 17:23).
- *Energetic and bold* – initially against the early church, but later used to excellent

effect to spread the 'gospel' (Philippians 3:6).

- **Determined** – disregarding his violent past, he concentrated solely on completing God's plans for his future (Philippians 3:13).
- **Focussed** – would not let others stop him from going to Jerusalem (Acts 21:14.)
- **Dual citizenship** – this enabled him to approach Jews, Romans and Gentiles (1 Corinthians 9:19-23).
- **Highly qualified** – he received excellent legal and theological training (Acts 22:3).
- **Insight** – Paul's knowledge of God was so deep that he even confused Peter! (2 Peter 3:16).

Even though our calling might be different to Paul's, God has given each of us distinct abilities and personalities to perform a particular task. Our challenge is to accept the way that He has made us and to run with the qualities we have been given.

Understanding that we're different

Someone once said that graveyards are the richest places in the world because they are full of people who have died and taken with them the treasures that God placed in them to use whilst on earth. Jesus told the parable of the talents[135] to demonstrate the importance of using our gifts and abilities. In this story, the master rewarded the servants who used their talents, but punished the servant who did nothing with his own. There are two interesting points to note. Firstly, when we discover and use the abilities and personality that God has given us, we will become increasingly fruitful and productive in our lives. The second point is that we are not all given the same number of talents. When we step outside of our limits and try doing things that do not match our abilities or personality, we can experience stress. If we are to be fruitful in what we do, it is important to know what we're good at doing and to recognise that we cannot excel at everything we choose.

A danger to be aware of is the temptation to compare ourselves with other people. When we do this, it is easy to become jealous of what others have and then to lose sight of what we actually do possess. A likely outcome of making comparisons is that we can concentrate on what other people have and do nothing with what we have been given. In this parable, we are told simply that the master gave talents, (which was a monetary unit like a pound or dollar) according to each of their abilities. The parable does not mention if the servants questioned the decision to give them unequal amounts. However, whilst the first two servants simply got on with using what they had been given, it is possible that the servant who received the least number of talents fell into the common trap of comparing what he had against others. It is conceivable that his 'laziness' was caused by him becoming envious and measuring his portion against theirs. However, the consequences of this inactivity were disastrous: he lost everything.

This is a trap that I have fallen into on more than one occasion. So, what has been my own experience? For a start, some would say that I am a 'typical' left-handed, middle child who developed educationally late in life. To compound it all, I have a high-achieving, older brother who experienced a smooth and seamless career, eventually being head-hunted and going to live in Monaco! We should resist the temptation to compare ourselves against anyone else because in doing so we will allow the devil to discourage us and to steal our joy.

Galatians 6:4   **Each one should test his own actions. Then he can take pride in himself, without comparing himself to somebody else.**

God's leading – our circumstances

God can also use our current circumstances to bring us guidance in our work situation. Different seasons in our lives can place specific demands on us that can radically affect what we decide to do for a job. For example, a friend was recently made redundant and, because his wife had been promoted to a senior level in her company, he decided that he would have to find a local job to enable him do the school-run for their children. Even though this would potentially limit the range of work he could apply for, he accepted that circumstances would heavily affect his next choice of job.

God is certainly in the business of bringing change to our situation, such as getting us out of unemployment. However, when we are considering what we should do next, we also need to look at our present circumstances and see if He is telling us that, for the time being, we need to balance our responsibilities. If we feel overwhelmed by our circumstances due to, for example, a disability, caring for a relative or not knowing how to gain relevant experience, we shall look at some practical ways of overcoming some of these difficulties in the appendices.

Sitting down to count the cost

As with the obedient servants in the parable, God wants us not only to be aware of our own gifts and abilities, but also to be searching for ways to develop them so that we can return to Him with more than we started out. It appears that God is never satisfied in giving us just a little, but wants us to be overflowing with good things[136]. However, there is also our side of the bargain: we have to act and actually work hard to develop the gifts and visions that He has given us. One of the main messages in the parable of the talents is that if we don't use the abilities that we've been given, we'll lose them. On the other hand, if we do use them, God will bring an increase. Paul gave his apprentice, Timothy, similar advice to use the gifts that God had given him.

1 Timothy 4:14–15   **Do not neglect your gift, which was given you…so that everyone may see your progress.**

What is the best way of discovering what we are able to do and then to develop these abilities? Jesus offered the following advice[137]: anyone intending to build a tower should first of all sit down and work out if they have sufficient funds. In a similar way, if we want to discover whether we are able to do a certain type of work, we too should sit down and count the cost to see if we have what it takes to perform a particular job. To help us determine whether we possess the skills, experience and personality to 'complete our tower' – to start a certain profession – there are a number of methods that we can use.

A) Make a self-assessment of what we can do

A good place to start in sitting down and counting the cost is by making an honest and frank assessment of what we think we actually can do. Paul in his letter to the Romans advised:

Romans 12:3   **…Do not think of yourself more highly than you ought, but rather think of yourself with sober judgment…**

An important part of writing a CV or completing a job application is to list our skills, abilities and achievements. If we haven't already done this, it could be a good idea to start now. It is easy to underestimate the skills we possess; everyone has skills that they use every day, probably without realising:

Getting children to school uses:
- Time management skills
- Conflict management skills
- Driving skills

Paying household bills uses:
- Organisational skills
- Budget and finance skills
- IT skills – if paying online

Sorting out disagreements uses:
- People skills
- Communication skills
- Problem-solving skills

Our task is to identify the skills we have and then 'sell' them to an employer. There are also, a number of skills assessment tools, on the internet, that we can use to help us gauge the abilities we possess, and Appendix 6 offers ways to identify and develop those skills that are important for employment.

B) Seeking confirmation and advice

Something else that we can do to enable us to 'sit down and count the cost' is to seek confirmation and advice from other people. Receiving advice and guidance for our career direction is a wise move. The Bible says[138] that plans fail as a result of receiving no or little advice, and if we are serious about seeking God's revelation and instruction, we too should seek advice.

Good advice can give us confirmation about our abilities and possibly shed some reality upon our intentions. A drawback of a self-assessment is that we can often find it difficult to be completely objective. Depending on our personality, we can either be too harsh on ourselves and downplay our abilities, or be unrealistic and exaggerate what we're able to do. When we receive honest advice from other people about what we can do, we gain greater assurance that we have the personality and ability to do a specific job. In particular, the right advice can be essential in our receiving the correct information before we make an important commitment to enter into a certain profession.

Proverbs 12:15   **The way of a fool seems right to him,**
                                   but a wise man listens to advice.

There are many instances in the Bible where advisers and counsellors were used. There were times when God raised up His own people to positions of influence in the courts of kings – Joseph in the palace of the Pharaoh and Daniel in the courts of Nebuchadnezzar. However, we should remember that not all advice is good advice, and the question that arises is: who should we seek advice from for our job situation? Despite being surrounded by court advisers, King Nebuchadnezzar didn't receive any revelation about his dreams until Daniel appeared. Similarly, we too should be selective in who we approach for advice, and should only choose those people who have our best interests at heart.

Who to seek for advice?

Some time ago, a survey discovered some surprising facts about who we are likely to go to for advice on our careers. The most popular group that were approached were families whilst, ironically, the least likely were careers advisers! The survey also showed that many people who give careers advice don't necessarily provide unbiased and informed views. Consequently, to ensure that we receive the right advice about our job situation, it is essential that we seek a range of views, including those from a professional careers organisation. In the table below, we evaluate the pros and cons of approaching certain groups of people for careers advice.

Group	Pros	Cons
Family	Know us well, so could provide useful feedback on how well they think we would fit into a job.	May have ulterior motives to their advice. Also, might not see us objectively enough.
Close Friends	Know us well, so could provide useful feedback on our suitability for a job. More likely to give an objective view than family.	May not want to offend by giving unwelcome advice. Also, may not be aware of important requirements of particular jobs.
Teacher / Lecturer	Will know our ability and something of our character.	Cannot be relied upon to give impartial advice – often pressured to direct into their subject area.
Manager at Work	Will know us quite well, including our ability and character at work.	Cannot be relied upon to be impartial – may be unwilling to give advice that would
Pastor / Church Leader	Should be able to give valuable spiritual guidance as well as practical advice	May not know us well enough to give balanced feedback. Also, may not have sufficient knowledge about the skills needed for a specific type of work.
Careers Adviser	Able to give professional and impartial advice, with access to up-to-date careers information and resources	Access to professional careers advice can be difficult and sometimes expensive (£60 - £100 p/h). Also, the quality of advice and guidance can vary.

Our task, then, is to seek people who can encourage us in a course of action, but who will also speak openly and honestly to us about ourselves. At times, this may involve hearing difficult truths about our ability or personality; however painful this might be, in the end it can be good for us to learn about our limitations. It can be a great advantage to consult professional organisations for careers advice, and Appendix 8 lists different agencies that offer this service; most, but not all, will offer a free service.

Proverbs 20:5 **The purposes of a man's heart are deep waters, but a man of understanding draws them out.**

The advantage of belonging to an active church

It is important that we don't take this 'walk' through our present wilderness on our own. The Bible tells us that we are part of the body of Christ[139], the church, and as such we are not designed to deal with life's issues on our own. We need the church to surround us in order to support us physically, encourage us emotionally and feed us spiritually.

Being guided by the prophetic

Another way that we can sit down and count the cost to see if we are able to do a job is through prophetic guidance. In the last section, we saw how God can speak to us through the advice that we receive from others. In addition to this, God can speak supernaturally to us through His Holy Spirit, and when He does so it is called the prophetic. The prophet Isaiah predicted a time when God's people would hear from Him and would be guided by His voice in all matters[140]. There are plenty of examples of the prophetic in the Bible. For instance, Agabus predicted that Paul would be bound and arrested if he travelled to Jerusalem[141]. Paul had to give a lot of guidance to the early church concerning prophecy, and he emphasised that we should only prophesy if it strengthens, encourages and comforts[142]. If we are part of a church and want to hear from God concerning our job situation, then we too can receive prophetic instruction for our next move. The following recalls one such occasion when I received prophetic guidance for my job.

I had been quietly suffering in a job for eighteen months; the pay was low, the job involved shift work and management was like that in the comedy series *The Office*. My work situation became a regular topic in our prayer group at church but, for many months, nothing appeared to change. One day, I heard about a couple in a church in north London who had started a furniture-recycling project in their neighbourhood. As soon as I heard this, I felt the Holy Spirit's 'finger' jab me in the ribs and say something along the lines of, 'Are you listening?' That night, I prayed for greater revelation. Was God asking me to start up my own furniture-recycling project? If so, where should I start? At that time I didn't even own a car let alone a van to collect and deliver items of furniture.

At the prayer group the following week, I shared what I thought God was asking me to do. My comments raised a few eyebrows and it was suggested that I take this to the church eldership for their wisdom. When I did so, one of the elders felt strongly that the Holy Spirit would open doors for me in this venture, and I left feeling encouraged that I had indeed been hearing correctly from God. I continued to pray for guidance, and began to look for the open doors that one of the elders had prophesied.

The year was 1997, and I was invited to a friend's house to watch the results come in for the General Election. It was a great evening because God decided that this would be the moment when He would open a door and lead me out of the wilderness. Just before the Enfield result was returned, I began a conversation with a person who turned out to be the manager of a local furniture-recycling project, and she was looking to employ someone fluent in a foreign language. As soon as she said this, I immediately knew that this was the job that I should apply for – not only because of the prophetic guidance but also because I spoke French! I attended the interview and promptly got the job. For me this was a great experience of how the prophetic gives not only a foretaste of things to come but also guidance on how to react when knowledge of a job offer arises. If the early church relied on being guided by the Holy Spirit, how much more nowadays should we rely on this form of guidance from God for all parts of our lives including our job situation?

However, it has to be recognised that some churches do not believe that God still speaks to His people in this way, believing, instead, that such guidance was only available for a limited period of time in the early church. If we are to hear God speaking to us prophetically, we need to be praying for this guidance and, importantly, be expectant to receive it.

Receiving encouragement

Another advantage of being part of an active church is that it can be a good place to receive the right sort of encouragement and advice. During his ministry to the Gentiles, Paul had Barnabas, whose name actually means *Son of Encouragement*, to accompany for this very purpose. Despite his outstanding ability to evangelise, Paul still needed to receive encouragement, particularly when faced with opposition and violence. In the same way, if we too feel 'hard pressed on every side' as a result perhaps of being out of work, then we also need to receive encouragement from close friends and family.

2 Corinthians 4:8–9

We are hard pressed on every side, but not crushed; perplexed, but not in despair; persecuted, but not abandoned; struck down, but not destroyed.

There can also be opportunities to network if we are part of a church. The more people we know, the more potential leads we will have for tracking down a job or performing voluntary work. We could even receive advice on how to gain access into a certain type of work, from others in our church who are in that profession. There is some truth in the old adage that tells us: *It's not what you know, but who you know.*

Encouraging others

The pain that we have endured whilst going through our career wilderness comes with its own unique value. The experience that has wounded us the most, often turns out to be the area in which we have most wisdom to help and advise others.

2 Corinthians 1:4

…who comforts us in all our troubles, so that we can comfort those in any trouble with the comfort we ourselves have received from God.

In many ways who better to encourage and advise someone experiencing depression than someone themselves who has dealt with this burden? Who better to help someone who is experiencing long-term unemployment due to a disability than someone who has also gone through the same thing? God sometimes allows us to go through painful situations because this places us in an unrivalled position to support others in a similar situation. When we share our own experience[143] of a career wilderness and how we reached the exit with greater faith and love for God, we automatically encourage others with similar issues. It should also be an encouragement to ourselves to know that people around us can hear from God about their jobs through what we tell them about our own journey across the wilderness. God can use our words to bring revelation and instruction to those in need.

Review of chapter

One way that we can hear from God about our jobs is for us to take an honest look at who we are as a person. The Bible says that God has given us everything we need to perform His will. If we are able to discover what we are good at and what sort of personality we have, then this will give us a good idea about what God wants us to do for a living. Jesus gave the parable of the talents to illustrate the importance of using and developing the gifts that he has given us. When we find a job that suits our abilities and personality, the Bible tells us that we will be fruitful in what we do and also experience a sense of peace.

God created us as unique individuals with different personalities and varying abilities. However, a temptation that we must resist is to compare ourselves with others, as when we do it will probably not only cause us to be jealous but also make us forget about our own qualities. A likely outcome of making comparisons is that we end up by not fully using our own abilities. God can also use our circumstances to speak to us about how we should proceed in our career. Even though God is fully able to turn our situations about, He can, nevertheless, use our present responsibilities and restrictions to guide us in our next choice of work.

It is essential that we take the time to evaluate our potential for employment. There are a number of ways that we can do this, including making a self-assessment and also seeking advice and confirmation from others. We should select people who will not only encourage us in a course of action, but also speak to us honestly about our strengths and weaknesses. A church can be a safe place to seek the right sort of advice and encouragement. An important way that Christians can hear from God is through prophetic guidance from trusted members of their church. Furthermore, in addition to receiving support, we can also encourage others who may be going through similar challenges. God can sometimes allow us to undergo painful situations because it places us in an unrivalled position to help others in similar circumstances. It can be the case that God will use our experience to bring revelation and instruction to those in need.

The following worksheet will enable you to address some of the issues that have been raised in this chapter. The exercise can be carried out on your own or alongside a prayer partner. Take time to consider each question as honestly as possible, and record your responses on a separate sheet.

Exercise 13

Part 1. Taking a Good Look at Who We Are – Knowing our Limits

God sets limits to the areas in which He wants us to be involved. When we find a job that suits our abilities and personality, we will have a sense of peace. However, when we step outside these limits, then we can experience stress.

For Prayer & Reflection

The following verses, which were used in the chapter, have been chosen to help you to focus on your own circumstances. Take some time to reflect on your situation through the questions that follow these verses.

Exodus 31:3 — **... and I have filled him with the Spirit of God, with skill, ability and knowledge in all kinds of crafts.**

Galatians 6:4 — **Each one should test his own actions. Then he can take pride in himself, without comparing himself to somebody else.**

1 Timothy 4:14–15 — **Do not neglect your gift, which was given you...so that everyone may see your progress.**

- **Can you think of any job you have held which:**

    ☞ **Suited you well and where you had a sense of peace?**
    ☞ **Didn't suit you, and you felt stressed?**

- **How could you benefit from this experience the next time you choose a job?**

- Each of us possesses different personality traits, and some are listed in Appendix 7. Ask yourself and others who know you well, which of these types best describes you.

We shouldn't immediately disregard a certain job or profession because of a lack of expertise. God may be asking us to get trained up and qualified in that particular area.

- Can you think of a job / career that you would like to get into but for which, at present, you lack the necessary skills and experience?

- If the answer is yes, then firstly find out as much as possible about that job. Secondly, discover how you can gain relevant experience to test out your interest.

- Turn to Appendix 1, which offers job information, entry requirements and opportunities for voluntary work.

It is important how we compare ourselves with other people as, at times, this can lead to envy, discouragement and loss of joy.

- Are you able to identify moments when you have compared yourself with others? Are you doing it now?

- On your own or with a prayer partner, invite the Holy Spirit to speak to you directly about the unique plans and valuable talents that God has placed inside you.

God can speak through our circumstances about our job situation. When we consider our next job, we need to look at our present circumstances and seek God about how to achieve a balance in our responsibilities.

- By looking at your present circumstances and responsibilities, is it possible to work out what God could be saying about your next job?

- What action do you need to take to strike the necessary balance between your aspirations and your responsibilities?

Part 2. Taking a Good Look at Who We Are – Counting the Cost

The Bible says that God has given us everything we need to perform His will. Jesus advises us to sit down and count the cost or, in other words, work out if we have what it takes to perform a certain job. If we are able to discover what we're good at doing, this may indicate what God wants us to do for a living.

For Prayer & Reflection

The following verses, which were used in the chapter, have been chosen to help you to focus on your own circumstances. Take some time to reflect on your situation through the questions that follow these verses.

Luke 14:28

'Suppose one of you wants to build a tower. Will he not first sit down and estimate the cost to see if he has enough money to complete it?'

Proverbs 20:5

The purposes of a man's heart are deep waters, but a man of understanding draws them out.

1 Corinthians 14:3

But everyone who prophesies speaks to men for their strengthening, encouragement and comfort.

The Bible tells us that plans fail for not taking advice. Advice can give confirmation about our abilities and essential information on which to base our future plans.

- **You have to be selective in your choice of the people you approach for careers advice. Your task is to seek those who can encourage you in a course of action, but who will also speak to you honestly about your ability, personality and circumstances.**

- **Take another look at the table in this chapter and make sure that those** who advise you know what they are talking about!

- **Turn to Appendix 8 for information on how to access professional careers advice.**

A church can be a good place to network. The more people you know, the more potential leads you might have for tracking down a job, performing voluntary work, or even receiving advice from others who are in a certain profession on how to access a type of work.

- **Try finding out what jobs people do in your church. Could they provide you with an opportunity to gain relevant experience or give you useful vocational information?**

The Holy Spirit can guide us as much today as during biblical times, and when He does it is called the prophetic. If we are in an active church then we too can receive prophetic guidance about our job situation.

- **With a prayer partner, ask the Holy Spirit to remind you of the plans that God has for your life**

- **Have you received prophetic words that still haven't become a reality? Ask the Holy Spirit to breathe new life into any prophecies that you may have received.**

God can use our own situation to enable us to empathise and encourage others who may be experiencing similar circumstances.

- **It can be an encouragement for us to know that people can hear from God through the words we speak. Look for opportunities to share your wisdom and experience of walking with God during a challenging job situation.**

Dreams and Plans

_____

_____

_____

_____

_____

_____

_____

_____

_____

_____

_____

_____

_____

_____

Chapter 14

The Desires of our Heart

This chapter will take a final look at how God can choose to bring revelation and instruction into our lives. We shall see that gaining an understanding of the true desires of our heart is an important and yet frequently overlooked way in which we can hear from God for guidance in our job situation.

God wants us to be full of His joy

I grew up with the common misconception that if I did what I *really* wanted to do then I would automatically be going against God. I held the mistaken view that unhappiness, sacrifice and even a degree of suffering were the *only* indicators of successfully following God's plan. Furthermore, I also believed that I couldn't pursue any occupation in which I could be happy because that would have been just too unspiritual. This type of thinking was prevalent in ancient Greek philosophy, where pleasure of any sort was associated negatively with the fleshly, carnal side of human nature, and consequently was evil. On the other hand, it was believed that the spiritual side of human nature could only be experienced through pain, sacrifice and discomfort. Simon Stylites, a Christian ascetic saint who lived in the fourth-century, is remembered for taking this philosophy to extremes. He believed that he could please God and become more holy by living on a small platform on top of a high pillar, which he did for a foot-numbing thirty-seven years!

However, if we take a look at what God has to say about the desires that we have in our heart, then we will learn something quite different from what I used to believe.

Psalm 145:19   **He fulfils the desires of those who fear Him;**
He hears their cry and saves them.

The words joy, gladness, happiness and fulfilment, are closely linked with the idea of the desires of our heart. When we are walking in a close relationship with God, He is in the business of making us joyful and giving us our heart's desires. The theme of *joy* permeates the whole Bible, where the word is mentioned over two hundred and fifty times! Whilst we would be correct in thinking that there are some fairly depressing stories in the Bible involving death and destruction, in fact most of these stem from humankind walking disobediently away from God. That is not to say that all suffering is a result of disobedience. In the early chapters of this book we saw that God can permit pain and suffering in our lives so as to allow good fruit to grow. It is often through our most difficult situations that God is able to do His most effective work. The joy and gladness that God wants to build up in us does not rely upon the level of comfort that we are experiencing. If this were the case then every time something difficult happened, such as a period of unemployment, the joy of God would evaporate like the morning mist.

2 Corinthians 8:2   **Out of the most severe trial, their overflowing joy and their extreme poverty welled up in rich generosity.**

The joy that God places in our hearts is supernatural in nature and is based on the love that exists between God and us[144], and remains with us through both good times and bad. It is also a 'taster' from heaven of things to come in eternity. In the letter to the Hebrews[145], we are told that Jesus was able to scorn the shame and endure His crucifixion because of the joy that was before Him. This joy did not arise out of His crucifixion but out of what was waiting for Him in heaven. Peter explained[146] to the early church that despite their hardships, their 'inexpressible and glorious joy' emerged from their faith in Jesus. Even though they had never actually met Him and were experiencing hardships, nevertheless, the early church was bubbling over with joy and gladness.

'Please Lord, please, please, please, can I have the latest porsche GT, with all optional extras? Oh, and don't forget the fluffy dice.'

What are the desires of our heart?

In our media-driven world, our senses are bombarded with images appealing to our desires: a desire to become a pop star, a desire to become famous, a desire to become a size 6, and the list continues. Sometimes the word 'desire' is even given a sinful connection, suggesting that if we give in to our desires we will, inevitably, do something 'naughty but nice'.

So what does God mean when He tells us that He will give us the desires of our heart? What we're talking about here are those deeply held desires that we have to do something. I am not referring to a lust, for example, to buy the latest Porsche or acquire a beautiful villa in the South of France. The desires of the heart are those that originate from deep within, and emerge like a crystal-clear spring or a mighty geezer shooting high into the air. According to the Bible, the profound desires of our hearts have been placed there by God Himself, and these can only be satisfied when we are in a loving relationship with Him. The devil will offer many counterfeits to this joy and satisfaction, and will try to fool us that we can satisfy these desires elsewhere. God, however, is clear that we can only be fulfilled when we are following Him.

Psalm 37:4   **Delight yourself in the Lord**
                     and He will give you the desires of your heart.

Our true desires will fill us with excitement

If we are aware of what our deep desires are, then we can take this as a good indicator of what God is asking us to do. This is because we are told that these same desires originate from Him in the first place. Our true desires are deeply personal, but it is essential that we don't deceive ourselves by trying to feel something that isn't there. For example, I spent many years convincing myself that I would be happy being a Catholic priest, until I realised that I was trying to force myself into a shape that wasn't me. Of course, God will indeed call others into the Catholic priesthood, but it wasn't my calling. The question that many of us may ask is: how will we know when we are walking according to our true heart's desires and God's plans? The answer is simple: we will know because when we think about these desires our minds will be filled with excitement, enthusiasm, energy, vitality, happiness and life! If what we're feeling does not fit with these descriptions, then we would do well to re-examine what we think we really want to do. If God is behind what we believe are the desires of our heart, then the outcome will always be joy and fulfilment, and not the opposite.

John 10:10   **The thief comes only to steal and kill and destroy; I have come that they may have life, and have it to the full.**

In the previous chapter we made a self-assessment of our abilities and personality, and once we are able to gauge these, it could give us a strong indication of what God intends for us to do. In a similar way, it is a good idea to identify those things that we really enjoy doing – subjects and activities that excite us and cause us to leap out of bed with enthusiasm each morning. It can also be helpful to ask others for their point of view on this matter to see in which situations they think we 'shine' and are more alive. To help us consider different job options and to find out how we feel about certain occupations, Appendix 1 gives useful websites for us to visit. The more we know about our deep desires, the closer we will be to achieving them.

It is also important to point out that when we have identified what we truly want to do, then God will line things up to enable it to happen. Our true desires, which have been given to us from God, reflect the plans that He has set for our lives. For this reason, God will adjust our ability, personality and circumstances to line up with these deeply-held and God-given desires.

God's joy is also our own joy!

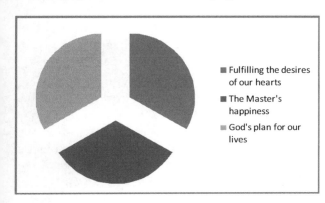

- ■ Fulfilling the desires of our hearts
- ■ The Master's happiness
- ■ God's plan for our lives

The Bible explains that there is a joy that we will come into only when we are doing what God created us to do. We will now pick up again on the parable of the talents.

Matthew 25:23 '**...I will put you in charge of many things. Come and share your master's happiness!'**

We have already established that it is God who places the deep desires in our hearts, and once we follow these, we automatically follow His plans for our lives. In this part of the parable Jesus introduces another dimension: when we follow God's plan we will also 'share in the Master's happiness'. In other words, when we are obedient to God's guidance, He will give us His joy. Somehow, when we obey His plans, our own joy and that of God become identical. Entering the Master's happiness and satisfying our own deep desires are synonymous – one and the same thing.

There is also amazing power available to us when our heart's desires line up with the will of God. Jesus told His followers[147] six times that if they ask for anything in His name, then it would be given to them. The fact that He repeated Himself so many times shows that He wanted them, and us today, to understand an important message: when we pray out of the desires of our hearts they will automatically line up with the will of God. Jesus explains the inevitable outcome of these kinds of prayer – they will always be answered and we will be filled with joy!

John 16:23–24

'...I tell you the truth, My Father will give you whatever you ask in My name...Ask and you will receive, and your joy will be complete.'

The reason why God tells us to ask for things in this manner is because He wants there to be an 'agreement' in the spiritual realm between what we want and what He wants. Paul talks about how God can do 'immeasurably more than all we ask or imagine'[148]. Even if we don't know how He is going to achieve this, when we ask and imagine then we enter into agreement with His promises. When this happens, the rest is up to God and anything can happen!

The killers of dreams

The imagination is where our dreams and the desires of our heart are acted out and given form in our mind. It is the task of the enemy to take these dreams away from us so that we miss the opportunity to pray for God's plans and to experience His joy in our lives. Peter tells us[149] that the devil prowls around like a roaring lion looking for people to devour, and to counter this, the church must stand firm and resist his schemes. It is important for us to acknowledge that the devil still prowls around today seeking to pick people off, and if we are to stand firm against his tactics then it is necessary that we too are aware of the strategies that he employs. A common tactic of the devil is to gradually wear us down. His arsenal for doing this includes three particular weapons that we must be on the look-out for, which we will call the 'killers of dreams':

- **Discouragement**
- **Fear**
- **Hopelessness**

Over a period of time, the enemy uses these either to persuade us to cut down on our dreams or to completely give up on them. Whilst God will be saying, 'Go on, go on', the 'killers of dreams' will cause us to look at our circumstances and believe that all is lost. Instead of standing firm, we end up conceding territory to the enemy and giving up on a dream or a deep desire – this could be to return to college, to start voluntary work or to enter into a certain profession.

After leading the nation of Israel out of the wilderness, Moses assigned leaders of the twelve tribes to explore Canaan and to report back to him on the quality of the land. All of them reported that the land was rich and flowing with 'milk and honey'[150]. However, most of the leaders were overwhelmed by the power of the Amalekites and became fearful. They allowed the 'killers of dreams' to cloud their perception and destroy their desire to possess this land. Despite God's clear plans for Israel to take ownership of this country, most of the leaders who had ventured into Canaan were now considering a full-on retreat – not only back into the Wilderness, but back into slavery in Egypt! Thankfully there were two particular leaders, Joshua and Caleb, who had also reconnoitred this territory and reported back on the fruitfulness of the land. However, in contrast to the other leaders, they had confidence in God's promise and, consequently, they were able to make a stand against the enemy's strategy to rob them of their dreams. Let us now compare the two reports given to Moses on the suitability of the land:

The other leaders' report:[151]

'But the people who live there are powerful, and the cities are fortified and very large…We can't attack those people; they are stronger than we are…We seemed like grasshoppers in our own eyes, and we looked the same to them.'

Joshua and Caleb's report: [152]

'We should go up and take possession of the land, for we can certainly do it.'

The outcome of their reports was decisive. God said[153] that because Joshua and Caleb had a different spirit to the other leaders, only they would be allowed to lead Israel into the land of Canaan. Everyone else who had shown fear and had doubted God's promises was kept from entering into this land and would eventually die in the wilderness.

The Spirit that takes us into God's plans

In a similar way to Joshua and Caleb, what brought David out of his wilderness was a spirit that refused to let go of God's promises. Whilst still on the run from Saul, David did not allow the 'killers of dreams' to destroy his desire to become king, and he cried out that God would fulfil His purpose for him[154]. His response to the temptation to give up on his dreams was not to despair but to declare God's promises over his life. As soon as he took the step of aligning his words to the will of God instead of to fear and discouragement, the victory was his. In this way, David allowed God to fulfil His purpose for him, and we too need to let God do the same in our own lives. If we hold on to the promises of God and speak of His might in the same way as Joshua, Caleb or David, then we also will be allowed to leave our wilderness and take up residence in the territory that God has prepared for us. The challenge of our faith is to declare God's promises out loud, despite all contrary evidence. The flip side to operating in faith is to speak and act out of discouragement, fear or hopelessness, which can prevent us from entering into God's plans and achieving the desires of our heart.

As we look over our lives we might become aware of deep desires that have remained in our heart untouched, ignored and forgotten. It may be possible that just like the leaders of Israel who gave a negative report to Moses, that we too have allowed discouragement, fear or hopelessness to destroy our dreams and desires. For us, this could be the result of not having received the right encouragement from our family when growing up – in fact - all we may have received was discouragement. On the other hand, we might have spent some or most of our lives in 'survival mode', and never held any precious dreams at all. It is also possible that at one time we did hold a desire to do something only for circumstances to rip it from our hands. There can be many reasons why our dreams and desires die, and some of us may be able to identify closely with Job after he had lost everything that he valued.

Job 17:11   **My days have passed, my plans are shattered, and so are the desires of my heart.**

The challenge for us is to exercise our faith, to disregard the 'killers of dreams' and to focus on what God's promises have to say. We cannot defeat the enemy by using our own words. Instead, if we speak the word of God with conviction, then not only will the enemy cease his attack, but we will also find that our God-inspired dreams will begin to take on life and become a reality. Once we do this, absolutely nothing can take away our deeply-held desires – not resources, age, qualifications or circumstances. If we align our words to those of God, it will only be a matter of time before His plans for our lives come to pass.

It is good to realise that if we have committed our lives to Jesus then, whatever our experience has been to date, there can always be a new beginning. If we have lost sight of our dreams and the desires of our heart, or have felt that we never held any, then there is exciting news: God is inviting each of us today to come to Him again so that He can renew and restart our dreams. Through these, God will guide us into what He has always planned for us to do.

Isaiah 60:1   **'Arise, shine, for your light has come, and the glory of the Lord rises upon you.'**

Review of chapter

An often overlooked way in which we can hear from God for guidance in our job situation is to gain a better understanding of the true desires of our heart. According to the Bible, these desires have been placed there by God Himself, and can only be satisfied through a loving relationship with Him. Because they come from God in the first place, these desires can serve as a guide as to what God wants us to do. Furthermore, we will recognise our true heart's desires and also God's plans because they will fill our minds with joy and excitement.

The parable of the talents teaches us that walking according to God's plans, experiencing His happiness and satisfying the desires of our heart are all one and the same thing. There is also power available to us when we pray out of the desires of our heart because, in doing so, we pray in line with the will of God. Jesus says that these kinds of prayer will fill us with joy and will always be answered.

However, the enemy will try to take these dreams away so that we miss our opportunity to pray for God's plans and to experience His joy in our lives. A tactic of the devil is to use the 'killers of dreams' – discouragement, fear and hopelessness – to force us to give up on our desires. We are told that what enabled Joshua and Caleb to make a positive report to Moses and to enter the 'promised land' was their different spirit. In a similar way, David's spirit allowed him to hang on to God's promises and his dream of becoming King of Israel. If we continue to declare the promises of God for our lives, then we too will enter into His plans and fulfil our dreams for our jobs and careers.

The following worksheet will enable you to address some of the issues that have been raised in this chapter. The exercise can be carried out on your own or alongside a prayer partner. Take time to consider each question as honestly as possible, and record your responses on a separate sheet.

Exercise 14

Part 1. The Desires of Our Heart – Gaining an Understanding

The desires of the heart are those that originate from deep within us. According to the Bible, the really profound desires have been placed there by God Himself, and these can only be satisfied when we are in a fruitful, loving relationship with Him. If we are aware of what our deep desires are then we can take this, with some confidence, as a good indicator of what God is asking us to do.

For Prayer & Reflection

The following verses, which were used in the chapter, have been chosen to help you to focus on your own circumstances. Take some time to reflect on your situation through the questions that follow these verses.

Psalm 37:4   **Delight yourself in the Lord,**
                                           and He will give you the desires of your heart.

2 Corinthians 8:2   **Out of the most severe trial, their overflowing joy and their extreme poverty welled up in rich generosity.**

Joy, gladness, happiness, fulfilment – these are words that are closely linked with the idea of the desires of our heart. God wants to make us joyful and give us our heart's desires.

- **What is your belief system? Do you believe deep down that God wants you to be full of joy and walking according to the desires of your heart, or do you believe that in order to please God you have to endure pain and suffering?**

- **This could be a good time to apologise to God about any wrong beliefs that you may hold. Ask Him to speak to you about His love for you and how**

He wants you to be full of joy.

We will be able to recognise our true desires because they should bring our hearts to life and fill our minds with excitement, enthusiasm, energy, vitality, happiness and life. If what we are feeling does not fit these descriptions, then we would do well to re-examine what we believe we really want to do.

- **How do you feel when you think about the desires of your heart? Does the thought fill you with excitement or the opposite?**

- **Spend some time going through Appendix 1, which gives some useful job information websites. How do you feel about some of the jobs that you were able to research?**

- **If you are unsure about your true desires, then ask God to show you. Once you have prayed, keep your eyes and ears open as you watch TV, read the newspaper and go about your daily routine. God will bring to your heart something precious to you.**

- **Ask people who know you well to tell you what appears to make you 'shine' and be more alive.**

Part 2. The Desires of Our Heart – Holding on to Our Desires

The enemy's intention is to take our dreams away so that we miss the chance to pray for God's plans and to experience His joy. It is important for us to look out for the 'killers of dreams' – discouragement, fear and hopelessness – that the enemy uses to force us to cut down or to completely give up on our dreams.

For Prayer & Reflection

The following verses, which were used in the chapter, have been chosen to help you to focus on your own circumstances. Take some time to reflect on your situation through the questions that follow these verses.

Matthew 25:23	'...I will put you in charge of many things. Come and share your master's happiness!'
Numbers 13:30	We should go up and take possession of the land, for we can certainly do it.

- Can you recall times in your life, no matter how long ago, when the 'killers of dreams' stole dreams from you and caused you to modify or to abandon your plans?

- As you look back, you might become aware of deep desires that have remained in your heart untouched, ignored or forgotten. This could have happened as the result of:

    - Never having received the right kind of encouragement as a child.
    - Having children very early on in life.
    - Being hit by ill health.
    - Finances drying up after having being made unemployed.
    - An abusive family situation.
    - A failed project or business venture, destroying your confidence.
    - Failure at school, resulting in low basic skill levels.

- Is it possible to identify some of the reasons that have taken away your dreams and desires?

- Bring these before God

    By making an effort to agree with God about His plans for his life, David allowed God to fulfil His purpose for him. In the same way, we need to allow God to fulfil His purpose for us. Our challenge is to exercise faith and to disregard the three dream killers and to focus on what God's promises have to say.

- There is always a new beginning in Jesus! On your own or with a prayer partner, present your dreams to God and ask Him to breathe new life into your dreams.

Dreams and Plans

_____

_____

_____

_____

_____

_____

_____

_____

_____

_____

_____

_____

_____

_____

_____

Chapter 15

Fragile Jars of Clay

In this chapter we shall look at how the word of God can help us overcome certain barriers that can prevent God's revelation and His purposes from entering our lives. These barriers include:

- Our perspective of ourselves

- Our self-doubt and insecurity

- Generational sin

Scripture contains many accounts of how God worked with ordinary people who displayed failings and weaknesses. Paul described us as fragile as jars of clay[155] into which God has placed the light of His word. It should be an encouragement for us to know that despite our frailties, God is able to include us intimately in His plans. To bring this into the context of our work, it is well within the capabilities of God to move us into a job or to develop a successful career even if, for example, we have spent a long time out of work. In fact, Paul was not shy about recalling his own flaws, saying[156] how on many occasions he was put under all kinds of strain for the sake of the gospel. He also described[157] having 'a thorn in my flesh', which was undoubtedly some sort of disability. Because of his infirmity, Paul was able to declare that God's power is made 'perfect in weakness'[158].

A Godly perspective of ourselves

The first barrier that can prevent God's revelation and purposes entering our lives is the way we view ourselves. God appears to have a different perspective on our weaknesses, as if He deliberately allows them so that He can display His power. In fact, Paul said that God went out of His way to work with those that the world would consider weak and inadequate in order to shame the strong and the wise.

1 Corinthians 1:27 | **Isn't it obvious that God deliberately chose men and women that the culture overlooks and exploits and abuses, chose these 'nobodies' to expose the hollow pretensions of the 'somebodies'? (*The Message*)**

Not only does God have a different perspective on our weaknesses, but He will also help us to change our own view of ourselves. To bring this into context, whatever our experience has been of developing a career, God wants us to base our expectations not on what has happened to us in the past, but on what He intends for us in the future. God didn't see Moses merely as a well-to-to, stuttering shepherd, but always saw him as a mighty man of faith who would lead the nation of Israel out of captivity in Egypt. However, like many of us, Moses required some help in accepting this new revelation into his life. Before God could use him to liberate His people, He needed to change Moses' own perspective of himself. How did He achieve this?

Exodus 4:2–4 | **Then the Lord said to him, 'What is that in your hand?' 'A staff,' he replied. The Lord said, 'Throw it on the ground.' Moses threw it on the ground and it became a snake, and he ran from it. Then the Lord said to him, 'Reach out your hand and take it by the tail.'…**

In this account, God asked Moses to move on from his old life of under achievement, and to lay down his identity of a humble shepherd – as symbolised by his staff. To ensure that Moses separated himself from his staff and all that it represented, God literally turned it into a snake and, unsurprisingly, Moses ran away from it. God's next command, for Moses to actually pick up the snake, appears to be strange. This was a test of his trust and faith in God's instruction and, as soon as he did this, the snake turned back into a staff. The test was an important step in helping Moses adjust the way he viewed himself. What was formerly 'a staff' in his hand and everything it represented – the old Moses – was now God's staff in his hand. Previously, Moses' staff merely guided and protected his flock of sheep; now it would guide and protect the nation of Israel on their journey to the 'promised land'. By picking up the snake, Moses didn't just show obedience but also confidence and faith in following God's word, however unusual that may have appeared. In the same way, when we follow God's instructions and apply His word over our lives, He will bring revelation and enable us to view ourselves as He sees us.

Breaking out of our self-imposed mould

In the gospel of John[159] we are given the account of Jesus meeting a man who had been an invalid for most of his life and, surprisingly, Jesus asks him if he wants to get better! Why did He ask such an obvious question? After all, the man had been living on the fringes of society for thirty-eight long years. The answer lies in the fact that he had become so consumed by his problems that his identity had become the disability itself. When Jesus asked him if he wanted to be healed, the disabled man didn't just answer a simple 'Yes', he just rewound the tape that he had been playing in his head for all those years – 'I have no-one to help me into the pool…'.

We can also easily become absorbed with our own issues, such as being out of work, up to the point that when Jesus actually offers a way out, we are not able to take it up. It is possible to entirely lose perspective and forget not only how we used to see ourselves but also how God views us. All we see is ourself with the problem superimposed, such as our lack of experience or qualifications. God wants to change our perspective so that we break out of what has been containing us and expect a change in our circumstances. By confessing God's word over our situation, we allow the Spirit of God to bring about this release.

In the book of Genesis[160], we read how Abraham also lost his perspective and became overwhelmed by the fact that he had no son to whom he could pass on his inheritance. To help him readjust his viewpoint, God took him out of his tent (his problem) and asked him to look up at the heavens. When Abraham did this, his focus switched from his own dilemma to God's promises. In a similar way, declaring God's word over our lives will enable us to move our gaze from our immediate situation to the plans that He has prepared for us.

Self-doubt and insecurity

The second barrier that can prevent God's revelation and purposes entering our lives is our self-doubt and insecurity. The calling of Moses and Gideon had something significant in common: their responses showed that they were both racked by insecurity and self-doubt. Each of their calls from God came during a period when Israel was 'under the cosh' and in need of a strong leader to deliver it from their enemy. However, when Moses was asked by God to return to Egypt to set the Israelites free, he reacted by panicking and being overwhelmed with doubt. Similarly, when Gideon received God's call to liberate Israel, he responded in the same way by protesting that he was simply not up to the task. What both of these men did was to speak out of their fear and insecurity rather than out of their faith in God. The following conversation records Moses' response to God's request for him to liberate Israel from the Egyptians:

The call of Moses[161]

God: So now, go. I am sending you to Pharaoh to bring my people the Israelites out of Egypt.

Moses: Who am I that I should go to Pharaoh...?

God: I will be with you. And this will be the sign to you that it is I who have sent you...

Moses: Suppose I go to the Israelites and say to them, 'The God of your fathers has sent me to you,' and they ask me, 'What is His name?' Then what shall I tell them?

God: I AM WHO I AM...Go, assemble the elders of Israel and say to them, 'The Lord, the God of your fathers...appeared to me and said...I will make the Egyptians favourably disposed towards this people...

Moses: What if they do not believe me...?

God: But if they do not believe these two signs or listen to you, take some water from the Nile and pour it on the dry ground... (it) will become blood on the ground.

Moses: O Lord, I have never been eloquent...I am slow of speech and tongue.

God: Now go; I will help you speak and will teach you what to say.

Moses: O Lord, please send someone else to do it.

The following conversation records Gideon's response to God's request for him to liberate Israel from its oppressor:

The call of Gideon[162]

God: The Lord is with you, mighty warrior.

Gideon: But sir, if the Lord is with us, why has all this happened to us?...But now the Lord has abandoned us and put us into the hand of Midian.

God: Go in the strength you have and save Israel out of Midian's hand. Am I not sending you?

Gideon: But Lord, how can I save Israel? My clan is the weakest in Manasseh, and I am the least in my family.

God: I will be with you, and you will strike down all the Midianites together.

Gideon: If you will save Israel by my hand as you have promised – look, I will place a wool fleece on the threshing floor. If there is dew only on the fleece and all the ground is dry, then I will know that you will save Israel by my hand, as you said.

(Early the next day, Gideon squeezed out the fleece and wrung out the dew)

Gideon: Do not be angry with me. Let me make just one more request...

These conversations not only show the insecurity of two men, but also show the grace of God. Despite His anger with Moses, God's reply sounds like a loving parent who is frustrated with a petulant child: 'What about your brother, Aaron...? I know he can speak well.' The Lord might have been justified in punishing both Moses and Gideon for their lack of faith by withdrawing their commission. Instead however, God overlooked their negativity, and patiently offered them one assurance after another to be with them at all times.

It can be argued that insecurity and faith in God are complete opposites, and the fruit that they produce are also poles apart. Insecurity demands something concrete that our senses are able to physically detect, and the fruit that it produces will invariably be negative and based on a fear of *possible*, rather than *certain* outcomes. Faith in God, on the other hand, does not demand something physical for our senses to detect, but is all about 'being sure of what we hope for and certain of what we do not see'[163]. This emerges when we are reborn spiritually and acquire a sense that enables us to detect the presence and promises of God. One translation defines faith as the 'essence' of things hoped for, and it is our spiritual sense that picks up this essence or aroma of hope that comes from God.

Many of us can probably identify with how both Moses and Gideon felt when God showed them His plans for their lives. With hindsight it is easy to point the finger at these two great men and suggest that they should have immediately stepped into God's commands. However, obeying God's commands was no easier for them than it is for us today. Are there insecurities in our lives that cause us to doubt and to be fearful when God speaks to us about His plans? There are some areas in my own life, such as my job situation, in which I now have a secure faith that has been tried and tested many times. However, there are other areas where I am still a work in progress, and my faith levels are less than secure.

Our employment situations can provide ample opportunity to display insecurity and fear. There can be many reasons for this, but it could be due to a disability or a low level of qualifications and skills. Our insecurity might also stem from a lack of relevant work history or complicated family commitments that appear to limit our chances of obtaining work. Whatever shape our insecurities take - if God is asking us to do something new regarding our work - then He will commend us for stepping out in faith[164]. When we do this, only victory awaits!

Hebrews 11:33–34

> **...who through faith conquered kingdoms, administered justice, and gained what was promised; who shut the mouths of lions, quenched the fury of the flames, and escaped the edge of the sword; whose weakness was turned to strength; and who became powerful in battle and routed foreign armies.**

Don't allow negativity to rule

Elijah provides us with one of the most tragic stories in the Bible about someone who did not fulfil his calling. Despite experiencing the dizzy heights of calling down God's fire and defeating the priests of Baal, he nevertheless allowed insecurity and fear to rob him of his ministry. In order to coax him out of his insecure mindset, God came to talk with Elijah personally when he was hiding in his cave. Despite this intervention, God decided that he was not going to change, so he took away Elijah's anointing and transferred it to Elisha. The story of Elijah gives us an important warning that if we continue to respond to God in a negative way, the call on our lives to do something will not necessarily remain with us indefinitely. At some stage, hopefully sooner rather than later, God expects us to step out in faith and take a risk with Him. In doing so, we should know that if we have accepted Jesus into our lives then we are the beloved of God and consequently can rest secure in His care.

Deuteronomy 33:12 **...'Let the beloved of the Lord rest secure in Him, for He shields Him all day long, and the one the Lord loves rests between His shoulders.'**

Comfort zones

A by-product of being insecure is the development of comfort zones. The main characteristics of a comfort zone are inactivity and a reluctance to move on, and they can prevent the plans of God becoming a reality in our lives. Comfort zones are a form of psychological conditioning that cause us to create and operate within set boundaries. Anyone who has established such a zone will tend to stay there and not step outside for fear of losing the unfounded sense of security that it brings. This way of thinking also persuades us to settle for what is merely good enough rather than what is actually best for us. When God appeared in the burning bush, Moses was well established in his comfort zone. After retreating to the desert following his failed attempt to liberate the Hebrews from Egypt, Moses had decided to settle down to work as a shepherd for the rest of his life. However, God had different plans and, despite his extensive protests, Moses eventually stepped out of his comfort zone and into God's plan for his life.

If we are to leave such a zone ourselves, it will always involve challenging established ways of doing things in our lives. If this is where we are at present, then God would ask us to adopt a new set of behaviours to enable us to enter more fully into his plans.

Romans 12:2 **Do not conform any longer to the pattern of this world, but be transformed by the renewing of your mind. Then you will be able to test and approve what God's will is – His good, pleasing and perfect will.**

Generational sin

The third barrier that can prevent God's revelation and purposes entering our lives is the effect of sin passed down through our family from one generation to another. God's purpose is to bless us, and the Bible tells us of the blessings that flow from being in a close relationship with Him – blessings that don't just remain with us but also pass on automatically through our family line. David tells us in one of his psalms[165] that the Lord's love and His righteousness is with both those who fear Him and also with their children's children. In a similar way we read in Exodus[166] that God shows His love to a thousand generations of those who love Him and keep His commands. The implications are that our descendants, many generations on, will benefit from how closely *we* are walking in the ways of God.

There is, unfortunately, a flip side to this. The Bible tells us that as with blessings, sin is also passed along our generational lines. This is a spiritual principle, though it can often be seen working through natural social patterns. For example, unfaithfulness in marriage gives a poor example to children and undermines their ability to trust a future partner or to be faithful themselves. Generational sin, like any other type of sin, is a rebellion against God. When we are born again by accepting Jesus into our lives, we are legally justified before God and are forgiven. However, we are not yet free from the consequences of sin[167], and this includes the effects of generational sin.

| Exodus 20:5–6 | **...For I, the Lord your God, am a jealous God, visiting the iniquity of the fathers upon the children to the third and fourth generations of those who hate Me, but showing mercy to thousands, to those who love Me and keep My commandments.** (*NKJV*) |

It is clear from the Bible that generational sin is not a punishment on future generations but is rather a consequence of the actions of our ancestors. We are told that the sins of our forefathers are *visited* on us, and this is a spiritual principle that can have a radical effect on our lives. Such sins can not only affect families, but also communities and even entire countries. In the book of Joshua[168] we have the account of Achan who, through disobeying God by stealing some plunder, caused the whole of Israel to suffer defeat in battle. God said that until this sin was dealt with, His presence and victory would not accompany Israel. This shows that Achan's sin didn't just affect him and his family, but also the whole of the nation of Israel.

Paul tells us in his letter to the Ephesians[169] that, in reality, our struggle is not against things that we can see but rather a battle against a whole array of spiritual powers and forces set against us by the devil. The mindset of the western world often struggles to accept the reality of unseen spiritual activity, relegating it either to fiction books or Hollywood films. However, many places in the developing world, such as Africa, have an acute understanding and awareness of the intense battle going on between God and His angels against the devil and his demons. In fact, Paul goes on to tell us[170] that what we see around us is not set to last forever, whereas that which is unseen in the spiritual realm is more real and will last for eternity. It is important to stress that the outcome of this battle has already been decided: Jesus won the victory by being raised from the dead[171]. However, until He returns to earth, the battle for our lives continues.

Freedom from generational sin

Generational sin can often be identified by looking at patterns of behaviour and recognising recurring problems in successive generations along our maternal or paternal lines. These behavioural problems can affect every part of our lives, and some common patterns include alcoholism, gambling, violence, financial or business failure, interest in the occult and certain forms of sickness. A further problem that can be passed down through the generations is long-term unemployment. We are not talking about a period of unemployment that can be a feature at some time in all of our lives. What we are referring to here is the situation where whole families haven't seen a single member work for many years. What we also have in mind are families that have no work ethic or aspirations to improve their lot in life and have had many generations who have been wholly dependent on the social security system. Welfare support is an important part of society and is a privilege that is not available in every country. However, many people suffer from the generational sin that keeps them trapped in long-term unemployment. It also results in a mindset that does not seek to improve their chances but instead encourages an unhealthy dependency on the state for survival.

During my time as a careers adviser in South London, I worked intensively on many housing estates that were experiencing substance misuse, poverty, vandalism and unemployment rates of over 70%. However, despite the desire of many people to get out of this situation, it was often very difficult to actually meet with them in the first place to help them to move on. When I delivered advice in community venues, I would count it a successful day if even one in five of my clients remembered or were able to keep their appointments. In many of our situations and in the lives of our families, God's blessings are often not getting through because of the sin that has been passed down. Jesus said[172] that the thief (the devil) comes into our lives in order to 'steal and kill and destroy'. The good news is that Jesus Himself wants to come into our generational line so that He can bring life into areas where there has been only pain and death. This means that in Him, we can free ourselves from the effects of sin in our family line and begin to walk unhindered with God. For some of us this issue could be very significant. At the end of this chapter there is an exercise which is designed to help us to take the necessary steps to break any generational sin that we might recognise in our own lives. The essential stages in the process are:

- identifying the root of this sin in our generational line.
- applying the 'axe' to this root through forgiveness and repentance.

Review of chapter

It should be an encouragement to know that despite our imperfections, God is able to include us in His plans. Whether our weakness is a lack of skills or long-term unemployment, He can always turn the situation around. God holds a different view of our weaknesses as though He allows them so that He can display His power.

God also wants to transform our own perspective of who we are, and to bring fresh revelation to view ourselves in the same way as He sees us. Not only this, He will enable us to move our gaze from our immediate situation to the plans that He has prepared for us. In the same way, God will also deal with any self-doubt and insecurities that might be preventing us from entering fully into His purposes. Our employment situations can provide us with plenty of occasions to display insecurity and fear. However, when God calls and we step out in faith – and not insecurity – then breakthrough awaits us.

The Bible tells us that God wants to bless us, and that these blessings pass on automatically to our descendants. We also learn from scripture that, in a similar way, the sins of our ancestors are also passed along our family line. Generational sin is the consequence of the actions of our forefathers that can have a major effect on our lives. However, the good news is that in Jesus, we can free ourselves from the fallout from generational sin and begin to walk fully according to God's plans.

The following worksheet will enable you to address some of the issues that have been raised in this chapter. The exercise can be carried out on your own or alongside a prayer partner. Take time to consider each question as honestly as possible, and record your responses on a separate sheet.

Exercise 15

Part 1. Fragile Jars of Clay – Changing Perspectives

God appears to have a different view of our weaknesses, as if He allows them so that He can display His power in our lives. When His word lives in us, He is able to include us in His plans. Our job situation can give us many opportunities to show insecurity and fear, but when God calls and we respond in faith, only victory awaits.

For Prayer & Reflection

The following verses, which were used in the chapter, have been chosen to help you to focus on your own circumstances. Take some time to reflect on your situation through the questions that follow these verses.

Exodus 4:2–4

> **Then the Lord said to him, 'What is that in your hand?' 'A staff,' he replied. The Lord said, 'Throw it on the ground.' Moses threw it on the ground and it became a snake, and he ran from it. Then the Lord said to him, 'Reach out your hand and take it by the tail'...**

Deuteronomy 33:12

> **...'Let the beloved of the Lord rest secure in Him, for He shields him all day long, and the one the Lord loves rests between His shoulders.'**

- **Are there any insecurities in your life, especially around your job situation, that fill you with doubt and fear?**

- **If you suffer from low self-esteem or have a poor self-image, God wants to change this. Take some time out and invite the Holy Spirit to speak with you personally of the Father's love for you.**

- **Ask close friends and family to remind you of some of your positive aspects.**

God wants to transform our perspective and bring fresh revelation to view ourselves in the same way as He sees us. He always saw Moses as a mighty man of faith who would lead Israel out of captivity. However, as with many of us, Moses needed help to accept this new revelation. The following exercise is based on Exodus 4:2-4.

1) *Casting away Moses' staff (old-self)*

- On a sheet of paper, write down any factors that may have caused you to be insecure and to doubt yourself. Examples may include: negative words spoken over you by others or by yourself, a lack of encouragement in your life, being stuck in a rut, a disability, a lack of career focus, a lack of education, a low level of skills, a feeling that even God has no great plan for your life.

- Together with a prayer partner, seek God's forgiveness for your own doubt and lack of faith, and also forgive those who have hurt you.

- Ask the Holy Spirit to bring God's healing into these areas.

- Take the sheet of paper and, like Moses did with his staff, throw it 'on the ground' – bin it!

2) *Taking up God's staff (new-self)*

- On another sheet of paper, write down any prophecies that you have received.

- Revisit scripture given in the previous exercises and, on the new sheet of paper, write down any that speak to you for your particular situation.

- Ask the Holy Spirit to breathe life into any scripture that speaks powerfully to you and also into any prophetic words or pictures that you have been given.

- Ask the Holy Spirit to give you His perspective of who you are in Christ – an heir and cherished child of God[173].

Comfort zones in our lives can be the result many different factors. The reason behind Moses' comfort zone was a lack of self-confidence and faith in God. However, there can be other reasons that can cause us to fall into such a zone. The Bible recognises this and, in particular, instructs us to be on the lookout for any of the following in our lives:

- **Stubbornness, disobedience**

    Psalm 81:12   **So I gave them over to their stubborn hearts to follow their own devices.**

- **Idolatry and love of the world**

  Matthew 6:32   'For the pagans run after all these things, and your heavenly Father knows that you need them.'

- **Laziness and lack of effort**

  Matthew 25:26   His master replied, 'You wicked, lazy servant! So you knew that I harvest where I have not sown and gather where I have not scattered seed?'

- **Are you in a comfort zone? Can you identify why this is so?**

- **If you have fallen into a comfort zone, it could be an opportunity to apologise to God. On your own or with a prayer partner, ask God to help you to adopt new ways of doing things, and also ask to be given new opportunities to step into.**

Part 2. Fragile Jars of Clay – Generational Sin

In many of our lives and those of our families, the blessings that God has planned are sometimes not reaching us because of the sin that has been passed down from one generation to another. This can often be identified by looking at patterns of behaviour and recognising recurring problems in successive generations. Issues surrounding unemployment can *sometimes* be the result of generational sin.

For Prayer & Reflection

The following verses, which were used in the chapter, have been chosen to help you to focus on your own circumstances. Take some time to reflect on your situation through the questions that follow these verses.

Exodus 20:5–6   ...For I, the Lord your God, am a jealous God, visiting the iniquity of the fathers upon the children to the third and fourth generations of those who hate Me, but showing mercy to thousands, to those who love Me and keep My commandments. *(NKJV)*

Psalm 103:17

But from everlasting to everlasting
the Lord's love is with those who fear Him,
and His righteousness with their children's children —

Exercise for freedom from generational sin

Freedom from all sin is found in the blood of Jesus and this is taken up through our faith, which results in repentance and forgiveness. The following exercise is designed to help us to break any generational sin that we might recognise in our own lives. Together with a prayer partner, invite the Holy Spirit to bring revelation and release as you go through each part of the exercise.

- **Come to God in prayer and ask the Holy Spirit to show you any patterns of generational sin in your family from your father's side or your mother's side.**

- **Using a family tree, make a note of everything that He shows you.**

- **It is important to come out of denial and recognise any hurt that was committed against you by your parents and your ancestors.**

- **Forgive those who have sinned against you – speak your forgiveness out loud.**

- **Acknowledge and repent of your own sin, which may include anger or fear, and accept responsibility for it (1 John 1:9).**

- **Also, repent of the sins of your forefathers   (Ezra 9:5-7 and Nehemiah 1:5-7).**

Ask your prayer partner to pronounce forgiveness over you (James 5:16).

- **Together with your prayer partner, pronounce the following: 'We break the curse of the law that has come on me through generational sin, on the basis that Jesus became a curse for me, through dying on the cross, so that I might instead inherit the blessing of Abraham, who God blessed in all things.' (based on Galatians 3:13,14)**

Source: Chester & Betsy Kylstra – Restoring The Foundations www.rtfi.org

Chapter 16

Head in the Heavenlies and Feet on the Earth

In this book we have looked at how God can use a career wilderness to introduce change in ourselves, and we have also examined the ways in which God can speak to us regarding our choice of career. In this final chapter we shall look at how to move forward with our jobs in a practical way once we have heard from God. The chapter will deal with the important matter of keeping our feet firmly planted on the ground whilst at the same time keeping our heads and minds in the heavenly realms.

Working hard without striving

After many years of trying to follow God, I have discovered that when I do obey His lead, I also have to work very hard. However, it has also been my experience that whenever I walk according to His plan, I never have to strive or struggle to achieve success. Even though God expects us to work hard and to use the gifts and abilities that He has given us[174], He doesn't expect us to strive in order to make things happen. Let us clarify an important difference between the economy of God and the economy of the world.

In the economy of the world there is no understanding or recognition that there is a heavenly Father with whom we can develop a close relationship[175] and, furthermore, can be relied on to help and guide us. In this economy we are very much dependent on our own strengths and strategies – not only do we have to work hard, but we also have to fight and contend with others in order to achieve our goals. On the other hand, in the economy of God we are certainly called to work hard, but there should never be any striving in what we do. It is amazing how much easier things become when we are walking closely with God, listening out for His voice and following His strategies. Before Adam and Eve were thrown out of the Garden of Eden they were put in charge of God's creation[176]. It was only after their fall and departure from the garden that they began to toil in their daily work[177]. If we have invited Jesus into our lives and are diligently following His lead, God's promise is that we will operate in His strength and not our own. If we do it this way, then there will be no need to struggle to get things done.

Zechariah 4:6	**'Not by might nor by power, but by My Spirit,' says the Lord Almighty.**

God promises that He will renew our strength and that we will not grow faint and become weary[178]. Finding a meaningful job that not only pays the bills but also brings a level of satisfaction can involve plenty of hard work. However, when we invite God into the situation, He will ensure that we do not end up striving in order to make it happen. I well recall an occasion when, out of desperation to leave a particular job, I attended no less than twelve interviews in a single month. Within a fortnight I had received rejections for every single position for which I had applied. In fact, some of the companies that had offered me an interview didn't even bother to contact me with the results, and I only discovered on the grapevine that I hadn't been successful. As soon as we become desperate and try to go forward in our own strength, we can set ourselves up for failure and disappointment. Once this episode was over and I had said 'sorry' to God, I distinctly remember Him saying to me something along the lines: 'Have you quite finished trying to make things happen on your own?' Within a year, I had been promoted three times in quick succession, and on each occasion my advancement in the company was totally unexpected. Even though I still had to go through the usual arduous interviews, at no point, during this process, did I feel that I had to strive to achieve success. When we walk closely with God and learn to move in His strength, then we will find joy, and not strife, in our work.

Psalm 28:7	**The Lord is my strength and my shield; my heart trusts in Him, and I am helped. My heart leaps for joy and I will give thanks to Him in song.**

God will enable us to make a start

The most difficult part of beginning something new, such as developing a career, is to get moving in the first place. Just like driving a car, once we have got started, momentum will assist in carrying us forward. However, it is when we are still stationary that is easy to stall and grind to a juddering halt. When we are following God's lead we might be surprised to learn that He is very practical and fully aware of what we need to do to start something new. Jesus said that our Father in heaven already knows all our needs[179], which includes how we should proceed to get things moving in our lives. Moses had great difficulty in launching off into God's plans, and spent time finding excuses why he couldn't lead the Hebrews out of Egypt[180]. If Moses had been driving a car at this time, we would have seen him stalling the engine and leapfrogging the car all the way down the road! Fortunately for him, however, God was gracious and decided to give some practical instructions to help him to get his task under way.

Exodus 4:15

> **'You shall speak to him (*Aaron*) and put words in his mouth;**
> **I will help both of you speak and will teach you what to do.'**

God reassured Moses that despite his difficulty with speech, he would still be more than able to achieve his purpose – to be the leader of Israel. The way that God got things moving was to offer Moses some very simple, practical and obvious advice: to get his brother Aaron to be his mouthpiece and speak on his behalf.

Exercising our faith

In the same way that Moses struggled to get moving with his mission, we too can sometimes fail to understand how to begin to move forward with God's plans. Our inability to move in the first place can often be due to our reluctance to take a 'risk' and to trust God. One of the best ways to express our faith in God's ability to transform our job situation is to be courageous and take some initial practical steps. We read in the book of James[181] that faith in God only has meaning if it is backed up with action. If we simply *say* that we believe that God will guide us and yet do nothing to act on this belief, then it is not real faith at all. True faith will always result in our taking a practical step to get started in the direction where we believe God is leading us. Later in this chapter we shall look at the example of Nehemiah and how he managed to overcome considerable opposition in his task of rebuilding the walls of

Jerusalem. In the same way as Nehemiah, we must develop a strategy that will enable us not only to start our task but also to bring it to completion – to find that job with our name on it. In the appendices we shall consider how to exercise our faith by developing practical strategies to move us into the jobs that God has prepared for us.

Moving forward when the direction is unclear

Our inability to get moving with God's plans can also be due to not being sure of what sort of job we should be going for. Much of this book has been about how to seek God's direction in regard to our future jobs and careers, and this revelation can either come all at once or gradually over a period of time. If we fall into this latter group, like I did, then there is a danger that we have to be aware of. The danger is this: because we sometimes don't know what it is that God wants us to do, or only a small part of it, we can become paralysed into inactivity and make no start at all. The trouble with standing still is that in reality, we never *just* stand still, but we end up going backwards without even realising it. If we are not going forwards, our marketability to employers – how much of an attractive prospect we appear – decreases with every passing year. In a similar way to running on an exercise machine, if we do not increase our pace, we can find soon ourselves going backwards. The problem that many people face is not so much a reluctance to obey God but rather a feeling that they haven't received enough revelation from Him to enable them to make a start.

In such situations, I am convinced from personal experience that it is best to make any start we can with the limited information that we have received from God. We might not have the full picture, but any start is better than none at all. If we hang around for God to bring us a crystal-clear message then we run the real risk of not only failing to go forward, but also of falling way behind the place where we are now. At this point in the book, it might be a good idea to revisit Chapter 12 where we discussed how God often waits for us to act before giving us further instructions. Even if we make the mistake of stepping out in the wrong direction, the Bible assures us that God will intervene to prevent us from losing our way.

Psalm 37:23–24   **If the Lord delights in a man's way,**
                                          He makes his steps firm;

though he stumble, he will not fall,
for the Lord upholds him with His hand.

Let me give a brief example from my own experience. From the age of fifteen I felt that God was calling me into the Catholic priesthood; however, this wasn't something that I was going to rush into. Once I had completed my A-levels, I decided to perform voluntary work for a year and also do some travelling abroad. In addition to keeping in close contact with the seminary, I also used this time to speak to different people about my plans, doubts and desires for the future. As a result of all these experiences, I came to an understanding that God wasn't in fact calling me to the priesthood. However, the consequence was that at the age of twenty, all my plans had stalled and I found myself in the confusing situation of not knowing what to do next.

The best advice that I was given at this time was to follow the desires of my heart, which included learning French. For me, this was very much a make or break time in my relationship with God, and I simply prayed that if He were real He would enable me to fulfil this dream. I hitchhiked to the south of France where I found a job in a hotel, and within six months I returned to the UK reasonably fluent in French. I took an intensive one-year A-level course that enabled me to start university the following year. One of the main lessons that I learnt during this time was to keep moving. As a result of my decision not to enter the seminary I could have allowed disillusionment and fear to have paralysed me, and I thank God for the advice that I received because it encouraged me not only to acquire a useful language skill but, most importantly, to keep moving forward. The Bible says 'that in all things God works for the good of those who love Him, who have been called according to His purpose'[182]. God can work with anything in our lives and turn it around for our good – even unintentional errors or disobedience.

Looking back, I can now see how God intervened at this stage in my life; firstly, by giving me the desire to learn French, and secondly, by the guidance that I received through a close friend. Little did I know that God's intervention would achieve far more than I could ever have expected. Not only did my French lead to my gaining a useful qualification, but most importantly my relationship with God was sealed with an unbreakable bond of trust. Out of desperation I had prayed to God and He responded by meeting my immediate and long-term needs. Money can't buy that sort of experience!

Keep moving forward

If we find ourselves in a position of uncertainty of where to turn to next, we should always try to keep moving forward. Just as with a car, where it is much easier to turn the steering wheel when the vehicle is in motion, we will find changing our own direction less difficult when we are taking action upon what we feel God is instructing us to do. We can achieve this by positioning ourselves where God can speak to us through the people we meet, the activities that we pursue and the situations that we experience. Also, it is always constructive to take another look at what we are good at doing and examine whether this lines up with any desires that we have. My desire had been to learn French and I pursued this subject as a way of escape from my state of indecision and confusion. At a later stage, this interest connected with another subject that I hadn't anticipated, namely business studies, which formed the second half of my honours degree. I do not recount this story to boast about my own ability, but rather to testify what God has been able to produce out of some of the most difficult parts of my life.

Rebuilding our city walls

Nehemiah lived in the fourth-century BC and led the return of the Jews back to Jerusalem from their exile in Babylon. However, after spending seventy years, in what is modern-day Iraq, the Jews found the city 'laid to waste' and in ruins. Nehemiah responded by challenging his people to demonstrate their faith in God by rebuilding the city. In a similar way to James in the New Testament, Nehemiah underlines the necessity of living out the practical side of our faith in God.

James 2:18   **But someone will say, 'You have faith; I have deeds.' Show me your faith without deeds, and I will show you my faith by what I do.**

Nehemiah can be an example to anyone whose situation, such as their career, resembles a city in ruins. He showed some admirable traits that God used to bring about the rebirth of the Jews as an independent nation. Nehemiah not only had the massive logistical task of rebuilding the city walls, but also faced fierce opposition from his neighbours. Yet despite all these challenges, he led a team that successfully reconstructed the city walls in just over fifty days, which then enabled them to get started on the city itself. The story is relevant today because the way in which Nehemiah approached his monumental task can serve as a model for the way we can face our own challenges. Despite the temptation to give in and seek the path of least resistance, Nehemiah persisted in his assignment and showed some fantastic qualities, without which Jerusalem would have remained a ruin. Let us now take a look at some of Nehemiah's excellent qualities that enabled him to run with God's plans to rebuild Jerusalem.

- *Firstly,* he had complete confidence in God, as opposed to his own ability. His book contains many prayers to God about the rebuilding of Jerusalem

Nehemiah 1:5   **...'O Lord, God of heaven, the great and awesome God, who keeps His covenant of love with thos e who love Him and obey His commands...'**

- *Secondly,* he continually spoke faith-filled words over the rebuilding of Jerusalem

Nehemiah 2:20   **...'The God of heaven will give us success...'**

- *Thirdly,* he showed courage in stepping out and obeying God.

Nehemiah 2:2–3   **...I was very much afraid, but I said to the king...**

- *Fourthly,* he developed a realistic strategy, by having some families building whilst others stood guard. Families also offered a more effective defence because they will fight more fiercely to protect each other.

Nehemiah 4:16   **From that day on, half of my men did the work, while the other half were equipped with spears, shields, bows and armour...**

- *Fifthly,* he refused to give up regardless of the opposition and sarcasm.

Nehemiah 6:11   **...'Should a man like me run away?...I will not go!'**

- *Lastly,* he finished the job.

Nehemiah 6:15 **So the wall was completed on the twenty-fifth of Elul, in fifty-two days.**

Many of us reading this book may feel that in regard to our work situation, our task is similar to that of the reconstruction of Jerusalem. Even though our challenges may not be based on bricks and mortar and the rebuilding of a city wall, nevertheless, God is able to bring us through our current wilderness period and provide for our needs. What is our equivalent to rebuilding the city walls? We might wonder where the money is going to come from to pay for a college course or how to find affordable childcare to free us up to return to work. Furthermore, we might be concerned that our disability would prejudice our job application. On the other hand, we could still feel confused about the kind of job on which to develop our career. Whatever the challenges surrounding our situation, God invites us today to live out our faith in a practical way like Nehemiah, and to move forward in the expectation that He will show us how to rebuild our own city walls.

And let's not forget that in our walk with Jesus, the whole world and everything in it, including our jobs, belongs to Him. When we pray according to His will, God loves the simple prayer: 'More Lord.'

Psalm 24:1,5,7 **The earth is the Lord's, and**
everything in it, the world, and all who
live in it;
He will receive blessing from the Lord
and vindication from God His   Saviour.
Lift up your heads, O you gates;
be lifted up, you ancient doors,
that the King of glory may come in.

Review of chapter

God wants to show us how to proceed with the practical side of our career plans. Even though he expects us to work hard and to use the gifts and abilities that He has given us, at no point does He expect us to strive in order to make things happen. In the economy of the world we are very much on our own, and consequently have to depend on our own strengths and strategies. On the other hand, if we operate in the economy of God, His promise is that we will work in His strength and not our own.

The hardest part of starting something new, such as developing a career, can be to get moving in the first place. Our struggle to get started can sometimes be due to our reluctance to take a 'risk' and to trust in God. One way to express our faith in God's ability to transform our job situation is to step out and take some first practical steps. However, the problem faced by many people is not so much an unwillingness to follow God's plans, but rather a lack of clear instruction on how to proceed to get started. If we find ourselves in this position, the best advice is to make any start we can with the limited information that we have received from God. Any start is better than none at all. We should place ourselves where God can speak to us through the people we meet and the activities in which we get involved.

The way that Nehemiah approached the task of rebuilding Jerusalem can serve as a model for the way we approach our own job-related situations. Whatever the challenge surrounding our jobs, God invites us today to live out our faith in the same way as Nehemiah, by keeping our head connected to heaven and by planting our feet firmly in the practicalities of Earth.

The following worksheet will enable you to address some of the issues that have been raised in this chapter. The exercise can be carried out on your own or alongside a prayer partner. Take time to consider each question as honestly as possible, and record your responses on a separate sheet.

Exercise 16

Part 1. Head in the Heavenlies and Feet on the Earth – Not Striving

Even though God expects us to work hard and to use the gifts and abilities that he has given us, He doesn't expect us to strive in order to make things happen. When we walk closely with God and operate in His strength, then we will find joy in our work.

For Prayer & Reflection

The following verses, which were used in the chapter, have been chosen to help you to focus on your own circumstances. Take some time to reflect on your situation through the questions that follow these verses.

Zechariah 4:6   **'Not by might nor by power, but by My Spirit,' says the Lord Almighty.**

Psalm 28:7   **The Lord is my strength and my shield; my heart trusts in Him, and I am helped. My heart leaps for joy and I will give thanks to Him in song.**

- **Can you think of something that you are doing in order to develop your job in which you are striving to achieve some sort of success?**

- **If you are striving, here are some possible explanations: the timing is not yet right; you have misunderstood what God is asking you to do; you have not invited God into this situation and you are trying to forge ahead in your own strength.**

- **On your own or with a prayer partner, ask the Holy Spirit to speak to you about how you should proceed. Recommit your plans to God and ask Him to lead you again.**

In the same way that Moses struggled to get moving with his vision, we too can get stuck and fail to understand how to get started in something God has asked us to do. Sometimes, this is not so much due to unwillingness or a lack of faith to follow God, but rather due to uncertainty about what sort of job He is telling us to go for. The best way to express our faith that God can transform our job situation is to step out and take some first practical steps.

- If you are experiencing a situation where you have stalled and are unable to move forward, can you identify the reason? Could it be due to:

    - **A lack of vision or understanding of how and where to go forward?**

    - **Unwillingness or a lack of faith to proceed?**

If we find ourselves in a position of uncertainty of where to turn to next, the best advice is to keep moving forward. We should place ourselves in a position where God can speak to us through the people we meet, the activities that we get involved in, the places in which we find ourselves and the experiences that we go through.

Part 2. **Head in the Heavenlies and Feet on the Earth – Moving Forward**

Nehemiah shows the importance of living out the day-to-day practical side of our faith in God. He provides an example to anyone whose career prospects resembles a city in ruins. Nehemiah is relevant today because the way that he approached his task serves as a model for the way we can approach our own challenges.

For Prayer & Reflection

The following verses, some of which were used in the chapter, have been chosen to help you to focus on your own circumstances. Take some time to reflect on your situation through the questions that follow these verses.

James 2:18   **But someone will say, 'You have faith; I have deeds.' Show me your faith without deeds, and I will show you my faith by what I do.**

Nehemiah 6:11   **…'Should a man like me run away?…I will not go!…'**

Philippians 2:13   **For it is God who works in you to will and to act according to His good purpose.**

Nehemiah's excellent qualities:

- **He had complete confidence in God**

  How confident are you that God can turn your situation around?

- **He continually spoke faith-filled words**

  Do you declare faith-filled words over your job / career?

- **He showed courage**

  It can take courage to follow God. Have you showed courage in obeying God's call?

- **He developed a realistic strategy**

  The Appendices give practical strategies for seeking employment. In addition to the practical side of finding work, you must also devise a strategy that is based on prayer, which is aimed at the unseen battle in the spiritual realms.

- **He refused to give up**

  If you have been tempted to throw in the towel and give up, then there is good news for you: God is the God of new beginnings. On your own or with a prayer partner, invite God to breathe new life into your job situation.

- **He finished the job**

  Invite the Holy Spirit to fill you with His strength and give you His strategies so that you do not need to strive. Remember, it is the Lord Himself who fulfils His plans for you.

Dreams and Plans

_____

_____

_____

_____

_____

_____

_____

_____

_____

_____

_____

_____

_____

_____

_____

Exercise 17

Before we take any big decision, we must first receive confirmation from a number of different sources that we are indeed hearing correctly from God.

The idea of the chart on the following page is to test the strength of your calling to a specific career, e.g. teaching. Each spoke on the chart denotes a different area of indication of potential suitability for you.

The more you know about the requirements of your desired job, the more useful you will find this exercise.

Scoring

Place a mark on a corresponding number level to show your relative strength. E.g. if you have a lot of relevant experience in your desired job, place a mark at level 5. If you have little experience, then place your mark lower down the scale.

Do the same for each of the eight categories and create a spider's web effect by linking up all the eight points.

What to make of chart?

The chart will provide a quick visual assessment of *some* of the indicators of your *potential* fit to a particular job / role.

If you have a low score, this could indicate a skills or qualifications gap, which can be rectified by taking a college course. On the other hand, it might indicate potential unsuitability for a certain career or role.

Don't forget to pray about it.

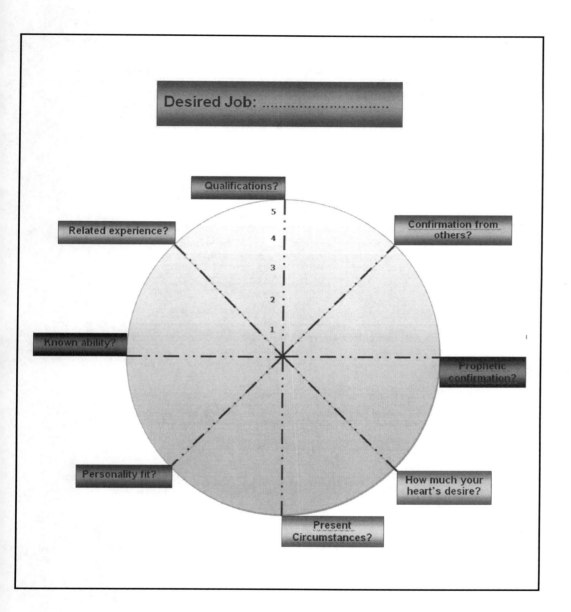

Desired Job: ....

Qualifications?

Confirmation from others?

Related experience?

5
4
3
2
1

Known ability?

Prophetic confirmation?

Personality fit?

How much your heart's desire?

Present Circumstances?

SECTION THREE

Appendices

Practical Careers Resources

APPENDIX 1 – ACTION PLANNING

How should we start to plan our course ahead to get us into a job or a desired career? The first thing we should start and continue doing as a daily discipline is to spend time with God and get into agreement with His will for our lives. This has been a topic that has been covered in detail in previous chapters. The second thing we should do is to write our goals down. The Bible gives the earliest advice in writing an action plan!

Habakkuk 2:2 **…write the vision and make it plain…**

Proverbs 16:9 **In his heart a man plans his course, but the Lord determines his steps.**

Goal-setting requires time, discipline, courage and perseverance. Between our goals and ourselves, we may well encounter setbacks of all sorts and the temptation to give in. Let's hang on to Nehemiah's determined words: '…should a man like me run away?…I will not go'[183].

Step 1. **Researching job / Careers information**

Finding a job or the developing of a career can be best viewed as being a series of stepping-stones crossing a river. We are on one bank and our desired job or career is on the far side. In the absence of a bridge or a boat, the only way to cross this river is to walk across these stepping-stones, one at a time, until we have reached the other side. Each stone in the river represents the skills, qualifications, work experience and personal circumstances that we have acquired to get into that job or career.

The first task in this process is for us to understand where exactly we are headed – do we know which job we want to go for? It is not sufficient to have a vague idea of the sort of job we would like to operate in, we have to be familiar with the many requirements of the job, such as:

- **Qualifications**
- **Skills**
- **Personal circumstances e.g. flexibility to travel that will take us away from home**
- **Relevant experience**

At this early stage in planning ahead we will benefit enormously by taking time to thoroughly research jobs that interest us. The following websites give us information about the resources of job / careers information that are freely available to us.

General job / vocational information
- http://nextstep.Direct.gov.uk/
- www.direct.gov.uk/careersadvice
- www.prospects.ac.uk
- www.advice-resources.co.uk/adviceresources/general/dir/jobprofiles/
- www.cvbuilder-advice-resources.co.uk/
- www.connexions-direct.com/jobs4u
- www.bbc.co.uk/learning/
- http://jobseekers.Direct.gov.uk/
- www.support4learning.org.uk

Computing, IT and Telecoms
- www.absolutecomms.co.uk
- www.computerweekly.com
- www.computingcareers.co.uk
- www.jobsdomain.co.uk
- www.justit.co.uk
- www.planetrecruit.com
- www.technicalresources.co.uk
- www.technojobs.co.uk
- www.thitjobboard.com

Art, Design and Fashion
- www.artsprofessional.co.uk
- www.the-aop.org
- www.bbc.co.uk/jobs
- www.leisurejobs.co.uk
- www.careersindesign.com
- www.designweek.co.uk
- www.fashionpersonnel.co.uk
- www.thestage.co.uk

Construction and Land Services

- www.architecturaljobs.co.uk
- www.anderselite.com
- www.buildingservicesjobs.co.uk
- www.careerstructure.com
- www.earthsciencejobs.co.uk
- www.w5recruitment.co.uk
- www.hunterdunning.co.uk
- www.jobsinsurveying.co.uk
- http://jobs.planningresource.co.uk
- www.ukcivilengineering.co.uk

Business and Administration

- http://jobs.careersinlogistics.co.uk
- www.legal-secretaries.co.uk
- www.governmentjobsdirect.co.uk
- www.h2office.co.uk
- www.principalpeople.co.uk
- www.jobsgopublic.com
- www.consultantsboard.com/mca
- www.officeangels.co.uk
- www.officerecruit.com
- www.pa-assist.com
- www.peoplemanagement.co.uk
- www.prweekjobs.co.uk
- www.researchresearch.com

Engineering and Manufacturing

- www.apgate.com
- www.jimfinder.com
- www.justengineers.net
- www.fisitajobs.com
- www.manufacturingjobs.co.uk
- www.thecareerengineer.com
- www.theengineer.co.uk/jobs

Drama, Music and Media

- www.bbc.co.uk/jobs
- www.creativepool.co.uk
- www.formula-won.co.uk
- www.justpeople.com
- www.starnow.co.uk
- www.spotlightcd.com
- www.thestage.co.uk
- http://uk.music-jobs.com

Finance and Selling

- www.cityjobs.com
- www.efinancialcareers.co.uk
- www.ft.com/jobs
- www.inretail.co.uk
- www.justpeople.com
- www.marketingweek.co.uk
- www.theworkbank.co.uk

Social Care

- www.allcarejobs.co.uk
- www.socialworkjobs.co.uk
- www.communitycare.co.uk/jobs
- www.greatsocialcare.co.uk
- http://mumandworking.co.uk
- www.ecarers.com
- www.workingmums.co.uk

Education

- www.vacancies.ac.uk
- www.fejobs.com
- www.jobs.tes.co.uk
- www.teachingtimesjobs.co.uk
- www.thes.co.uk
- www.education-jobs.co.uk

Government and Politics

- http://careers.civil-service.gov.uk
- www.governmentjobsdirect.co.uk
- www.jobsgopublic.com
- www.lgjobs.com
- www.jobs.ac.uk/sector/polictics
- www.publicjobsdirect.com

Transport and Logistics

- www.aviationjobsearch.com
- www.careersinlogistics.co.uk
- www.cruiseshipjob.com
- www.jobsintransport.co.uk
- www.jobs-in-transport.com
- www.justpeople.com
- www.railwaypeople.com
- www.roadtransport.com
- www.supplychainrecruit.com

Healthcare

- www.123doc.com/pub_cgi/jobs.pl
- www.bdjjobs.com
- www.emedcareers.co.uk
- www.flamehealth.com
- www.wales.nhs.uk
- www.healthcarejobs.co.uk
- www.healthjobsuk.com
- www.nhsjobs.com
- www.nursefindersuk.com
- www.nursingnetuk.com
- http://www2.nmc4jobs.com

Sciences

- www.access-sciencejobs.co.uk/
- www.chemicalsearch.co.uk
- www.earthsciencejobs.co.uk
- www.earthworks-jobs.com

- www.pharmajobs.co.uk
- www.pharmaceuticaljobs.com
- www.phdjobs.com
- www.sci-search.com
- www.tcetoday.com

Sport, Leisure and Tourism

- www.adventurejobs.co.uk
- www.hcareers.co.uk
- www.leisurejobs.com
- www.leisureopportunities.co.uk
- www.caterer.com
- www.travelindustryjobs.co.uk

Step 2. **Finding our way into a job**

Once we have learned more about our desired job, our next task is to negotiate our way across the 'river'. Where direct entry into a job is not possible for us, there are often a number of ways to get into a job or a particular career, such as gaining a new qualification or performing voluntary work. Also, sales experience could lead to a career in marketing or voluntary work may increase chances of getting into a social work position.

The following exercise is designed to help us plan ahead and work out which stepping stones we have to walk onto in order to get into our chosen job.

1.   The left-hand column offers some possible stepping stones to help us to our job. Please add others if necessary.

2.   In the other columns, please enter those jobs that interest you.

3.   Using the list of stepping stones in the left hand column, identify which could help you into a particular job

This task may be difficult to complete if we haven't first completed Step One, and gained sufficient information about a job/s.

Stepping Stones	Type of work where you have shown an interest			
	e.g. Hotel Management	Job 1	Job 2	Job 3
Full-time training.	✓			
Part-time training while working in a different area of work.				
Voluntary work.				
Enter a new job at a lower level and then aim to work your way up.				
Get yourself established in a job in an organisation then transfer to different area /department that you prefer.				
Go into a company as a consult-ant or as a temp and wait for job opportunities to arise				
Other				

Once you have reviewed your interests and how to get there, which route do you prefer to take? What action is required for you to start moving towards your chosen job?

Step 3. **Seeking further careers advice**

There are many different organisations that we can approach to help us negotiate these stepping-stones and reach our desired job or career. Getting the right information and advice can help us make decisions about our future by linking personal interests and skills to a job or career.

Connexions – www.connexions-direct.com/
Youth support service for thirteen to nineteen-year-olds and for those with learning difficulties up to twenty-five years old. This service is managed locally by local authorities working together with key youth support agencies.

Nextstep – www.direct.gov.uk/nextstep
Nextstep offers both a face-to-face and a telephone advice service – offering a source of impartial advice on courses, careers, funding and more. To book an appointment to meet a careers adviser *or* to receive careers advice over the phone, visit the website or call free: 0800 100 900

Direct.gov – University and Higher Education

http://www.direct.gov.uk/en/EducationAndLearning/UniversityAndHigherEducation/index.htm

A service that helps people to consider the steps necessary to enter Higher Education (HE). The website offers links to information on HE courses around the country, how to apply to university, financing studies, student life and how HE can drive forward your career.

Higher Education – HE

Each university will have a careers department, which will have trained careers advisers able to give advice on courses and related careers information. To contact a complete list of universities in the UK visit www.ucas.ac.uk

Colleges of Further Education – FE including Adult Education Colleges

All FE colleges and adult education colleges will have a careers department that will have trained careers advisers able to give advice on courses and related careers information. To locate a course at your local college visit: www.direct.gov.uk/nextstep (visit *find a course*)

Libraries

Libraries are excellent places to find out what careers advice services may exist in your area. To find your local library visit www.direct.gov.uk

APPENDIX 2 – JOB SEARCH TIPS

What is the best way to find a job? For a start, you have to develop an effective strategy that will enable you to find a suitable job as quickly as possible and with the least amount of trouble and effort. If your strategy is not working, you need to review the way you're looking for a particular job

It is said that only 30% of job vacancies are openly advertised to the public. This leaves an amazing 70% of jobs that are left to be found in the 'hidden job market'! The question that arises is: with the limited time you have got, where do you look for a job? Is there a best method or strategy when conducting a job-search?

Experts say that one in every three job-hunters become unsuccessful because they abandon their job hunt prematurely. When asked why, many would say: 'I never thought that this would take so long and I ran out of energy.' As a result, it's wise to invest what energy you do have into a job-hunting strategy where the odds are more favourable. Which strategy should you adopt for job hunting? The answer is: **A varied approach**!

The 30% visible job market

1)   **_The Internet_** is now an essential method to consider when making job searches and applications. Application forms and CVs can be submitted via the WWW and e-mail. However, it is worth remembering that no standards exist to guarantee information content or levels of service on the internet. You may need to satisfy yourself that the company is bona fide before sending your personal details through to a website.

Many employers are now advertising their vacancies online, and ask applicants to apply online, and they will often tell you whether or not you have been successful by e-mail. In some cases, this is now the only way that some employers fill their vacancies.

- **78% of recruitment companies advertise job vacancies online.**

- **There are currently around 1000 online Job Boards in the UK.**

- **To make sure you keep up with the latest vacancies, you will need to:**

    1.   Find ways of having access to the internet.

    2.   Have your own e-mail address.

    3.   Know how to find vacancies and fill in applications online.

Using the internet to find job boards

Jobs are usually advertised on Job Boards, which are like electronic newspapers. Generally, there are three types of Job Boards:

- Niche Job Boards are dedicated to particular professions or industries.
- General Job Boards advertise all types of vacancies.
- Local Job Boards advertise all types of jobs in the area they cover.

You can search for the right job boards by using a search engine (for example Google or Yahoo), which can be saved in your favourites list of websites.

Finding internet access

If you have access to the internet at home, then it's easy. If not, here are a few suggestions:

- You can use UK online centres, which are based in the community, such as in internet cafés, a public library, a college, a community centre or a village hall. Some even move around from place to place to give more people the chance to go online. You can find your nearest UK online centre in England by phoning 0800 77 1234

A list of online career and recruitment sites

www.activate.co.uk	www.graduate.com
www.doctorjob.co.uk	www.insidecareers.co.uk
www.eurograduate.com	www.jobs.ac.uk
www.get.hobsons.co.uk	www.mbajobs.net
www.graduate-recruitment.co.uk	www.milkround.co.uk
www.grb.uk.com	www.prospects.ac.uk
www.fish4.co.uk/jobs	http://3wjobs.com
www.gisajob.com	www.agencycentral.co.uk
http://jobs.guardian.co.uk	www.alljobsuk.com
	www.brookstreet.co.uk
www.jobsin.co.uk	www.reed.co.uk
www.jobsite.co.uk	http://jobs.telegraph.co.uk
www.jobsworld.co.uk	www.timesonline.co.uk
www.jobexpress.co.uk	www.totaljobs.com
www.jump4jobs.co.uk	www.workcircle.co.uk
www.manpower.co.uk	www.workthing.co.uk
www.monster.co.uk	www.hays.com
www.jobs1.co.uk	www.hotrecruit.com
www.jobsfor.co.uk	www.jobs.co.uk

- Your local library may have computers that are connected to the internet.
- You may have friends or relatives who are happy to let you use their computer to go online.

2) **Jobcentre Plus** advertise job vacancies on public display boards. If you identify a job that you are interested in, a Jobcentre Plus adviser can provide more details and make appointments for interview. Visit www.jobcentreplus.gov.uk for more details. To make a new claim for benefit call 0800 0 55 66 88

3) **Local and National Newspapers** are a good source of vacancies. It's a good idea to find out what day your local paper comes out and for larger newspapers find out which days they advertise certain jobs. For example The Guardian advertises IT jobs on Mondays. Newspapers also keep you up-to-date on which companies are moving into your area and creating new jobs.

4) **Professional and Trade Journals** relate to particular sectors of work, and can be an excellent source of vacancies, e.g. for jobs in the advertising sector look in the Journal Campaign and for nursing look in the Nursing Times. Popular trade journals and magazines can be available either in your local library or newsagents.

5) **Recruitment Agencies** have the advantage of working closely with employers. Anyone can register with a recruitment agency to look for work but they will only match you to a job if you have what an employer is looking for. Agencies offer both full-time, part-time work and temporary work. Some agencies deal with specific vacancies such as catering, whilst other agencies cover a variety of different occupations, from unskilled to managerial.

Agencies will require information from you relating to your past experience, qualifications, skills and possibly references, and this is where a good CV will come in useful. Details about different agencies can be found in the Yellow Pages or other local directories, which can be found in libraries. If you are looking for senior management and executive level vacancies, there are fee-paying agencies that provide advice and counselling as well as possible job vacancies.

How do I get the most out of a recruitment agency?

To get the most out of a recruitment agency, it is important to remember to sell yourself to them so that they understand what skills and attributes you have to offer the employers on their database.

To make the most out of your recruitment agency, make sure you:

- Keep in regular contact with them.

- Give them all the information they need (including all your contact details and references).

- Are honest in the details that you give them about yourself.

- Keep your CV accurate and up-to-date.

- Tell them if there is a particular type of job you don't want (be up-front and save time).

- Listen to any advice from your consultant about improving your CV (remember they are professionals and they want to help you get a job).

- Talk to your agency if they are not finding you work. It may be because there is not enough of the type of work you want and you might want to think about other types of work you are willing to do. Or, you could register with another agency that offers the type of work you are looking for.

6) *Job and Careers Fairs* can provide information about recruiting trends, career options and current openings in specific organisations. They will also give you the opportunity to develop your network of career contacts. Remember to take copies of your CV, dress as you would for an interview and collect as many business cards as you can so that you can follow them up at a later date.

The 70% hidden job market

1) *Networking/using your contacts.* Many vacancies are never actually advertised but rely on staff already working in the organisation to spread the word. Ask your friends and relatives to keep a lookout for you in their companies. Networking is one of the most successful ways of finding employment and does not necessarily involve

asking your friends for a job. It could form part of your job research – who works where, who knows who, who can tell you what it is like to work for a particular company, who can give you advice about your career path etc. You will be surprised at how many people you really know!

You can either make contact by picking up the telephone or by writing a personal letter. When telephoning choose a time of day when people are usually less busy – for example, immediately after lunch. Ask if it is convenient to talk – and be prepared to call back if necessary. It is not advisable to ask for a job, just ask for advice, say what you are interested in and that you are looking for information, and would they be prepared to spend quarter of an hour with you? You may be surprised at how helpful most people are when asked for advice (it's often quite flattering). They may suggest you speak to someone else and your contact list will grow.

Prepare what you are going to ask them – research the area you are interested in:

- What types of jobs do people do?

- What does the job involve?

- What sort of career structure does the job have?

- Are there any professional organisations you could contact?

- What about qualifications and training?

- Who are the potential employers?

- What are their specialities?

- Which ones are you going to target?

- Who are you going to contact there?

If you have a clear objective of what you would like to get from the conversation or meeting you will give a good impression and show that you are taking a business-like approach. Keep a record of the company, the name of the person you spoke to and the outcome.

Always write or telephone afterwards to thank them for their time and help, and if they have been supportive let them know about any successful outcomes.

Using the internet to network

The internet gives us unprecedented access to large numbers of people in our own country and across the world. There are many different internet sites that can give you an excellent chance to network and discover who is out there working in an organisation that you would like to get into. It can be a big help if you can create a link with someone who could act as an introduction for you into their organisation. They could also give you valuable information about the organisation, which you could use to your benefit during a job interview.

LinkedIn – www.linkedin.com/

LinkedIn is a business-oriented social networking site and is mainly used for professional networking. In early 2010, LinkedIn had more than 60 million registered users in over 200 countries worldwide. This networking site offers professionals exceptional potential for networking and career development through new and existing contacts.

Some other useful site to develop your presence:

* www.facebook.com/
* twitter.com/

2)   ***Speculative Approaches.*** This is an excellent way of approaching companies of particular interest to you. You could send them your CV together with a well thought-out covering letter to ask if they have any vacancies at present or expect to have any in the near future. It may be worth finding out where they advertise and how often vacancies for which you are suited occur.   Yellow Pages Directory, www.yell.co.uk and www.thomson-directories.co.uk will identify potential employers.

Your local chambers of commerce will also be able supply you with a list of local businesses, which could indicate likely companies for you to target.

3)   ***Voluntary Work.*** Make a contribution to the local community by working free of charge during the day, evenings or weekends, e.g. by working in a caring environment or manning a telephone nightline or a hospital radio station. Voluntary work is good for your self-esteem, it will impress any potential employer and, of course it will help other people.

Voluntary Work offers an excellent way to gain work experience, and is also viewed by employers as being potentially as valuable as paid employment. It can offer a much needed break to get you into a particular job sector.

How to find voluntary work?

- Contact local Volunteer Centre or visit: www.do-it.org.uk
- Contact organisations directly
- Do a Google search for voluntary opportunities

4) **Work Experience/Work Shadowing** – visit www.jobcentreplus.gov.uk and view information on work experience schemes such as 'Work Prep'.

5) **Self Employment**

Starting up your own business could be a solution to your hunt for employment. Use your initiative to sell your skills, a product or service e.g. IT consultancy or childminding. Your local Business Link will also advise on all aspects of starting up a business i.e. grants, business planning, finding premises etc. They may also run training programmes to assist you. For further information, visit: www.businesslink.gov.uk

You can also get information and advice from the small business adviser at most high street banks. If you need legal advice on how to set up a business, the Law Society provides an initiative 'Lawyers in Business'. Telephone 020 7405 9075 for a list of lawyers operating the scheme in your area who will give you a half-hour free consultation.

The trick with developing an effective job search strategy is do some of each of the above. Don't spend too much time and effort with those job search strategies where the odds are less favourable.

Extending your network

Think about all the people you know or who you have met, who could help you find out more.

Contacts	Name	Phone / email
Current business colleague		
Ex business colleague		
Ex bosses/employers		
Suppliers/reps you have dealt with		
Fellow members of trade associations		
Your old clients/customers		
Solicitor/bank manager/accountant		
Contacts in your church		
Family friends		
Social friends/neighbours		
School, College or University friends		
Your partner's contacts		
Others		

Keeping track of your job search activity

Vacancy title	Employer's name, address, phone number etc.	Where and when vacancy seen	Date details requested and how	Date details received	Date completed application returned	Copy taken?

APPENDIX 3 – WRITING A WINNING CV

Ten top tips for a winning CV

1. ### A two-page CV is best

   A CV that is either too long or too short is cited as one of the main reasons for rejection of CVs.

2. ### Tailor your CV to the job

   When you write your CV, make sure it contains words that relate to the skills, experience and qualifications that are required in the job. A CV that is tailored to a specific role will stand a far higher chance of being selected than a generalist CV, which is not focussed on the job. If you are applying for a variety of different jobs you may need to draw up several CVs.

3. ### Chose a format to impress

   Make sure your presentation is perfect, avoiding grammatical errors and spelling mistakes.

4. ### Be conservative in your presentation

   If you go over the top in your format it can put many employers off. Photos, coloured paper, creative fonts and humour can often lead to rejection of a CV.

5. ### Use 'power' words

   Make sure that you use words that create an impression of power and achievement (see later in this section), and avoid repetition.

6. ### Don't include too much information

   A CV isn't a place to write your life's history. If you include too much information it will crowd out the important facts that an employer wishes to know. The parts of your CV should include: a profile, achievements, work history and duties in job role, qualifications, and contact details (especially mobile phone number). You can mention at the end that references are available upon request.

7. ### Reverse chronological CVs are most popular with employers.

   However, there are other formats, such as functional (where the focus is on your skills rather than on your work history) which can be very effective. Which format you choose will depend on your circumstances.

8. *Highlight your achievements*

It is critical that you highlight your achievements in your CV. A person who comes over as being successful will stand a better chance of being selected for a job interview. Where possible, make sure that your achievements are quantifiable (e.g. you increased sales by 30% in one year) and you demonstrate how this related to your role.

9. *E-CV's*

Today, many employers and recruitment agencies prefer you to email your CV because it allows them to electronically scan the document for key words that contain information about your skills.

10. *Covering letters*

When replying to an advertised position, make sure that your CV is accompanied by a covering letter. Your letter should be brief and factual, stating how your skills match the role requirements, and why you would like to work for their organisation.

If you are sending your CV speculatively, your letter should explain more fully the reason for you contacting them, and clearly highlight how you could be an asset to their organisation.

The different parts of a CV

It is important to point out that there is no single best way to write a CV. The format we choose will depend upon our experience, skills and qualifications. A CV is a chance to highlight our strengths and downplay our weaknesses. The following list includes some common sections to be included in a CV.

1) *Personal details*

Full name, address and mobile / telephone number. Date of birth, nationality, gender and marital status are optional. This can be placed at the top of the CV or at the bottom.

2) *Personal profile*

Employers like a CV to start with a strong personal profile. This should be approximately four lines in length, and should highlight relevant experience and skills for the job you're going for.

3) *Key Skills or achievements*

Employers want to look for particular skills or personal qualities, such as the ability to use a computer keyboard, good organisational and communication skills (with business clients and colleagues), language skills, ability to use initiative, flexibility, teamwork and the ability to cope with pressure. When you apply for a job, make sure you look at the job specification, identify the skills required and clearly demonstrate in your CV that you have them.

4) *Employment History/Work Experience*

This section should include full-time / part-time work and voluntary work. For each job include the name of the employer, dates, job title and duties/responsibilities undertaken. Experience should run in chronological order (most recent job or work experience first). You could also include your achievements in this section – please see above.

People with a great deal of work experience, with similar employers, may want to list their jobs, the companies they have worked for and the dates and then explain all their work achievements in one section entitled 'Work Activities and Achievements'. Others may want to list all their work experience separately and list the duties in point form. Also, try to avoid unexplained gaps of time.

5) *Education and Qualifications*

School/College/University, that you attended, starting with the most recent and working backwards. Include the qualifications you gained, with grades and dates. You can also include in this section any relevant professional qualifications that you have gained. If your education is stronger than your employment history then this should be placed first. Juggle the order of headings around to show yourself to your best advantage.

6) *State that references are available upon request*

Before sending your CV to a prospective employer, you must check your CV for spelling, grammar and layout carefully. Ask someone to look through your final copy to double-check for mistakes.

Different Types of CV

1) *Traditional / Chronological CV*

This is the traditional approach to CV writing, and it revolves around presenting education and work experience typically in reverse chronological order – most recent first. The emphasis is on qualifications and job titles.

Advantages:	Don't use it when:
• Useful in traditional settings.	• Work history is patchy.
• Shows steady growth development.	• Periods of unemployment.
• Shows impressive job titles.	• Lots of career changes.
• Shows name of prestigious last employer.	• Lots of job-hopping.

2) *Functional CV*

This approach is based around emphasising skills and strengths and accomplishments rather than job titles. The information that you include is not in chronological order.

Advantages:	Don't use it when:
• Emphasises capabilities.	• Entering traditional occupations e.g. teaching, accountancy.
• Good when changing careers or when entering the job market.	• When not sure about what you have to offer.
• When work history is patchy.	

3) *Targeted CV*

In this approach a CV is tailored for a specific job or opportunity and presents strengths related to this goal.

Advantages:	Don't use when:
• Good for applying for a very specific job or role.	• Starting a new career or entering the job market and have little experience.
• Use when you have several job directions and maintain a different CV for each.	• When not sure about what you have to offer.
• Can give emphasis to abilities gained outside paid employment.	

Action words for CVs

The words that you choose to include in a CV will determine what sort of image you create about yourself, and is one of the keys to successful job hunting. The list below will help you chose effective words for your CV, which will have an impact on an employer.

Power words

Achieved	Communication	Co-ordinated	Delivered
Determined	Developed	Established	Identified
Improved	Initiated	Introduced	Investigated
Learned	Managed	Motivated	Negotiated
Obtained	Organised	Participated	Performed
Planned	Prepared	Proposed	Provided

Supervised

Personal qualities

Able	Accomplished	Achieved	Adaptable
Articulate	Capable	Committed	Competitive
Conversant	Consistent	Diplomatic	Effective
Efficient	Enterprising	Enthusiastic	Experienced
Expertise	Flexible	Knowledge	Positive
Practical	Proactive	Proficient	Qualified
Resourceful	Skilful	Solely	Specialised
Successful	Tactful	Trained	Versatile

Resourcefulness

Achieving	Advancing	Awarding	Challenging
Continuity	Correcting	Diverting	Eliminating
Fulfilling	Initiating	Instigating	Introducing
Improving	Identifying	Pioneering	Prioritising
Progressing	Providing	Rectifying	Revitalising
Solving	Strengthening	Surpassing	Transforming
Targeting	Unifying	Widening	Winning

Public relations & human resources

Advising	Appointing	Balancing	Collaborating
Consulting	Counselling	Employing	Encouraging
Facilitating	Grouping	Guiding	Handling
Hiring	Integrating	Monitoring	Motivating
Recruiting	Sponsoring	Strengthening	Training

Advertising & promotion

Accounting for	Convincing	Generating	Improving
Influencing	Launching	Marketing	Persuading
Presenting	Promoting	Recommending	Representing
Securing	Selling	Trading	

Techniques

Acquiring	Analysing	Arranging	Applying
Budgeting	Cataloguing	Comparing	Compiling
Completing	Computing	Correlating	Decreasing
Distributing	Enlarging	Ensuring	Examining
Expanding	Generating	Increasing	Indexing
Improvising	Inspecting	Manufacturing	Providing
Purchasing	Raising	Redesigning	Reorganising
Restructuring	Reviewing	Revising	Scheduling
Systematising	Transferring	Translating	Utilising
Verifying			

Research & analysis

Automating	Accurately	Advancing	Amending
Classifying	Determining	Developing	Differentiating
Disseminating	Equating	Evolving	Experimenting
Interpreting	Investigating	Quantifying	Observing
Processing	Relating	Searching	Studying
Solving	Theorising		

Quantifiers & other useful words

Accelerating	Benefiting	Channelling	Combining
Concise	Doubling	Enriching	Excelling
Extending	Foundation	Gaining	Incentive
Key	Minimising	Maximising	Notable
Significant	Stretching	Substantially	Superseding
Tripling			

Technical & practical

Analysing	Assessing	Balancing	Built
Calculating	Constructing	Crafting	Creating
Delivering	Designing	Drafting	Drawing
Eliminating	Engineering	Evaluating	Joining
Manufacturing	Measuring	Operating	Processing

| Printing | Programming | Relaying | Styling |
| Testing | Wiring | | |

Communications

Approving	Authoring	Counselling	Demonstrating
Disseminating	Documenting	Editing	Facilitating
Informing	Instructing	Interviewing	Mediating
Moderating	Negotiating	Participating	Presenting
Presiding	Reporting	Serving as	Writing

Handling of information

Analysing	Calculating	Checking	Communicating
Copying	Collecting	Collating	Comparing
Compiling	Composing	Computing	Creating
Designing	Detailing	Disseminating	Documenting
Filing	Issuing	Listing	Organising
Preparing	Presenting	Processing	Recording
Reviewing	Simplifying	Summarising	Systematising
Storing			

Systems

Controlling	Converting	Correcting	Creating
Designing	Directing	Driving	Evolving
Implementing	Maintaining	Manipulating	Operating
Phasing	Piloting	Planning	Producing
Recovering	Repairing	Restoring	Running
Setting			

Management

Administering	Appointing	Attaining	Assigning
Authorising	Commissioning	Conducting	Contracting
Controlling	Co-ordinating	Deciding	Directing
Enacting	Establishing	Exceeding	Executing
Expanding	Heading	Implementing	Incorporating
Initiating	Instituting	Maintaining	Managing
Masterminding	Obtaining	Organising	Performing
Producing	Reducing	Repositioning	Retaining
Revising	Spearheading	Stipulating	Streamlining
Strengthening	Supervising	Trimming	Turning Around
Undertaking			

Negotiations

Assuring	Closing	Collaborating	Consolidating
Determining	Discussing	Evaluating	Formalising
Investigating	Negotiating	Mediating	Proposing
Sorting	Stabilising		

Relationships with people

Assisting	Communicating	Coaching	Co-operating
Contributing	Delegating	Directing	Educating
Encouraging	Guiding	Instructing	Leading
Liaison with	Motivating	Negotiating	Persuading
Recruiting	Selecting	Selling	Supervising
Supporting	Training		

Creativity

Arranging	Conceiving	Creating	Designing
Developing	Devising	Enabling	Enhancing
Formulating	Innovating	Inverting	Originating
Packaging	Realising	Refining	Reshaping
Resolving	Solving	Structuring	Visualising

APPENDIX 4 – SUCCESSFUL APPLICATION FORMS

Many organisations and recruitment agencies use standard application forms (SAF) as a way of selecting people for interview. It enables them to get the information they require, rather than what you want to give them. Although the information requested can vary widely, the same rules apply as with CV and letter writing. The application form should get the reader interested enough in you to want to meet you or recommend you for interview so that you can have the opportunity to sell yourself to them face-to-face.

Important: When writing your application form, put things in the right places as neatly as possible, and where possible obtain an electronic version of the form and type your answers. It will look a lot neater and create a more professional image.

Points to Remember:

- Read the instructions carefully e.g. use black ink, bold capitals where asked.
- Be careful with date of birth - don't put today's date!
- If it asks where you heard about the vacancy – you must complete the box provided. Leaving it blank shows a lack of attention to detail.
- Big open white spaces on forms are to be avoided. Give as much detail as possible.
- Grades should be specified for last qualification. Play down any mid-career ones if not good.
- Thin employment experience should be expanded. Details of work undertaken would add interest.
- Full sentences in Hobbies/Interests section would give an idea of personality i.e. In my spare time I enjoy team sports – badminton, tennis.
- Any other relevant information is the ideal place to show enthusiasm for the work applied for and to mention key skills and abilities. Leaving this blank shows lack of enthusiasm or a rushed application.
- Common examples of omissions include: only one referee detailed and no signature. This lack of care of attention to details will speak volumes to the employer.
- Check spellings and grammar. Get a friend to read it through.
- Use an envelope large enough to take the form unfolded.

Carefully follow this step-by-step procedure

- Read through the advert carefully, and pay close attention to the job description and specification.

- In the section where you are invited to describe your suitability for the post, it is essential that you base your answers on the key points in the job specification. If you do not address these points then you may miss your chance to 'sell' yourself to the employer.

- Decide on key skills, abilities and personal qualities and match them to the employer's requirements.

- Use strong action/positive words where possible to show your enthusiasm.

For higher level jobs, applicants are expected to show a greater knowledge of the company or organisation – not just what is in the employer's literature. You can gain more information on the company through reports, the internet and any informal contacts you might have. To help you in your job search, the Graduate Career Directory – Hobsons – provides information on a wide range of graduate employers. This information will be essential not only for the interview stage but also for the application form where there may be a chance to show this knowledge.

Unless told otherwise you could send a covering letter with your application form. It gives you the opportunity to provide extra information in support of your application and to convey your enthusiasm and motivation for the job. You never know, in doing so, it may help sway the employer in your favour.

APPENDIX 5 – JOB INTERVIEWS

A job interview is all about selling yourself to the employer and convincing them that you're the right person for the job. If you don't do this, no-one else will do if for you! A job interview typically lasts anything up to forty-five minutes. However it takes on average only 90 seconds to make a first impression, and selectors often make up their minds about a candidate's personality within just the first four minutes of an interview. You should then make the best use of those crucial first few minutes to create the right sort of impression.

Points to remember:

1. *Prepare well beforehand*

- Research the employer – visit their website, read the company brochure and annual report. Also, try linking in with someone on a social networking site who works for the company to get some inside information.

- Make sure you know 'inside out' the skills the employer is looking for – check the information given on the job advertisement and in the job specification.

    Make a list of key points you want to get across.

Don't forget the skills that employers want:

- Communication skills – presenting, listening.

- Organisation and planning skills – being able to prioritise your workload and work unsupervised.

- Working in a team – listening to other people's points of view, being constructive and joining in with ideas.

- Problem-solving – being able to find alternative solutions.

- Flexibility – being able to adapt to changing working environments.

- Time management – being able to prioritise and organise.

Overleaf there are examples of interview questions and also questions that you could ask. If you can answer their questions fully and evidence your answers to these, then you should do well.

2. *On the day of the interview*

- Dress appropriately, be clean and tidy – a dark business suit is usual. Remember to polish your shoes!

- First impressions count – from the moment you walk through the door and are greeted by the receptionist. They could be asked for their impression of you.

- Smile and give the interviewer a good, firm handshake.

- Be prepared for any questions and give good examples to back up your claim.

- Make sure you answer the questions asked!

- Give yourself time to answer. If you don't understand say, 'Can you clarify the question please?'

- Answer as fully as possible. Make it easy for the selector to see that you are right for the job, but don't talk too much.

- Watch your body language – don't fidget! Try and remain calm and confident.

- Keep eye contact with the interviewer.

- Be enthusiastic and as natural as possible. It will show in your voice and in your face.

- Remember to smile, shake hands and say 'thank you for seeing me' at the end of the interview.

Interview questions

The bulk of the interview will be taken up with their questions, but a good interviewer will always leave time for you to ask questions of your own – it is a two-way process. While the interviewer is trying to decide whether you're right for the company, you need to think 'Is this job right for me?' By asking questions of your own you will obtain the information you need to make the right decision if the job is offered to you. Not only is this an essential way of extracting information, it's another opportunity to make yourself look good by highlighting your strengths, showing off your research efforts and demonstrating your enthusiasm. If you don't ask questions it will look as if you are not interested.

Questions you could be asked:

- What do you know about this company/industry?

- Why are you interested in working for the company?

- What experience have you had of working in teams?

- What have you found the most enjoyable aspect of your course?

- What positions of responsibility have you had?

- What are your strengths and weaknesses?

- What can you offer us?

- What is your greatest achievement to date?
- What work experience have you had?
- What did you learn from it?
- Why are you interested in this line of work?
- Where do you see yourself in three to five years' time?
- What are your long-term career ambitions?
- What do you like to do in your spare time?
- Tell me about yourself.

Questions you could ask:

- What are the key tasks and responsibilities of this role?
- Where do you see this role fitting in with the rest of the organisation?
- Will the job involve travel?
- Do you run an induction programme?
- What training and development do you offer?
- What are your performance review procedures?
- What are your key criteria for promotion?
- How would you define your company culture?
- What are your strategies for growth?
- When do you expect to make a decision?

After the interview

Feedback

It is useful to obtain feedback from your interview performance and whether you have been successful or not. The employer will have assessed your performance objectively and you will be given specific examples of how you demonstrated effective or ineffective behaviour. This feedback will highlight your strengths and areas for further development. If you are receiving telephone feedback, make sure that you have pen and paper handy so that you can take notes.

If at first you don't succeed

It is often difficult to accept that you have been unsuccessful in your application for a job – it may be that you performed well but lost out to a better candidate on the day.

We live in a very competitive market and there will obviously be occasions when you are unsuccessful, but as long as you apply for work for which you have the necessary qualifications and experience then eventually you should succeed.

It may be useful to ask yourself the following questions:

- Am I applying for the wrong sort of jobs?
- Am I being too narrow in my search for a job?
- Have I customised my CV for the job I am applying for?
- Do I need to review my interview/presentation techniques?
- Where am I going wrong in selling myself?
- Am I researching and preparing enough for the interview?
- What image am I presenting to the interviewer/assessor?
- Is my body language assertive or passive?

Enlist some help from a work colleague, friend or a careers adviser. Show them your CV, the job applied for and go through your interview technique with them. They will be more objective than you and will be able to offer constructive support.

APPENDIX 6 – SKILLS AND WHY WE NEED THEM

Nowadays, employers require a flexible, adaptable and multi-skilled workforce that can fulfil many different roles. Businesses need to be sure that the people working for them can do the tasks necessary for the operation to run smoothly and effectively, and so enable them to keep ahead of the competition. The best way for you to stay marketable in an increasingly competitive and fast-moving world is to ensure that your skills are regularly reviewed and improved.

What are skills?

The Learning and Skills Improvement Service (LSIS) provides an excellent website that helps people make informed choices about their chosen profession. The following website contains many multimedia and interactive resources designed to explain which skills are needed in certain professions.
www.excellencegateway.org.uk/employability

Skills can be broadly divided into the following:

- **Key skills** ensure that your ability in reading, writing and arithmetic cover your everyday needs.

- **Transferable skills** are the ones you can take with you from one job to another, and can be used in any role in life. They build upon key skills, but are broader in their scope. They are also known as 'core skills or 'soft skills' and they are thought of as necessary to enable you to pass from one job to another. Transferable skills include those that can be measured such as, information technology or language skills, as well as less tangible attributes such as self-motivation and initiative.

- **Employment skills** are those you build up through studying and gaining experience in a job. They combine key and transferable skills and any specific skills you need for a particular job. They are made up of a range of talents and abilities and they enable you to be more self-reliant and to cope effectively in a changing world.

For example, if you want to become an accountant you are going to need more than just basic literacy and numeracy. As well as some of the above transferable skills, you will also have to posses relevant professional qualifications, which will give you the particular skills you need for that job. It is possible now to get work-based skills formally recognised via training and certification (NVQ's). Certification confirms a skill level and can act as a stepping stone to improve your career prospects.

The skills and qualities employers are looking for

The top 25 attributes

Rank order of importance	Attribute	Employer ratings of importance %
1	Willingness to learn	93
2	Commitment	88
3	Dependability/reliability	88
4	Self-motivation	88
5	Teamwork	87
6	Oral communication skills	87
7	Co-operation	86
8	Written communication skills	86
9	Drive/energy	84
10	Self-management	84
11	Desire to achieve/motivation	84
12	Problem-solving ability	83
13	Analytical ability	83
14	Flexibility	83
15	Initiative	83
16	Can summarise key issues	82
17	Logical argument	82
18	Adaptability (intellectual)	81
19	Numeracy	81
20	Adaptability (organisational)	80
21	Can cope with pressure/stress	80
22	Time management	80
23	Rapid conceptualisation of issues	79
24	Enquiry and research skills	79
25	Self-confidence	78

Source: Employer Satisfaction: Summary, Lee Harvey and Diana Green, QHE Project, University of Central England 1994.

It may be helpful to put the above in your own order of preference. This will help you to identify your own personal need and values.

How to develop your skills

There are a number of ways of developing your skills and the most obvious course of action to take is to start a college / university course, where you can receive training and gain a skill in a certain area. Appendix 1 offers information about organisations that offer careers information and advice that could help you decide which area to get trained in, and how to get started:

- Connexions - www.connexions-direct.com/

- Nextstep - www.direct.gov.uk/nextstep

- Directgov - University and Higher Educatuion www.direct.gov.uk/en/EducationAndLearning/UniversityAndHigherEducatio n/index.htm

- Voluntary work - www.do-it.org

Writing your skills profile

An essential part of finding and securing a job is the ability to know the skills that you possess. If you don't know which skills and attributes you have to offer an employer, how are they going to know? If you recognise a significant skills gap in your life, it is important that you take advice on how to gain the requisite skills and abilities. The above list of advice agencies will provide valuable careers information to help you to increase your chances of gaining employment in your chosen area. The following section offers exercises to enable you to review the skills and qualities that you possess.

Exercise - Knowing your strengths and weaknesses

This exercise will help you reflect on your strengths and areas for development. Look at the list of words below and tick those you feel best describe you. It may be that some apply only in certain circumstances, in which case tick them anyway.

Active Busy/Willing to be involved	**Lazy** Not willing to work	**Friendly** Pleasant to be with	**Dedicated** Willing to give time and energy
Thoughtful Considerate of others	**Caring** Understanding/ Sympathetic	**Shy** Uncomfortable with people you don't know	**Confident** Certain of your abilities
Independent Happy working on your own	**Communicative** Able to write and speak effectively	**Reflective** Able to think over a situation	**Uncertain** Unsure of what to do
Sociable Like meeting people	**Ambitious** Desire to be successful	**Focused** Able to centre attention on a problem/idea	**Self-starter** Able to work without Supervision
Promoter A good organiser	**Humour** Able to see the funny	**Steady** Reliable	**Persistent** Determined to succeed
Consistent Unchanging/ constant	**Ambitious** Desire to be successful	**Dependable** Solid/supportive	**Creative** Ability to think of new ideas/ways of working
Methodical Careful/orderly	**Practical** Able to see the possibility of a solution	**Instinctive** To act or know without thinking about	**Logical** To reason/to think through a problem
Impulsive To act without thinking	**Persuasive** To be able to convince	**Leader** To direct/to show the	**Follower** Happy to be told what
Indecisive Uncertain/unsure	**Networker** Identify and make contacts	**Influential** The power to affect another person	**Decisive** To be clear/certain
Competitive Ambitious to want to succeed	**Flexible** Able to work with different situations	**Motivated** Desire to do well	**Organised** To work in an orderly way

Pessimistic	Open-minded	Optimistic	Cynical
To expect the worst	To see the bigger picture	To be positive	To always see things negatively
Enthusiastic	Team worker	Stubborn	Energetic
Full of interest for a project/task etc.	Able to work with other people	To be unwilling to change a viewpoint	To be active/to get involved

When you have done this, look at the list above and sort out the words you have ticked under the following headings:

Happy about – Put an S for Strengths

Not happy about – Put a D for Development

<u>e.g.</u>
Enthusiastic S	Competitive D
Networker S	Flexible D
Instinctive S	Focused D

You may have found this exercise difficult. However, as job advertisements tend to ask about your personal qualities as well as your qualifications and relevant experience, it is a necessary exercise in any job search process. Employers want to know about you – the 'all round person'. It may be helpful to seek the views and opinions of others. Ask friends and family to look through the list, they may have other suggestions.

Recognising the skills you possess

Think about your strengths and weaknesses. What do you enjoy doing? For example:

- **Are you the kind of person who always gets a bargain?**
- **Do you mind asking for a discount on goods?**
- **Do you enjoy bartering in markets when you are on holiday?**
- **Do you find yourself with the best seats in a restaurant?**
- **Do people always agree with your suggestions (without you being bossy)?**

If the answer is **Yes** it could be because you have effective:

- **Negotiation and persuasive techniques**
- **Communication and interpersonal skills**
- **Leadership skills**

Exercise - Skills profile

This exercise will give you a skills profile, which pinpoints the skills you have, at what level and where you need to develop further. Make an honest assessment of your current skills, which can be used every day, at work and in your personal life. Give yourself a mark out of four for each main skill.

e.g.   1 = poor   2 = satisfactory   3 = good   4 = excellent

Your Skills	How have you developed this skill? Give an example
Self-awareness • Do you know yourself? • What are your strengths and weaknesses? • Can you cope with criticism?	
Self-management • Are you good at managing your time? • Can you work to deadlines when required? • Can you get things done without being constantly asked? • Are you good at planning and seeing plans through?	
Interpersonal skills • Are you good at judging just the right thing to say without putting your foot in it? • Can you put people at their ease quickly? • Do you mix well with all kinds of people?	
Flexibility • Can you assess the demands of different and difficult situations? • Can you adapt well to different situations? • Do you see new ways of approaching problems?	
Communication • Are you good at writing letters and reports? • Can you get your message across both on the telephone and in face-to-face situations • Are you sensitive to other people's moods and problems? • Are you a good listener as well as a good speaker?	

Problem-Solving • Can you collect and analyse information? • Do you see all sides of a problem? • Can you reach creative solutions that work?	
Team-Working • Are you good at building and maintaining relationships with other people? • Are you willing to listen to other people's suggestions? • Can you develop ideas with other people?	
Business Awareness • Do you appreciate the need for business development? • Can you identify areas which are cost effective? • Do you understand business 'politics'? • Do you understand when to maintain a confidentiality?	
Networking • Are you good at identifying people who might be useful to you? • Are you good at making contact with them? • Do you keep up links you have made?	
Negotiation • Do you know what you are aiming for when you start a discussion? • Are you assertive without being aggressive? • Can you give in gracefully?	
Computer Literacy • Can you use a spreadsheet? • Are you good at word-processing? • Can you use a computer package (e.g. MS Publisher) for presentation slides? • What about databases?	
Language Skills • Do you have a qualification in another language? • Can you use the business vocabulary of that language? • Are you confident enough to speak to prospective clients?	

Exercise – What motivates you?

It is important to know what sort of factors, which are attached to a job, motivate you. The following list provides you with aspects of a next job that you might consider to be of importance.

What do you want from a job?	Essential	Important	Unimportant
• Clear career progression			
• Structured training			
• Good salary			
• Early responsibility			
• Recognition of efforts			
• Variety of work			
• Working on long-term project			
• Working on short-term projects			
• Travel			
• Freedom to make my own choices			
• Relaxed working environment			
• Working autonomously in a team			
• Opportunity to be creative			
• Producing reports			
• Offering a service			
• Helping others			
• Working in a particular field/sector			
• Ability to be entrepreneurial			
• Developing a specialism			
• Long holidays			
• Sufficient time for pastimes			
• Other (add anything else you can think of)			

APPENDIX 7 – THE TYPE OF PERSONALITY WE HAVE

In order to be successful in the workplace, different behaviours are required in different jobs. For example, an operator in a nuclear power station is legally obliged to adhere to set procedures, and the personality required for this job will be poles apart from that needed by someone working in PR or marketing, which requires innovation and creativity. The behaviours that you need to use to be successful in a certain job, depend to some extent on your profession and not on what your personality preferences are. If you enjoy innovating, you may find it frustrating to work as an operator in a nuclear power station because you would have to keep within the confines of many legal rules and regulations. If you enjoy making sure that a job is done in a well-defined, correct and professional manner, you may find it exasperating working in a marketing agency. In this environment there can be a lot of ambiguity and change, and also a need to innovate constantly. In these examples, the frustration is due to a tension, or tug-o-war, between your personality preferences and the demands of your job.

Myers-Briggs® Model of Personality

Myers-Briggs Types[184]

ISTJ Introverted Sensing and Thinking	ISFJ Introverted Sensing with Feeling	INFJ Intoverted iNtuition with Feeling	INTJ Introverted iNtuition with Thinking
ISTP Introverted Thinking with Sensing	ISFP Introverted Feeling with Sensing	INFP Introverted Feeling with iNtuition	INTP Introverted Thinking with iNtuition
ESTP Extraverted Sensing and Thinking	ESFP Extraverted Sensing with feeling	ENFP Extraverted iNtuition with Feeling	ENTP Extraverted iNtuition with Thinking
ESTJ Extraverted Thinking with Sensing	ESFJ Extraverted Feeling with Sensing	ENFJ Extraverted Feeling with iNtuition	ENTJ Extraverted Thinking with iNtuition

MBTI, Myers-Briggs Type Indicator. Myers-Briggs are registered trademarks of the MBTI Trust, Inc

The Myers-Briggs model of personality is one of many such models designed to help you to orient yourself and find your way around your personality and identity. This model is based on four preferences (E or I, S or N, T or F and J or P) and you combine the preferences to give your Myers-Briggs personality type. For example, having preferences for E and S and T and J gives a personality type of ESTJ. There are sixteen Myers-Briggs personality types listed in the table, and even though you may exhibit a leaning towards a certain personality type, you may still show many others traits in the table.

The four preferences

1)

   a) ***E – Where, primarily, do you prefer to direct your energy?***

      If you prefer to direct your energy to deal with people, things, situations, or 'the outer world', then your preference is for Extraversion. This is denoted by the letter 'E'.

   b) ***I –*** If you prefer to direct your energy to deal with ideas, information, explanations or beliefs, or 'the inner world', then your preference is for Introversion. This is denoted by the letter 'I'.

2)

   a) ***S – How do you prefer to process information?***

      If you prefer to deal with facts, what you know, to have clarity, or to describe what you see, then your preference is for Sensing. This is denoted by the letter 'S'.

   b) **N –** If you prefer to deal with ideas, look into the unknown, to generate new possibilities or to anticipate what isn't obvious, then your preference is for Intuition. This is denoted by the letter 'N' (the letter I has already been used for Introversion).

3)

   a) **T – How do you prefer to make decisions?**

      If you prefer to decide on the basis of objective logic, using an analytic and detached approach, then your preference is for Thinking. This is denoted by the letter 'T'.

   b) **F –** If you prefer to decide using values and/or personal beliefs, on the basis of what you believe is important or what you or others care about, then your preference is for Feeling. This is denoted by the letter 'F'.

4)

   a) **J – How do you prefer to organise your life?**

      If you prefer your life to be planned, stable and organised then your preference is for Judging (not to be confused with 'Judgmental', which is quite different). This is denoted by the letter 'J'.

c) **P** – If you prefer to go with the flow, to maintain flexibility and respond to things as they arise, then your preference is for Perception. This is denoted by the letter 'P'.

When you put these four letters together, you get your personality type code, and there are sixteen combinations. For sources of jobs to match specific personalities visit:
www.teamtechnology.co.uk/careers/careers.html

An example of someone with the personality code EDFP:

Your most important preferences are Extraverted Intuition. Your 'dominant function' is Intuition, oriented towards the outer world. You promote exploration of new and better ways of doing things, to uncover hidden potential in people, things or situations. You break new ground, and are often looking one step beyond the current situation to pursue unexplored avenues, until all the possibilities have been exhausted. You often challenge the status quo and experiment with the introduction of change, to see if the situation can be improved or new potential uncovered.

An example of someone with the personality code ENFJ:

Your most important preferences are Extraverted Feeling. Your 'dominant function' is Feeling, oriented towards the outer world. This means you focus on building harmony in the world around you. You like to build rapport with people and create a positive atmosphere. You look after people's welfare. You naturally want to motivate others and make sure they are happy in each situation. You value other people's contributions, seek to develop the role that others play, and invest a lot of effort in building positive relationships. You try to overcome differences of opinion and find ways in which people can agree.

Source: With permission of Steve Myers   www.teamtechnology.co.uk

APPENDIX 8 – USEFUL ORGANISATIONS TO CONTACT

Where to Get Help if Going through Redundancy

- **The Advisory, Conciliation and Arbitration Service** (Acas) offers free, confidential and impartial advice on all employment rights issues. You can call the Acas helpline on 08457 47 47 47 from 8.00 am to 6.00 pm Monday to Friday.
  www.acas.org.uk

- **The Labour Relations Agency** (LRA) offers free, confidential and impartial advice on all employment rights issues for residents of Northern Ireland. You can contact the LRA on 028 9032 1442 from 9.00 am to 5.00 pm Monday to Friday.
  www.lra.org.uk/

- Your local **Citizens Advice Bureau** (CAB) can provide free and impartial advice. You can find your local CAB office in the phone book or online.
  www.citizensadvice.org.uk/

- If you are a member of a trade union, you can get help, advice and support from them.

- The **Department for Business and Enterprise and Regulatory Reform** have produced a guide to redundancy at:
  http://www.berr.gov.uk/files/file47510.pdf

Business Start Agencies

- **www.businesslink.gov.uk** (Also includes business start-up advice for disabled people)

- **http://www.start.biz/home.htm**

- **www.startups.co.uk**

- **www.fredericksfoundation.org** (Business start-up advice for disabled people. Covers most of Southern England)

- **www.adp.org.uk** (The Association of disabled Professionals)

- **www.fsb.org.uk** (Federation of Small Businesses)

- **www.smarta.com** Start-up business advice from Entrepreneurs

Careers Advisory Services

- **Connexions – www.connexions-direct.com/**

Youth support service for thirteen- to nineteen-year-olds and for those with learning difficulties up to twenty-five years old. This service is managed locally by local authorities working together with all the key youth support agencies.

- **Nextstep - www.direct.gov.uk/nextstep**

Nextstep offers both a face-to-face and a telephone advice service – offering a source of impartial advice on courses, careers, funding and more. To book an appointment to meet a careers adviser *or* to receive careers advice over the phone, visit the website or call free: 0800 100 900

- **Direct.gov – University and Higher Education** http://www.direct.gov.uk/en/EducationAndLearning/UniversityAndHigherEducation/index.htm

A service that helps people to consider the steps necessary to enter Higher Education(HE). The website offers links to information on HE courses around the country, how to apply to university, financing studies, student life and how HE can drive forward your career.

Miscellaneous

- **Jobcentre Plus** advertise job vacancies on public display boards. If you identify a job that you are interested in, a Jobcentre Plus adviser can provide more details and make appointments for interview. Visit www.jobcentreplus.gov.uk for more details. To make a new claim for benefit call 0800 0 55 66 88

- **General Job / vocational information to help you develop job ideas**

  - http://nextstep.direct.gov.uk/
  - www.prospects.ac.uk
  - www.advice-resources.co.uk/adviceresources/general/dir/jobprofiles/
  - www.cvbuilder-advice-resources.co.uk/
  - www.connexions-direct.com/jobs4u
  - www.bbc.co.uk/learning/
  - www.jobseekers.Direct.gov.uk/www.support4learning.org.uk
  - www.excellencegateway.org.uk/employability

APPENDIX 9 – STARTING UP YOUR OWN BUSINESS

Starting a new business is an option that many people take when faced with watershed moments in life such as being made redundant, experiencing long-term unemployment or, more positively, after hitting onto a winning and a profitable idea. Before you commit time and finances to a business idea the first step is to seek some professional advice. There are many business support agencies that provide excellent resources that can help guide your first tentative steps to becoming self-employed.

Business Start-Up Agencies

- www.businesslink.gov.uk (Also includes business start-up advice for people with a disabilbity)

- http://www.start.biz/home.htm

- www.startups.co.uk

- www.fredericksfoundation.org (Business start-up advice for people with a disabilbity. Covers most of Southern England)

- www.adp.org.uk (The Association of disabled Professionals)

- www.fsb.org.uk (Federation of Small Businesses)

- www.smarta.com (Start-up business advice from Entrepreneurs)

Starting a new business is both exciting and rewarding, but it is also full of challenges. The level of commitment that you will need should not be underestimated. The success of your business will partly depend on your attitude and skills. This means being honest about a range of issues – your knowledge, your financial status and the personal qualities that you can bring to your new business. Commitment, drive, perseverance and support from family and friends will go a long way towards transforming your business idea into reality and will be especially important during the early days.

This guide will help you decide whether you have what it takes to set up a new business. It also provides a look at the day-to-day reality of starting a business and outlines the skills and qualities that you will need.

1) The entrepreneurial quality check

Research has shown that there are certain qualities commonly found among successful business people. A typical entrepreneur will have the following key qualities:

- Self-confidence – a self-belief and passion about your product or service - your enthusiasm should win people over to your ideas.

- Self-determination – a belief that the outcome of events is down to your own actions, rather than based on external factors or other people's actions.

- Being a self-starter – the ability to take the initiative, work independently and to develop your ideas.

- Judgement – the ability to be open-minded when listening to other people's advice, while bearing in mind your objectives for the business.

- Commitment – the willingness to make personal sacrifices through long hours and loss of leisure time.

- Perseverance – the ability to continue despite setbacks, financial insecurity and exposure to risk.

- Initiative – the ability to be resourceful and proactive, rather than adopting a passive 'wait and see' approach.

2) Are you ready to start up?

- The day-to-day reality check

Setting up your own business requires your full commitment. One way to find out about the day-to-day realities of running a business is to talk to people who are in business already. Here are some of the challenges you need to think about.

- Personal sacrifice

The physical and emotional demands of starting up in business should not be underestimated. Starting a business is a life-changing event and will require hard work and long hours, especially in the early stages.

- Financial insecurity

There can be times of financial uncertainty and this may have a knock-on effect for both you and your family. For example, you may have to forgo holidays. You may have invested personal savings or used your family home as security and in the worst case scenario you risk losing your investment or even your home.

- Loss of company perks

Setting up your own business means that you will no longer be able to take advantage of the usual benefits associated with a permanent job. This includes the loss of 'safety net' benefits such as pension rights, sick pay, paid holiday and other company perks.

- Pressure on close relationships

You will need the support of your family and friends. They should be aware from the outset of the effect starting up a business will have on your life and it is crucial that they are right behind you. Their emotional backing may also need to be complemented by a practical 'hands on' approach. Discussing these issues before they arise will help.

- Isolation

Being your own boss can be a satisfying experience. However, shouldering all the responsibility for the success of the business can prove lonely. Unless you develop a network of contacts, there will be no one there to bounce ideas off.

3) Find out if you have got what it takes

Starting up a business requires a considerable investment of time, funds and energy. Before you begin, you need to honestly assess whether you really have what it takes and how well you think you might handle the risks involved.

You may want to consider the following questions:

- Are you prepared for the personal demands of setting up a new business?
- How well do you handle uncertainty?
- Do you have a positive attitude?
- Are you prepared to take chances and gamble on your ideas?
- Do you have any of the key qualities of a typical entrepreneur?
- Do you have an absolute determination to succeed?
- Can you bounce back from setbacks?
- Are you able to delegate?

- Do you have core business skills?
- Are you prepared to spend time carrying out in-depth market research?
- Do you have sufficient funds to set up a new business?
- Are you willing to draw on expert help when you need it?

Very few entrepreneurs can claim to be strong in all of the areas required. The key is to make the most of your assets and take action to address any gaps. This could include learning new skills yourself or drawing on outside help by delegating, recruiting or outsourcing.

Ultimately, you are the only person who can decide whether you have what it takes to make your dream of starting a business into a reality.

4) The business skills check

As a business owner you need core skills to execute your ideas to ensure that your new business survives in the long term. You should start by assessing your own skills and knowledge. This will help you decide whether you need to learn new skills or draw on outside help by delegating, recruiting or outsourcing.

- **Financial management**

This includes having a good grasp of cashflow planning, credit-management and maintaining good relationships with your bank and accountant.

- **Product development**

The ability to make long-term plans for product development and identify the people, materials and processes required to achieve them. In order to make such plans you will need to know your competition and your customers' needs. See our guides on how to understand your competitors, know your customers' needs and develop new products and services.

- **P eople management**

This includes managing recruitment, resolving disputes, motivating staff and managing training. Good people management will help employees to work together as a well-functioning team. See our guide on skills and training for directors and owners.

- **Business planning**

The ability to assess the strengths and weaknesses of your business and plan accordingly. See our guide on how to prepare a business plan.

- **Marketing skills**

A sound marketing approach will help you set up and oversee sales and marketing operations, analyse markets, identify selling points for your product and following these through to market. See our guides on how to write a marketing plan and market research and market reports.

- **Supplier relationship management**

The ability to identify suppliers and positively manage your relationship with them. See our guides on how to manage your suppliers and choosing the right suppliers.

- **Sales skills**

Without sales your business cannot survive and grow. You need to be able to identify potential customers and their individual needs, explain your goods and services effectively to them and convert these potential customers into clients. See our guide on how to reach your customers effectively.

5) The market research check

You need to research your target market and your competitors carefully. A common misconception is that entrepreneurs who have failed simply lacked sufficient funding or did not put the right team in place. In many cases new businesses fail because they have not spent enough time on researching their business idea and its viability in the market.

There are certain criteria you can use to establish this:

- Does your product or service satisfy or create a market need?

- Can you identify potential customers?

- Will your product or service outlive any passing trends or capitalise on the trend before it dies away?

- Is your product or service unique, distinct or superior to those offered by competitors?

- What competition will your product or service face - locally, nationally and globally?

- Is the product safe?

- Does your product or service comply with relevant regulations and legislation?

- Can you sell the product or service at a price that will give you sufficient profit?

Market research can play an important role in answering many of these questions and increasing your chances of success. How much research you do will depend on the time and funds you have available. You could:

- Informally canvass the opinion of friends

- Talk to industry contacts and colleagues

- Survey the public about whether they would use your product or service

- Ask customers of competing products what improvements they would like to see

- Set up focus groups to test your product or service

- Monitor what your competitors are doing

- Look at what has and hasn't worked in your industry or market niche

- Study wider economic and demographic data

The more information you have, the better placed you will be to make your business idea a success.

6) Overview of legal structures

To put your business on a proper footing with HM Revenue & Customs (HMRC) and other authorities, you need to make sure that it has the right legal structure. It's worth thinking carefully about which structure best suits the way that you do business, as this will affect:

- The tax and National Insurance that you pay

- The records and accounts that you have to keep

- Your financial liability if the business runs into trouble
- The ways your business can raise money
- The way management decisions are made about the business

There are several structures to choose from, depending on your situation. This guide will help you understand the differences between them. If you are not sure which legal structure would best suit your business, you can get advice from an accountant or solicitor.

- Sole trader

The advantages of being a sole trader include independence, ease of set up and running, and the fact that all the profits go to you.

The disadvantages include a lack of support, unlimited liability and the fact that you are personally responsible for any debts run up by your business.

- Partnership

The advantages of being in a partnership include its ease of set up and running, and the range of skills and experience that the partners can bring to the business.

However, problems can occur when there are disagreements between partners. There is unlimited liability and, as a partner, you are personally responsible for any debts that the business runs up.

- Limited liability partnership (LLP)

LLPs retain the flexibility of a partnership and your personal liability is limited. At least two members must be 'designated members' - the law places extra responsibilities on them.

The formation of an LLP is more complex and costly than that of a partnership and problems can occur when there are disagreements between the members. If the number of partners is reduced, and there are fewer than two designated members, then every member is deemed to be a designated member.

- Limited liability company

In a limited liability company your personal financial risk will be restricted to how much you invest in the business and any guarantees you have given in order to obtain financing.

However, you should remember that this type of company also brings a range of extra legal duties, including the maintenance of the company's public records, eg for the purpose of the filing of accounts.

- Franchise

The major advantage of a franchise is that it takes advantage of the success of an established business and support networks.

However, your freedom to manage the business is limited by the terms of the franchise agreement. Also franchisees often pay a share of their turnover to the franchiser, which reduces overall profits.

- Social enterprises

A social enterprise is a business with primarily social objectives. Any profits are largely reinvested in the business or in the community, rather than given to shareholders and owners. There are many different types of social enterprises, including:

- Community development trusts

- Housing associations

- Worker-owned co-operatives

- Leisure centres

Social enterprises may take a number of different business structures – the most common are companies limited by guarantee, companies limited by shares, and industrial and provident societies.

7) Your next step in setting up your business

There are many other important considerations that you need to make when going through a business start-up. For a continuation of this business guide visit: www.businesslink.gov.uk or call Business Link Helpline 0845 600 9 006.

84 John 16:13
85 Luke 24:13–35
86 Nielsen Media Research, Inc.
87 Study produced by the Kaiser Family Foundation
88 Mark 7:21
89 Col. 3:16
90 Jer. 29:11
91 Deut. 28:1–14
92 Mal. 3:10
93 Rom. 10:10
94 Matt. 16:15–18
95 Ps. 103:20
96 Rom. 8:31
97 Rom. 1:16
98 Heb. 6:12
99 Eph. 6:17
100 Isa. 54:17
101 Eph. 6:10–13
102 1 Sam. 17:28–29
103 Matt. 12: 36
104 Heb. 4:12
105 Heb. 12:15
106 Eph. 4:26–27
107 Eph. 6:11
108 Rev. 19:20
109 Prov. 19:20
110 Rom. 8:11
111 Acts 16:9
112 John 10:4
113 1 Kgs 19:12–13
114 Rom. 8:17
115 John 15:14–15
116 Heb. 4:16
117 John 5:30
118 Rom. 8:15–17
119 John 5:19
120 Rom. 12:2
121 Rom. 8:15
122 Eph. 6:12
123 An advertising campaign by the British Humanist Association in 2009 on some UK buses claimed: 'There's probably no God. Now stop worrying and enjoy your life.'
124 1 Cor. 2:9–12
125 Jer. 29:13–14
126 Exod. 20:4–5
127 John 2:17
128 Matt. 27:46; Ps. 22:1
129 Rom. 5:10
130 Luke 11:23
131 Gen. 32:24–28
132 Matt. 6:9-13
133 1 Pet. 5:6
134 Heb. 13:21
135 Matt. 25:14–30
136 Mal. 3:10
137 Luke 14:28
138 Prov. 15:22
139 Eph. 4:12
140 Isa. 30:21
141 Acts 21:10–11
142 1 Cor. 14:3
143 Rev. 12:11
144 John 15:10–11
145 Heb. 12:2
146 1 Pet. 1:8
147 John 14–16
148 Eph. 3:20
149 1 Pet. 5:8–9
150 Num. 13:27
151 Num. 13:28,33
152 Num. 13:30
153 Num. 14:24
154 Ps. 57:2
155 2 Cor. 4:7
156 2 Cor. 4:8
157 2 Cor. 12:7
158 2 Cor. 12:9
159 John 5:1–8
160 Gen. 15:5
161 Exod. 3:10 – 4:13
162 Judg. 6:12–16, 36–39
163 Heb. 11:1
164 Heb. 11:39
165 Ps. 103:17
166 Exod. 20:6
167 1 John 1:8
168 Josh. 7:1
169 Eph. 6:12
170 2 Cor. 4:18
171 Col. 2:15
172 John 10:10
173 1 John 3:1; Rom. 8:17
174 Matt. 25:21
175 John 16:26–27
176 Gen. 2:15
177 Gen. 3:17–19
178 Isa. 40:31
179 Matt. 6:25–34
180 Exod. 3:10 – 4:13
181 Jas 2:18
182 Rom. 8:28
183 Neh. 6:11
184 MBTI, Myers-Briggs Type Indicator, Myers-Briggs are registered trademarks of the MBTI Trust, Inc.

1 Jer. 29:11–12

2 From the mid-1990s up until 2008 there was a downward movement in the unemployment figures in Britain. However, this disguised a worrying trend in the number of people claiming Incapacity Benefit, a number that is not included in the unemployment figures. There are an estimated 10 million disabled adults in Great Britain covered by the Disability Discrimination Act, which equates to over one in five of the adult population. (DWP 2004) Of this number 1,224,230 receive Incapacity Benefit and a further 1,193,480 are in receipt of various forms of Income Support related to a disability (DWP 2007). People on Incapacity Benefit tend to remain claimants for the longest periods of time. The average time spent on Incapacity Benefit is now nine years, which has increased from an average of three years in 1985. (DWP 2008)

3 Research by the Department of Work and Pensions has shown that long-term worklessness is one of the greatest known risks to health:

- Health risk is equivalent to smoking 10 packs of cigarettes per day.(Ross 1995)
- Suicide rate in general increases six-fold in longer-term worklessness.(Bartley et al, 2005)
- It possesses a greater health risk than most dangerous jobs.(Construction & North Sea)
- Children of unemployed parents suffer with more chronic ill health.

4 Matt. 27:46

5 The Collins Concise Dictionary

6 Eph. 3:19

7 Ps. 139:1–4

8 Rom. 8:28

9 Nick Kochan, The Independent 25th January 2007

10 Matt.15:18–19

11 John 10:10

12 Rom. 7:14–25

13 John 14:23

14 Rev. 2:4–5

15 Exod. 33:15–16

16 John 16:25–27

17 Rom. 5:8

18 1 John 4:19

19 Rom. 8:30

20 1 John 3:1

21 Acts 13:22

22 Ps. 63:5

23 John 15:16

24 Exod. 20:5

25 Acts 1:14

26 Acts 5:34–39

27 Heb. 11:6

28 Rom. 5:1–2

29 Rom. 15:13

30 John 14:1

31 Rom. 1:16

32 2 Pet. 3:18

33 Heb. 6:17; 13:8

34 Matt. 7:24–27

35 1 John 3:20

36 Job 37:16

37 Isa. 46:5

38 1 Cor. 2:10–11

39 Matt. 6:8; 10:30

40 Rom. 16:27

41 Isa. 28:29

42 Ps. 104:24

43 1 Cor. 1:24–25

44 Jas 1:5

45 John 14:16

46 Gen. 1:27

47 2 Sam. 7:28

48 John 17:17

49 Luke 18:19

50 Ps. 34:8

51 1 John 4:8

52 Rom. 5:8

53 Matt. 22:37–38

54 Ps. 84:11

55 John 16:24

56 Isa. 40:12–31

57 Heb. 4:12

58 www.hubblesite.org

59 Oxford online dictionary – Dictionary lot.com

60 1 Cor. 15:33

61 Rom. 15:7

62 Eph. 5:25

63 Col. 3:13

64 Gal. 5:16–21

65 Gal. 5:22–23

66 1 Pet. 2:19–21

67 Jas 1:2–4

68 Matt. 5:48

69 1 Pet. 1:3–9

70 2 Pet. 1:3–4

71 Heb. 12:10

72 Prov. 16:9

73 Heb. 11:8–10

74 Acts 16:9

75 Phil. 3:8

76 John 16:14

77 Spread The Fire Issue 2 – 2005

78 Exod. 33:11

79 John 16:13

80 BBCi 19th March 2004

81 Luke 11:2

82 Col. 3:16

83 2 Tim. 3:16

BIBLIOGRAPHY

Bruce, F.F. The Spreading Flame (Carlisle, The Paternoster Press, 1995)

Carson, D.A., R.T. France, J.A. Motyer, G.J. Wenham, eds. New Bible Commentary 21st Century Edition (Leicester, England Inter-Varsity Press 1998)

Grudem, G. Systematic Theology (Leicester, England Inter-Varsity Press 1994)

Warren, R. The Purpose Driven Life (Michigan Zondervan 2002)

Bible version used, unless stated otherwise in the book: New International Version (London, Hodder and Stoughton 2000)

Illustrations by Bongo Clive Edwards: www.bongoclive.net

Oasis Business CIC

Charles Humphreys is a founding Director of Oasis Business CIC (OBCIC), a social enterprise that runs a number of projects in the UK and Africa that are designed to work positively with different vulnerable groups. In the UK, OBCIC is actively engaging with the Government's Big Society by running an IT-oriented training and coaching project called the Media Lab. This recycling-based project offers a radical solution to long-term unemployment among vulnerable groups, most notably NEET (young people).

OBCIC emerged out of Oasis Church in Colliers Wood, London SW19 (though OBCIC operates as a separate entity) as a way to enable its members to demonstrate their Christian beliefs to business communities around the world.

For further information visit: www.oasisbusiness.org

Send in your testimony

There is great power in giving our testimony (Revelation 12:11). When we leave our career wilderness and are able to tell of how God has broken through in a situation, then nobody, not even the enemy, can take away from us the absolute conviction of this revelation in our lives. Our testimonies are precious and are effective in encouraging and empowering others who have yet to see such a break through.

Please send in your testimonies of how the Father, through our Lord Jesus, has turned your job situation around. www.hope4acareer.com/Contactus.aspx

INTRODUCTION

By late 1942 the German armed forces had brought about an unparalleled sequence of victories, and Germany dominated Europe.

On 1 September 1939, Poland was attacked by 1.5 million soldiers in fifteen armored and motorized divisions, comprising 3,600 armored vehicles, and thirty-seven infantry divisions, supported by 6,000 artillery pieces and 1,900 aircraft. The Polish army was considered the strongest army in Europe after those of France and the Soviet Union. It comprised 1.3 million men in thirty-seven infantry divisions, eleven cavalry brigades, and one armored brigade, with 750 armored vehicles, 4,000 artillery pieces, and 900 aircraft.

Incredibly, only three weeks into the campaign the main Polish armies were shattered, despite their courageous defense. Warsaw surrendered on 29 September, and by 6 October, the campaign was over. In just over a month, the *Wehrmacht* had defeated what was generally thought to be a formidable opponent. German casualties were 14,400 dead and missing and 3,000 wounded. Polish casualties were 70,000 killed in action, an unknown number of missing, and over 700,000 prisoners.

Immediately after the Polish campaign, the OKH[1] initiated an inquiry into the effectiveness of the army in its first large-scale combat operation since the end of World War I. Although the campaign could be considered an outstanding success, the higher command had serious reservations. German officers were not reticent in truthfully pointing out any deficiencies in their units.

Although the Polish campaign confirmed the effectiveness of the tactics employed, there was considerable room for improvement. Some important general principles were re-emphasized: At all levels, effective leadership must be from the front; accurate and concise reports needed to be forwarded as commanders tended to exaggerate losses, terrain difficulties, and enemy strength; finally, troops were not adequately prepared for reconnaissance and security duties.

In addition, cooperation between the infantry and artillery was in many cases poor, as was the coordination of infantry and *panzers*. In heavy terrain and night fighting, the infantry did not meet the standards required. In many cases officers were far too cautious and failed to take advantage of immediate opportunities.

---

1. *Oberkommando des Heeres:* Army High Command.

Of particular concern was the performance of reservists, as they were not able to undertake the extended marches required and lacked the training and unit cohesion to carry out the prescribed elastic defensive tactics. Strenuous efforts were made to increase training in order to bring the reserve divisions up to regular army levels of performance.

These lessons and numerous others were applied to the training programs in order to ready the army for the campaign in the West. It was the willingness for considered self-criticism that constituted one of the major factors that enabled the German Army to perform at such high levels during the war.

Unfortunately, requests from the commanders of regular infantry units for more motorization, armored vehicles, and armored artillery vehicles could not be fulfilled. Because of a lack of production capacity, these scarce assets were largely allocated to the armored, mechanized, and motorized formations. Therefore, the infantry divisions were forced to rely on horse-drawn transport for supplies and moving artillery.

The hard lessons of the Polish campaign were successfully applied to the campaign in the West. Norway and Denmark were invaded on 9 April without warning. Denmark was immediately overrun and all the initial German objectives were secured quickly. The Norwegian campaign continued until 9 June when Allied forces evacuated Narvik due to the impending collapse in France.

France and the Low Countries were attacked on 10 May, and when on 20 May Guderian's *panzers* reached the Channel, the Battle of France was effectively over. The influence of the German infantry on the battle has been largely overlooked, with the focus on the *panzer* divisions and the *Luft-waffe*. In fact, it was the hard-marching infantry divisions that rapidly followed up on the advances of the armored units, providing flank protection and allowing the French and Allied forces no respite. Of the 141 German divisions employed in the attack, only 10 were armored, with the majority consisting of non-motorized infantry divisions.

The campaign in the West was a stunning victory that surprised even the Germans. The static slaughter of World War I was avoided and an old enemy utterly defeated in a scant six weeks. After suffering casualties in the millions in the previous conflict, the German army sustained losses of 28,225 killed, 116,592 wounded, and 13,595 missing.

Next it was the turn of Yugoslavia and Greece to succumb after being invaded on 6 April 1941. Yugoslavia surrendered unconditionally on 17 April and Greece on the twenty-eighth. Crete was taken in a very costly airborne assault that commenced on 20 May and concluded with the surrender of 18,000 mainly Commonwealth troops on 31 May.

In order to come to the rescue of his Italian ally, a small force commanded by *General* Erwin Rommel was sent to North Africa on 12 February 1941. On 24 March, Rommel went on the offensive with one *panzer* and two Italian divisions, steadily driving the British and Commonwealth forces back.

On 22 June 1941, over 3 million men comprising 17 armored divisions, 13 motorized divisions, 6 mountain divisions, and 101 infantry divisions attacked the Soviet Union. Complete surprise was achieved and the three army groups advanced rapidly. As in the previous campaigns, the armored and motorized divisions slashed through the Soviet defenses, ranging far ahead of the infantry divisions that were soon lagging far behind.

Massive pockets of trapped Soviet forces were created at Bialystok on 30 June and Minsk on 9 July; both pockets contained almost 300,000 men and thousands of armored vehicles. At Smolensk on 16 July, another 300,000 Soviet soldiers were trapped, and in the south at Umlan, 100,000 prisoners were taken on 4 August.

An even larger disaster for the Soviets occurred when Kiev fell on 19 September, trapping a staggering 665,000 men in the pocket.

However, these were not easy victories, and the infantry suffered significant numbers of casualties in both closing the pockets and preventing a breakout. In July and August 1941, the Germans lost almost 88,000 killed, over 273,000 wounded, and 17,000 missing. A large proportion of these casualties were attributable to the prolonged battle for Smolensk that lasted from 10 July to 10 September. This was twice as long as the whole campaign in the West.

Similarly, at Bryansk and Vyazma, another 650,000 men were trapped but continued to fight. Once again, the infantry sustained large numbers of casualties in reducing the pocket. The Soviet soldier proved himself to be brave, skilled, stubborn, and resourceful. Despite over 3 million casualties sustained by October 1941, the Soviet army continued to fiercely resist. The fighting was brutal and the distances covered were vast. This was a different kind of war from that in the West, something the *Wehrmacht* was not adequately prepared for.

The winter offensive before Moscow, launched on 5 December, caught the German forces completely by surprise. The confidence of the high command, as well as that of the ordinary German soldier, was severely shaken. At times it looked as though the whole German front was on the verge of disintegrating. However, for a number of reasons, this did not occur, and despite withdrawals, the front held. Not the least of these reasons was the steadfastness and courage of the lowly infantryman, fighting in unfamiliar and appalling conditions.

The Germans began their summer offensive on 28 June 1942 and, once again, completely deceived the Soviet high command (STAVKA). Instead of resuming the drive on Moscow, Army Group A (Weichs) headed south with the intention of capturing the oil fields of the Caucasus. Army Group B (List) was to attack southeast, with the taking of Stalingrad tasked to the 6th Army of Paulus. The initial advance was rapid, but the situation was not the same as the early months of Barbarossa in 1941. The coordination of the *panzers*, artillery, infantry, and the *Luftwaffe* was again highly effective, and staff work was as usual of a high standard. The Soviets were forced to rapidly retreat, and the *panzers* ranged far and wide. However, the retreat did not turn into a rout, no large pockets were formed, and no mass surrenders occurred. Every kilometer of the advance was usually bitterly contested. The Soviet high command and their soldiers had learned the lessons of the previous year well. Space was traded for time as the direction of the German advance was determined with reinforcements from other fronts and reserves were directed to the threatened areas.

By August, all still seemed to be going well for the Germans; however, the signs were increasingly ominous both on the Eastern Front and in North Africa.

In Africa Rommel's forces were almost at the gates of Alexandria and seemingly poised to capture both the Suez Canal and the vital Middle East oil fields. However, Rommel's advance was checked at the first battle of El

Alamein in July. Rommel intended to make his final push to Alexandria in August.

In southern Russia, Paulus's 6th Army was seemingly on the verge of driving the remaining Soviet defenders from the rubble of Stalingrad.

This was to be the limit of German conquests. Germany and its allies dominated western and central Europe, the Baltic states, the Balkans, and a large portion of North Africa. The German advance was first checked at Stalingrad and second at El Alamein and then remorselessly driven back. From that high water mark in August–September 1942, what followed was, with few exceptions, a long and bitter retreat ending with unconditional surrender.

The German common soldier had nevertheless performed prodigious feats of arms in a wide variety of theaters and conditions, from the green fields of Western Europe and the parched desert to the "endless" steppes and the frigid winter wastelands of Russia. The "*Landser*," as he called himself, was mostly a conscript, largely apolitical (members of the armed forces were not allowed to vote), highly disciplined, and well equipped, trained, and led. The retreat in the winter of 1941–42 had caused a crisis of confidence in the higher command that the army never fully recovered from. The exceptionally high morale exhibited at the end of the campaign in the West and the early weeks of the attack on the Soviet Union never returned. Most of the German soldiers fought for the same basic reasons as all other soldiers: for their country, their family, their comrades, and, ultimately, for their survival.

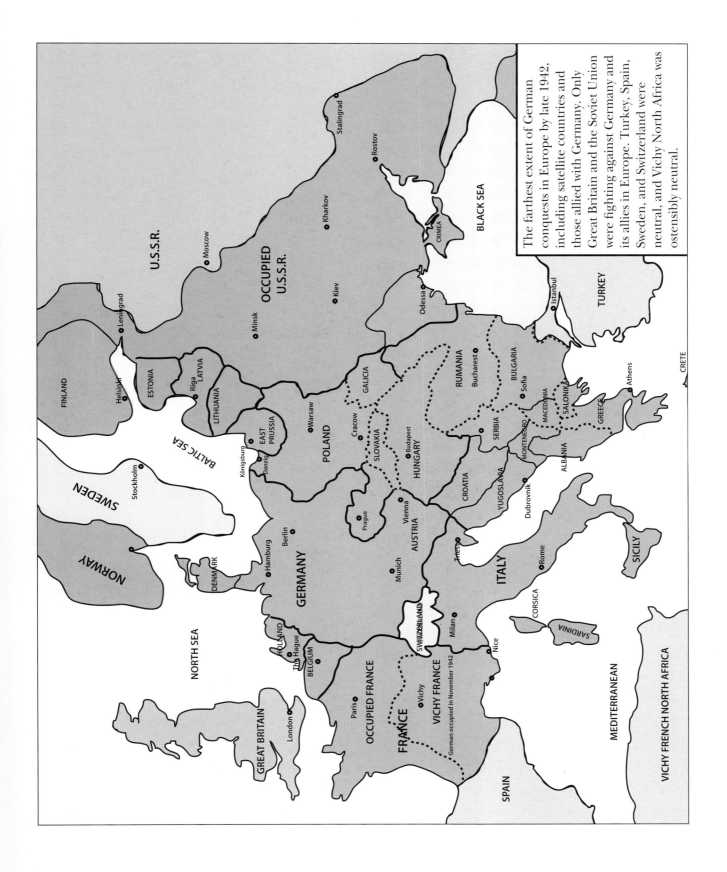

The farthest extent of German conquests in Europe by late 1942, including satellite countries and those allied with Germany. Only Great Britain and the Soviet Union were fighting against Germany and its allies in Europe. Turkey, Spain, Sweden, and Switzerland were neutral, and Vichy North Africa was ostensibly neutral.

THE INFANTRY

An infantry squad on patrol. The soldier in the foreground appears to be checking compass bearings.

Various aspects of the uniforms such as the pleated pockets, green collar facings, and immaculate full-length marching boots indicate that this is a very early war photograph.

The gruesome results of a direct hit on a bunker.

A primitive hut constructed from blocks of dirt or clay. German troops were shocked by the primitive living conditions they encountered.

Senior officers plan the next stage of the campaign. It was expected that even generals were to remain close to the front lines in order to react to changing conditions and take advantage of unexpected opportunities.

Infantry from a *Luftwaffe* Field Division. Jealous of the *Waffen SS,* the head of the *Luftwaffe,* Hermann Göring, fielded twenty-one divisions of *Luftwaffe* troops. Although lavishly equipped, these divisions were a failure in combat as the soldiers were poorly trained and led. The divisions were eventually either disbanded or handed over to the army.

Elite ski troops of a mountain division (*Gebirgsjäger*) training in the Austrian alps.

The wearing of the M1943 field cap, which was approved for general issue in June 1943, dates this photograph from the later war period.

Digging in, one of the most disliked tasks for an infantryman, even if it was essential to survival.

Weapons inspection. The soldiers are wearing the lace-up ankle boots and gaiters. The canvas gaiters were unpopular and nicknamed retreat gaiters as they were introduced when the German army was on the defensive and retreating.

Supplementing field rations with fresh meat. The soldier on the right is wearing canvas magazine pouches for the MP 38/40 machine pistol. Each pouch contained three thirty-two-round magazines.

Luftwaffe Flak crews relax beside their 4-meter *EmR 4m* range finder, the standard range finder for heavy antiaircraft guns.

Three newly awarded Iron Cross, Second Class, recipients. The actual medal was only allowed to be worn on the day it was awarded, subsequently replaced by a ribbon.

Cutting logs for the construction of the bridge pictured below. Due to the numerous water crossings in Russia, German engineers became very skilled at constructing expedient bridges.

It appears that even officers became involved in manual labor when the need arose.

The solid construction indicates that this bridge will be used for light vehicles as well as foot traffic.

The numerous swampy areas of the Soviet Union required the construction of extensive corduroy roads. Fortunately, there was usually plenty of timber available.

A *Luftwaffe* Flak crew with a *Kommandohilfegerät* 35 antiaircraft gun director.

The neverending paperwork associated with command or, more likely, war correspondents filing their articles to help bolster morale at home. Both war correspondents and photographers were very prevalent at the front.

Mountain troops (*Gebirgsjäger*) distinguished by their mountain caps (*Bergmütze*), *Edelweiss* shoulder and cap badge insignia, and mountain boots (*Bergschuhe*). Mountain divisions were deployed in northern Russia and the Caucasus.

More *Gebirgsjäger* relaxing behind the front lines. The soldier in the foreground above appears to be a Russian volunteer known as a *Hiwi* (*Hilfswilliger*).

A respite from the strain of combat operations, no matter how brief, is always welcome.

German soldiers took an oath of allegiance not to their country but to Adolf Hitler: "I swear by God this holy oath that I will render unconditional obedience to the *Führer* of Germany and of her people, Adolf Hitler, the Supreme Commander of the Armed Forces, and that as a brave soldier, I will be prepared to stake my life for this oath."

An award ceremony for recipients of the Iron Cross, Second Class. The German Army made extensive use of various decorations and awards for exceptional performance in combat in order to boost morale.

The standard *Wehrmacht* mortar, the 81.4mm *8cm Granatwerfer 34*, a battalion-level support weapon. Sturdy, reliable, and accurate, this weapon remained in production until the end of the war.

Weapons training for *Luftwaffe* troops with the standard bolt-action *7.92mm Kar 98k*.

An inspection by high-ranking officers at a permanent barracks (*Kaserne*).

A patrol prepares to head out.

Pistol practice with the iconic 9mm *P08 Luger*. The soldier on the right appears to be carrying a Walther *7.65mm PPK*.

Luftwaffe troops in a humorous moment. The soldier in front appears to have been awarded the Wound Badge in Black.

Mountain troops in an unfamiliar urban environment. These elite soldiers were sometimes used as assault troops.

The firepower of the infantry is based on the machine gun in both light and heavy configurations, in this instance the *MG 34*. The riflemen are to provide protection for the machine-gun team.

Relations between civilians and combat troops were often quite cordial, even in Russia. During the winter months, many soldiers lived with Russian families. In exchange for shelter, the soldiers provided food.

Bicycle troops of an infantry division reconnaissance section negotiate a pathway across swampy ground.

Another interminable river crossing is planned. Difficult to advance across under fire and relatively easy to defend, rivers often became the linchpin of defensive positions.

Members of a motorized supply section pause for a group photograph. The deplorable state of the roads in the Soviet Union is evident.

Officers at rest. The soldier on the right is wearing a relatively rare variant of the marching boot with a buckle arrangement at the ankle.

Occupation troops in Poland; they are considerably older than frontline soldiers.

Junior officers at Danzig *Kaserne* (barracks). The soldier second from the right wears the "piston rings" of a *Spieß*, the equivalent of a Master Sergeant in the U.S. Army.

A *Luftwaffe* lieutenant flanked by army officers. All have been awarded the Iron Cross, First and Second Class. The officer on the left has also received the Tank Battle Badge and the Wound Badge in Silver; the pilot wears his Pilot's Badge and Operational Flying Clasp; the officer on the right has received the Infantry Assault Badge and the Wound Badge in Black.

Recreation facilities with food and other amenities were set up in all major towns, where soldiers could relax when on short-term leave. They were also used as collection points for combat troops in emergency situations.

Two views of senior officers in conference. Note the pennant on the staff car. Liaison between the commands of various formations was generally extremely effective. In the photograph below, a military policeman stands guard.

Mountain troop comrades. The soldier on the left is wearing the very effective felt boots and appears to have been awarded the War Merit Cross, First Class.

Comrades in arms at the front and on leave. The shared experience of combat and the hardships of life at the front produced a bond that was incredibly strong.

Staff officers walk through a Russian village. Following at a small distance are what appear to be two armed guards. Partisan activity increased markedly after the first months of the invasion, and large areas of the countryside were virtually controlled by Soviet guerrilla forces.

The raising and lowering of the national flag is an important ceremony for all military forces. Even in the remote areas of an enemy country, the tradition must be observed.

Putting the finishing touches on a solidly constructed bunker. The two soldiers on the right are *Obergefreiter* (corporals); both have been awarded the Iron Cross, First Class. The soldier in the middle has also received the Iron Cross, First Class; the Infantry Assault Badge; and the Wound Badge in Black.

Noncommissioned officers enjoy a lighter moment. They are all wearing mountain boots; however, no mountain troop insignia is visible. The NCO in the middle is wearing the War Merit Cross that is rated one level below the Iron Cross, Second Class.

Another humorous moment as *Luftwaffe* NCOs ham it up for the camera. In Russia such moments were rare.

A very sharp photograph of NCOs. A wide variety of footwear is evident: shoes, marching boots, felt boots, and straw overshoes. Five members of the group have been awarded the Iron Cross, Second Class. The NCO second from the left is wearing trade and specialist insignia for equipment administration on his right sleeve.

No respite from the mountains of paperwork that any military organization generates.

Below and the next page: Camaraderie was considered by the *Wehrmacht* to be essential in promoting combat efficiency and fostered as much as possible. *Wehrmacht* unit cohesion was generally excellent. It was a matter of policy that personnel for units were recruited from specific geographical areas (*Wehrkreis*). Every effort was made to send sick and wounded soldiers back to their original units.

Constructing what looks to be a memorial or gravesite (note the flowers at bottom left).

Building a very solidly constructed log hut utilizing plentiful local materials.

Two officers outside their well-constructed command bunker. In the first months of the campaign, no permanent fortifications were necessary. This was to change after the winter of 1941–42 and particularly after the defeat at Stalingrad.

These NCOs are displaying the elaborately decorated walking sticks that became very popular with infantry units. The corporal in the center is wearing the War Merit Cross with Swords. The badge worn by the corporal on the right is difficult to discern; it may be a mountain guide badge.

On 21 August 1942, climbers from the 1st and 4th Mountain Divisions planted the German war flag on the peak of Mount Elbrus, the highest mountain in Europe. The highest of its twin peaks is 18,510 feet (5,642 meters). Although of no military value, this was a daring operation and useful for propaganda purposes.

A commanders conference held in the shade. The seated officer facing the camera is wearing the Knight's Cross of the Iron Cross.

The regimental band, a highly regarded means of entertaining the troops. It was also used to help win over the civilian population of conquered towns.

A combination of office and sleeping quarters. The M43-style cap made from camouflage material has been tailor made. German uniform regulations in the later war years were quite lax.

A reassuring photograph for the family that everything is fine at the front. Soldiers usually concealed the horrors of war from family members, particularly when the Allied bombing campaign intensified and the war came to the home front.

The welcome respite of home leave. However, in many cases the soldiers on leave were quite keen to return to their comrades as only they understood how they felt.

Above and below: A contrast in accommodations: a hastily constructed dugout and a solid hut that looks to have been built recently.

The face of courage—a highly decorated soldier. He has been awarded the following: the Knight's Cross of the Iron Cross; the German Cross in Gold; the Iron Cross, First and Second Class; the General Assault Badge; and the Wound Badge in Silver. This a very impressive array of decorations.

Another mountain soldier, wearing winter trousers that were reversible, usually gray, and worn over the uniform trousers. In the first winter on the Russian Front, the mountain troops were obviously far better equipped than their infantry counterparts. Even so, further specialized winter clothing was introduced in 1942.

In the quiet(er) sectors of the front, every effort was made to give the soldier a degree of normalcy and a respite from the harsh conditions at the front. The birthday celebration at right is a good example of this. Extra rations, particularly of alcohol, were distributed to improve morale.

Not as hospitable as the accommodations on the previous page, but all soldiers make do with what they have.

A sniper and his spotter. The German Army did not have a specialized sniper rifle as the excellent *Kar 98* was more than adequate for the task. In the sniper role, it was usually fitted with the *ZF 39* telescopic sight.

Sorting and packing ammunition supplies, a tedious but essential task.

Supplementing the sometimes inadequate field rations with local supplies.

The weary advance continues. If the soldiers were lucky, they would be given a ride in a truck like those in the background. However, as the German Army was nowhere near fully motorized, as the British and American armies were, this was a rare occurrence.

A temporary pontoon bridge for the infantry enables the advance to continue. German combat engineers were very adept at swiftly overcoming the numerous obstacles found in Russia.

Some idea of the distances traveled by the standard, non-motorized German infantry divisions can be ascertained from the two following maps. These trace the movements of the *1. Infanterie-Division* during the Western Campaign and the opening months of Barbarossa.

In the Western Campaign, the division was part of the *6. Armee* of Army Group B. Army Group B was commanded by *General* Bock and its task was to advance against the Netherlands and Belgium, drawing the bulk of the Allied forces forward. This facilitated the main thrust by Army Group A with its forty-five divisions, including seven *panzer*, to attack out of the supposedly impassable Ardennes against minimal opposition. However, the attack in the north, by itself, succeeded in pushing the Allied forces back.

1. Infanterie-Division partcipated in the advance into Belgium, battles on the French and Belgian frontiers, and the pursuit of defeated Allied forces. In the second phase of the campaign that began on 5 June, the division was part of the successful breakthrough against French forces defending on the Somme. The advance was rapid, with only minor engagements. From Partenay on 27 June, the division was transported by rail to the border of France and Spain, where it performed security duties until 10 August.

For Operation Barbarossa, the division was part of *18. Armee* of Army Group North that was tasked with an advance through Lithuania, Latvia, and Estonia, eventually taking Leningrad. Despite a lack of motorized and *panzer* divisions, Army Group North advanced both farther and faster than the other two army groups. The infantry divisions were regularly marching up to twenty miles a day. By the end of the month, the Dvina had been crossed and the Luga River by 14 July. The final assault on Leningrad was ready for implementation on 20 July but delayed due to increasing resistance and the the requirement to assist Army Group Center on the right flank.

Novgorod was reached on 16 August and the Volkhov crossed. Soviet forces encircled in the Luga pocket were destroyed by the middle of September and Leningrad was effectively encircled. Rather than a direct assault on the city, it was decided to starve Leningrad into submission. From 8 August 1941 to 28 December 1943, the *1. Infanterie-Division* participated in the siege of the city and defensive battles in the Wolchov area.

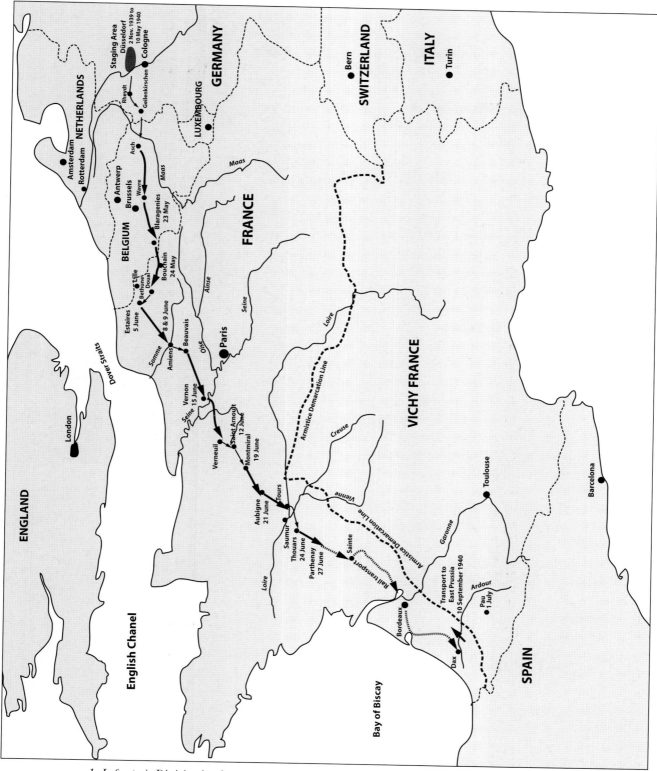

1. Infanterie-Division in the Low Countries and French campaign, May to June 1940.

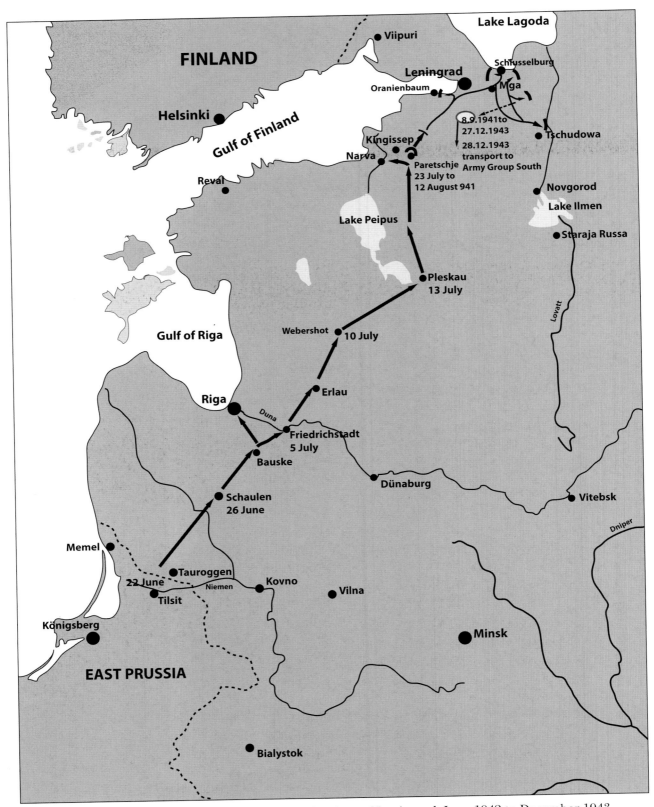

1. Infanterie-Division in Northern Russia and the siege of Leningrad, June 1942 to December 1943.

This page and the next two: Dramatic scenes of an 88mm *Flak* battery at night. Some of the guns are in revetments and others are on open ground.

The deadly quad-barrel 2cm *Flakvierling 38*, scourge of low-flying Allied aircraft. Rate of fire: 700 to 800 rounds a minute. Effective ceiling: 2,300 meters (7,500 feet).

Loading an 88mm antiaircraft gun.

Luftwaffe officers inspect an optical range finder, the 4-meter *Em.R. 4m*, the standard range finder for heavy antiaircraft guns. The range finder is served by a crew of four: range taker, layer for line, layer for elevation, and range reader.

The devastating dual-purpose "88" deployed in the ground role. Capable of destroying the heaviest Allied tanks at long range, even late in the war.

The "88" in the antitank role. The height of the gun was a disadvantage in this situation, and it was dug in if possible. However, this was a time-consuming task.

Another shot of the "88" in the ground role. The crew and the gun are quite exposed and vulnerable to high-explosive rounds.

The towed 10.5cm howitzer in the foreground is a *leichte Feldhaubitze 18*, usually abbreviated as *le FH 18*, the standard light field gun of the *Wehrmacht* divisional artillery during the war. It had a maximum range of 10.6 kilometers and a sustained rate of fire of up to six rounds a minute. The shells were separately cased with up to six charges, with the high-explosive round weighing 14.8 kilograms and the armor-piercing round 14.25 kilograms.

Le FH 18 being prepared for transport.

This page and the next three pages: Further views of the *le FH 18*. A stable and reliable weapon, it remained in service until the end of the war.

A *10.5cm le FHM*, a 1940 modification intended to increase the range out to more than 13,000 meters by using a more powerful charge. The additional force imposed on the howitzer was countered by a modified recoil system and a muzzle brake.

An earlier version of the *le FH 18* being prepared for firing. The maximum range of this variant was 10,675 meters, well below the maximum range of the British 25-pounder and the Soviet 7.62cm field guns, both of which could fire out to more than 13,000 meters.

An abandoned Soviet 152mm 1910/34 howitzer with its fully tracked tow vehicle. In general, Soviet artillery was far more mobile than its German counterparts as most of the German artillery was horse drawn.

An overrun Soviet artillery battery consisting of 122mm howitzers, most likely Model 1931 variants. Soviet artillery was extremely well designed and manufactured. The substantial numbers of these weapons captured in the early years of the war saw extensive service with the German Army.

An early-model Soviet 152mm howitzer Model 1910/30.

A really oddball piece, this is a 30.5cm Mrs (t)/Mrs 638 (j) produced in 1916 by Skoda and in service with the Czech and Yugoslav armies after 1918. Six of these heavy mortars were used during the 1941–44 siege of Leningrad.

The 30.5cm heavy mortar. The shell weighed 290 kilograms (639 pounds).

The 30.5cm heavy mortar in action firing on Leningrad.

Loading a 5cm *PaK 38* antitank gun. Firing a standard armor-piercing shell, 78 millimeters of armor plate of zero-degree slope could be penetrated at 500 meters range. This was not enough to knock out either the KV-1 or the T-34 frontally. Nonetheless, the *PaK 38* was a generally effective weapon and remained in service throughout the war.

A *PaK 38* just after firing. As it had a relatively low silhouette, it was easy to conceal, unlike the bulky "88." The *PaK 38* was superceded but never entirely replaced by the more powerful 7.5cm *PaK 40*.

The *21cm Mörser 18*, along with the *17cm K18*, was the standard heavy artillery piece for the German Army in World War II. It had a maximum range of 18,700 meters and a sustained rate of fire of one round a minute. Designed with an ingenious dual-recoil system in which both the barrel and top carriage recoiled on firing, considerably dampening recoil stresses and thereby making the gun platform very steady. Production of the *21cm Mrs 18* ceased in 1942 in order to concentrate on the *17cm K18*, with some 700 produced.

The gun crew of a *Mörser 18*, with a good view of the breech mechanism.

The *Mrs 18* in action. Note the massive shell casings. Various ammunition and propelling charges were developed for this gun.

The standard heavy howitzer of divisional artillery for the German Army in World War II, the *15cm schwere Feldhaubitze 18*. The *sFH 18* had a maximum range of 13,250 meters and a sustained rate of fire of up to four rounds a minute. Its separately cased shells weighed 43.5 kilograms, and the artillery piece called for a crew of twelve. Although outclassed by some Allied heavy artillery, the reliable and effective *sFH 18* was produced throughout the war, although demand always exceeded supply.

Another view of an *sFH 18*, in this instance more elaborately camouflaged. German gun crews had to be wary of the very effective Russian counterbattery fire.

A very exposed battery position with the ready-use shells in their protective wicker casings.

A view of *sFH 18s* in the firing position.

A good view of the business end of an *sFH 18*. The army was not entirely satisfied with the performance of the *sFH 18*, particularly when compared to Soviet equivalents. Attempts were then made to either redesign the weapon or improve the existing weapons, but none came to fruition before the end of the war.

A 60cm searchlight, a portable unit of 135 million candlepower and a range of 5,500 yards (5,000 meters). Usually linked to antiaircraft guns such as the 20mm and 37mm automatic *Flak*.

A substantial bunker destroyed by either heavy artillery or special "bunker-busting" bombs (PC-500), usually delivered with pinpoint accuracy by *Ju 87B Stukas*.

ARMORED AND MOTORIZED VEHICLES

The standard German armored personnel carrier of World War II, the *Sd.Kfz. 251* half-track, here an *Ausf. B* model. Speed was 32 miles an hour (52 kph) and weight was 8 tons. The *Sd.Kfz. 251* was produced in over twenty variants.

A burnt-out *Panzer IV Ausf. B* or *C*. Note the canisters for spare road wheels on the hull sides. The early *Panzer IVs*, with their low-velocity main gun and thin (30 mm) armor, were no match for T-34s and KV-1s.

Panzerjäger (tank hunter) *4.7 cm PaK(t)* on a *Panzer I Ausf B* chassis—a means to give self-propulsion to the Czech 4.7cm antitank gun, utilizing an obsolete fully tracked chassis. The first of many such conversions mounting increasingly heavier guns. First entered service in 1940 in France and Belgium.

An early-model *Panzer IV B* or *C* crosses a water obstacle on a twenty-seven-ton "K" bridge.

Panzer III Ausf. G or H, loaded with extra equipment, head to the front while supply trucks return to their depot. The Panzer III was the standard German medium tank at the beginning of Barbarossa. Most of the Panzer III were armed with the improved 50mm KwK L/42 rather than the far more effective L/60 as originally ordered by Hitler. The Panzer III was completely outclassed by the Soviet medium tank, the revolutionary T-34. Even the fitting of the high-velocity KwK 39 L/60 did not improve matters much.

"Dragon's teeth" antitank obstacles, effective at stopping tanks if they were covered by antitank guns, minefields, and supporting infantry. Otherwise, they were fairly easily demolished.

Panzerkampfwagen 38(t) move into battle. The *Czech Pz.Kpfw. 38(t)* was an important part of the equipment of the *panzer* divisions. It was a small vehicle weighing only some ten tons and armed with a 3.7cm main gun. From July 1941 all models of the *38(t)* served in Russia. The chassis and drivetrain were very reliable and formed the basis of several models of self-propelled antitank guns and artillery.

Recovery of a *Panzer III* from marshy ground. Compared to the T-34 and KV, German tanks had narrow tracks designed for European conditions, not the snow and mud of the Soviet Union. In response the Germans outfitted the *Panzer III* and *IV* with wider tracks and track extensions for winter and muddy conditions of spring and fall.

A *kleine Panzerbefehlswagen Sd.Kfz. 265* light armored tracked command vehicle. From 1941 to 1942, in service with higher headquarters. Also served with the signals battalions and observation batteries of artillery regiments in the *panzer* divisions.

Destroyed German light half-tracks.

A captured British A13 Cruiser tank mounting a 2-pounder gun.

The bane of the *panzer* forces, the dreaded T-34, with its high-velocity 76.2mm main gun (particularly the F-34 model), thick sloped armor, large-diameter road wheels, wide tracks, and lightweight but powerful diesel engine. Until the upgunned *Panzer IV* and the heavy *Tiger* and *Panther* helped to restore German tank superiority in 1942 to mid 1944, the T-34 was a markedly superior vehicle.

Officer's M36
Field Tunic

Soldier's M36
Field Tunic

Standard Steel Helmet

M37 Feldmütze
Officer's Field Cap

Soldier's M34
Overseas Cap

Iron Cross, 2nd Class

Infantry Assault Badge

Wound Badge
Silver—3 Wounds

Soldier's Identity Disc

M1931 Bread Bag

Soldier's Personal Items

Soldier's Pay and
Record Book

M35 Map/Dispatch Case

M1931 Mess Kit

M1931 Canteen
and Cup

Leather
Marching Boots

MG-34 Machine Gun with
7.92 x 57mm Ammunition Belt
and Case

Tellermine 35 Antitank Mine
with Carrying Case

Gear and Webbing Harness
Typically Worn by Infantry Soldiers

KAR98k Bolt-Action Rifle 7.92mm

Bayonet and Five-Round
Ammunition Clips

P08 Luger

P38 Walther 9mm

Walther 7.65mm PPK

MP40 with Magazine Pouch
and Luger Holster

KAR98k Ammunition Pouch

Entrenching
Tool

M1928 Stick Grenade

Gas Mask Canister

THE PANZERTRUPPEN

Collar Tabs worn
by Panzermen

M38 Officer's Field Cap

Panzer Crash Helmet
with Cloth Beret Covering

Panzer "Wrap" for Officer
in Armored Reconnaissance

THE WAFFEN SS

Runic Collar Tab
Worn on Right Side
of SS Uniforms

M38 "Palm Pattern"
Camouflage Smock

Officer's Field Cap
(missing chin cord)

Officer's M40
Overseas Cap

Steel Helmet

M40 "Palm Pattern"
Camouflage Smock
with Army Splinter
Camouflage Repairs

SSH 39
Combat Helmet

M35 Soldier's
Gymnasterka,
Sappers, Infantry

M36 Combat Helmet

Wrist Compasses

Tanker's Padded
Helmet

Russian Order of
the Red Banner

Soviet Order of the Red Star

ZOMZ 6x Binoculars with Case

THE BRITISH ARMY

Mark II Steel Combat Helmet

Visor Cap Made of Olive Drab Wool (badge is of The King's Royal Rifle Corps)

Overseas Cap Made of Khaki-Colored Twill

Battledress Tunic for Lieutenant Colonel of the Royal Engineers

Entrenching Tool and P37 Pattern Carrier

Mark V Gas Mask

P37 Pattern Bren Gun Ammo Pouch

P37 Pattern Large Webbed Canvas Haversack

Lee Enfield Mark 1 .303 Bolt-Action Rifle

Vickers Water-Cooled .303 Machine Gun

Bren .303 Light Machine Gun

THE FRENCH ARMY

MAS Model 1936 7.5mm Bolt-Action Rifle

M1886 8mm Lebel Bolt-Action Rifle with Bayonet

Hotchkiss 8mm Heavy Machine Gun

FM 1924 M29 7.5mm Light Machine Gun

Infantry Soldier's Forage Cap

Artillery Corporal's Forage Cap in Bluish-Gray Wool

1936-Style Infantry Officer's Tunic

M26 Adrian Steel Helmet
(used by the artillery as evidenced by the crossed cannons on the front)

M1938 Infantry Soldier's Breeches

Composite Paper Leg Wraps

Gas Mask Carrying Bag

M1935 Mess Kit

Leather Cartridge Belt and Ammunition Pouches

A T-34 with the F-34 main gun. The slogan on the turret reads, "For the Motherland."

An abandoned early-model T-34 with the lower-velocity F-11 main gun. Note the spare transmission attached to the top of the engine compartment. A fragile transmission was a significant weak point of this tank. In the early months of the campaign, numerous T-34s were lost due to mechanical failures.

Very likely a 1942 series production T-34 from the No. 183 Factory as indicated by the twin turret hatches. There is still no commander's cupola, which was finally introduced in the fall of 1943.

Despite the shock caused by the appearance of the T-34 and KV-1, the Germans, as usual, were quick to react. The new Soviet tanks were countered by superior command and control allowing the *panzers* to outmaneuver them with 88mm *Flak* and the 10cm field gun being used in the antitank role. In addition, the far more effective 5cm *PaK 38* was introduced and the very powerful 7.5cm *PaK 40* was rushed into service. Large numbers of captured Soviet 7.62cm field guns were also impressed into antitank service by the Germans, where they were designated the *PaK 36(r)*. Also, the *Panzer III* and *IV* were quickly up-gunned and up-armored.

Above and next page: The T-34, for all its good features, was hardly the perfect tank as portrayed in some literature. In addition to the fragile transmission mentioned previously, there was the lack of 360-degree vision commander's cupola, clumsy roof hatches that also limited the commander's vision, substandard optics for the sights, and lack of radios for command and control. The most serious fault in design was the cramped two-man turret that forced the commander to act as the loader, thus significantly reducing his effectiveness.

The very wide tracks of the T-34 compared to the *Panzer III* and *IV* are evident.

An interesting photograph of a dummy T-34 being used for antitank training with a smoke round simulating an armor-piercing round.

A knocked-out forty-five-ton KV-1 main battle tank variant, with its 7.62cm main gun, was superior to anything the Germans fielded at the time in terms of armor, armament, and maneuverability, sometimes requiring one hundred or more hits from the relatively puny German tank and antitank guns before the vehicle was rendered inoperable. "88s" and field guns firing over open sights were the only ground weapons at the time that could penetrate the frontal armor of this tank. However, it also suffered from serious design flaws that allowed it to be outmaneuvered by superior German command-and-control measures. In particular, it suffered from some mechanical unreliability and a typical Soviet lack of visibility. As a forty-five-ton vehicle, it was too heavy for the inadequate Soviet road network of the time, making it difficult to deploy the vehicle.

Two three-ton medium supply trucks and a motorcycle and sidecar combination. Opel and Mercedes Benz were the main manufacturers of these vehicles.

A light cross-country personnel car (*Kfz. 1*) of a half-track towed 7.5cm antitank gun unit (6th Battery).

In the winter snow and ice, in the spring and fall a sea of mud, in the summer soft dirt and sand. The truck driver in Russia never had it easy.

The neverending supply convoys wending their way to and from the front. As the campaign continued, the threat to convoys from partisan units increased until all convoys required some sort of escort. Here the convoy is approaching a checkpoint.

The vehicle second from the right is a six-wheel medium cross-country truck (open).

A medium motorbus configured as a workshop truck. The masses of spare parts required for a combat formation to function are evident. This vehicle carried only a limited selection of the most basic items.

Only the *panzer* divisions and those of the motorized infantry were allocated motorized transport, and even these units did not receive their full complement of vehicles. The infantry divisions had to make do with horse-drawn vehicles for supply and the towing of artillery. A wide variety of horse-drawn vehicles were produced, such as this supply wagon being loaded aboard a ship.

The top sign indicates the way to Moscow and the *Rollbahn* sign indicates a major supply route—in this instance the Minsk–Moscow highway, one of the few major all-weather, sealed highways in the Soviet Union.

Above and next page: What a typical *Rollbahn* really looked like—difficult to drive on in good weather and nearly inpossible to traverse in the spring thaw and fall rains.

The German Army began the war with a chronic shortage of motor transport. Because of the short duration of the campaigns in Poland and Western Europe, this shortage was not critical. However, Barbarossa, with the long distances involved, highlighted the problem. There were too many different types of vehicles in the *Wehrmacht* inventory—add to this captured vehicles from other countries and the result was a quartermaster's nightmare. Thousands of vehicles were lost due to a lack of basic spare parts. Also, many of the trucks were based on commercial vehicles and initally were two-wheel rather than four-wheel drive.

A heavy motor truck (open), *schwerer Lastkraftwagen offen (O)*. This vehicle appears to be a *Büssing-N.A.G.* 4.5-ton diesel with a payload of 8,000 pounds.

A commercial vehicle impressed into service as an ambulance. To alleviate the shortage of vehicles, many commercial vehicles were commandeered. The sign reads "Aschinger also in Poland."

A heavy truck chassis fitted with a bus-type body. The maximum payload was five tons.

An *Sd.Kfz 7* eight-ton half-track towing a *15cm sFH 18* howitzer over an eighteen-ton rated bridge.

Engineers complete a substantial bridge, suitable for heavy vehicles, while a half-track and a supply truck ford the river.

Senior officers oversee the construction of a light sectional bridge with a capacity of over thirty tons.

A supply convoy of medium cross-country 6x4 trucks. The leading vehicle is towing a medium open trailer.

A vehicle park with light cross-country personnel cars with snow chains on the rear wheels and 6x4 light trucks.

Italian *Bersaglieri* (sharpshooters) appear happy to be receiving a ride. Although German trucks were well engineered and reliable, they were completely outclassed by the superb U.S. GMC Model CCKW350 2.5-ton 6x6. The GMC trucks carried a heavier payload and had a far better cross-country capability. Thousands of these trucks were supplied to the Soviet Union, allowing factories to concentrate on armored vehicle production.

Wherever possible, heavy weapons were transported by rail to reduce the reliance on mortorized transport.

Three-ton supply trucks of the *Schell-Programm* type cross a pontoon bridge while a stream of refugees, carrying their meager possessions, flee the fighting.

Two views of a pontoon ferry being used to carry supply trucks over a wide river. German engineers were extremely skilled in quickly providing expedient means to keep the advance continuing.

A railhead and supply dump, illustrating the logistics of the supply system. The unloading area was located as close to the front as possible so that the supplies were distributed in a timely manner.

What passes for a "good" road in the Soviet Union. In the muddy seasons, tracked vehicles had to be used as tow vehicles to keep the urgently needed supplies moving.

Establishing a communications link with a radio truck (*Kfz. 72*) on the chassis of a medium cross-country truck. The transmitter is probably an 80- or 100-watt unit with a range of 125/200 miles key or 45/70 miles talk.

Either establishing or moving an 88mm battery. Note the number of chairs in the back of the truck on the right.

Standardized S-class three-ton trucks. Realizing that the vehicle parts supply system was chaotic, the *Wehrmacht* in 1940 introduced a program to standardize light, heavy, and medium trucks. Opel, Daimler-Benz, Magirius, Büssing-NAG, and Borgward were the principal builders of these vehicles. The three-ton class was the most numerous built, the best known being the Opel *Blitz* (lightning).

A medium cross-country truck picks up its load at a railhead.

A destroyed Soviet convoy. Soviet trucks looked somewhat antiquated, but they were well suited to the rough roads of the region.

A light cross-country personnel carrier. Obviously, conditions are somewhat dusty!

S-class trucks and other vehicles on railway flat cars. The sign at the right warns of dangerous flammable materials and forbids smoking.

GRAVEYARDS

German graveyards were often quite elaborate, as far as circumstances would allow. Death in combat was considered an honorable, heroic sacrifice for both the Fatherland and family. Nazi propaganda continuously emphasized this philosophy.

Appropriately, this graveyard is located next to a church. If possible, all gravemarkers were inscribed with the soldier's rank, name, unit, and day of death.

Hastily dug graves, but a concerted effort has been made to mark them appropriately. It was expected that the deceased would be moved to a more permanent gravesite.

"Our Heroes."

Another view of the elaborate cemetery.

The Iron Cross motif, along with the Christian cross, is prevalent at the majority of gravesites.

Fallen French soldiers. At least in Europe and Africa, the Germans were respectful to fallen enemy combatants.

An isolated and neglected graveyard.

Even in the early days of the invasion of the Soviet Union, *Wehrmacht* fatalities were in the tens of thousands. By September 1941, battle casualties (dead, wounded, P.O.W.) amounted to over 500,000.

The Nazi Party was not overly successful in providing solace to grieving families. For all the incessant propaganda about heroism and honor, the average Germans still turned to their religious beliefs for consolation.

Destroyed on the ground: I-16 (above) and I-15/153 (below) fighters. Both types were far inferior to the *Luftwaffe Bf 109E/F* fighters. In particular the I-15/153, as it was a biplane and hopelessly obsolete.

Further remains of I-15/153 fighters. In the opening days of Barbarossa, most of the Red Air Force losses were on the ground. Ironically, this saved the lives of trained Soviet pilots.

A totally destroyed Pe-2 twin-engine fighter and fighter-bomber. The Pe-2 was superior to the *Bf 110* and was in service throughout the war.

A destroyed SB-2 medium bomber. Its performance was similar to the German *Dornier Do 17*. The SB-2 stood little chance against the *Bf 109*, and when flown at low level against German antiaircraft fire, they were massacred.

The result of a *Luftwaffe* strike against a VVS airfield. On the first day of Barbarossa alone, close to 1,500 VVS aircraft were destroyed on the ground and, by the end of the first week, over 4,000.

German soldiers inspect a dreaded Soviet Il-2 Sturmovik ground-attack aircraft. Heavily armored and difficult to destroy, these aircraft carried a variety of bombs and rockets.

The workhorse of the *Luftwaffe*, the Junkers *Ju 52/3m*. Although obsolescent at the start of the war, the *Ju 52* performed admirably all through the war. Although slow, having a maximum speed of 170 miles per hour, the aircraft had legendary ruggedness and reliability.

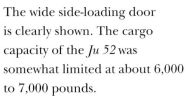

The wide side-loading door is clearly shown. The cargo capacity of the *Ju 52* was somewhat limited at about 6,000 to 7,000 pounds.

The *Ju 52* was very vulnerable to fighters, and efforts were made to increase its defensive armament. In this instance, a formation of *Ju 52s* flies low over the ocean for protection from fighter attack from below.

The upper manually operated 13mm *MG 131* heavy machine gun is apparent as is the beam gun position for the 7.92mm *MG 15*. Against a determined fighter, this defensive armament was inadequate.

On missions to reinforce the Tunisian bridgehead from February to May 1943, scores of *Ju 52s* were shot down by Allied fighters.

The standard *Luftwaffe* medium bomber in the early years of the war, the *Heinkel He III*. The elliptical wings are very apparent in the photograph below.

The deadly yet vulnerable *Junkers Ju 87B Stuka* was given a new lease on life in the early months of the campaign in the East. However, once Soviet fighter opposition increased, losses mounted.

The *Fieseler Fi 156 Storch* (Stork) possessed exemplary short takeoff and landing qualities. It was an ideal short-range reconnaissance and liaison aircraft.

The fate of thousands of *Luftwaffe* aircrew.

Soviet prisoners of war. In the first six months of the campaign, over 3 million Soviet prisoners had been taken. Due to the chaotic conditions in the camps with food and medical supply shortages, a deliberate policy of allocating minimum rations, and sickness, often brought about by malnutrition, by December 1941 over 1.3 million prisoners had died.

As the Soviet Union was not a signatory to the Geneva Convention regarding humanitarian treatment of POWs, there was no legal obligation to feed these prisoners. However, the moral obligation is undeniable.

Perhaps not surprisingly, tens of thousands of Soviet POWs volunteered to assist the *Wehrmacht* as auxiliaries. These foreign volunteers, or *Hiwis* (*Hilfswilliger*), received the same rations as the soldiers and were generally well cared for. In return, they performed their duties reliably and were steadfast and loyal. As the war situation deteriorated for the Germans, every effort was made by the soldiers to keep the *Hiwis* out of the hands of the Soviet authorities as death was almost certain.

Large columns of refugees were common during the early months of Barbarossa. Due to the speed of the initial German advance, most of the civilian population was not able to escape into the East.

Regardless of how the local populace felt about the German occupiers, a living still had to be made.

Colorful local inhabitants are a source of interest.

The death of anyone so young is paricularly tragic. Whether this child is a direct victim of the war cannot be ascertained.

The life of a rural peasant did not improve markedly as the tsars gave way to the Communists and then to the Nazis. One type of tyrant replaced another and life was as hard as ever.

Mountain troops with colorfully costumed soldiers. This is most likely a scene from the Tyrol or northern Italy. The feathers on the hat appear to be black Capercaille feathers usually found on the headgear of elite Italian *Bersaglierie.*

Children are always fascinated by soldiers, in this instance a mountain trooper.

Fraternization with the civilian population was strictly forbidden, and the penalty for doing so was harsh. However, the order was often ignored—particularly since, during the winter, soldiers were billeted with families.

A mountain trooper corporal has his studded mountain boots (*Bergschuhe*) cleaned by a local street vendor.

The Soviet Union covered a vast territory with numerous and varied ethnic groups, each with its own customs and religious affiliations. Despite forced collectivization, confiscation of crops, starvation, and bloody purges, the hardy and stoic peasant endured. The ability to overcome such hardships made the Soviet soldier such a formidable opponent.

These two photographs appear to show the recruitment of local citizens for service with the German armed forces either as auxiliaries or combat troops. The headgear seems to indicate Cossacks, who served in large numbers with the German Army. Eventually, two Cossack divisions were formed late in the war.

The novelty of having one's photograph taken is universal, particularly for these children who may never have seen a camera.

A study in contrasts: well-dressed Soviet schoolchildren and poorly clothed peasant children.

TOWNS AND LANDSCAPES

The Soviet landscape was vast, varied, harsh, and unforgiving. For many German soldiers, the psychological effect of this strange and forbidding country was severe depression.

Directional signs indicating headquarters, administrative services, and unit locations.

Elaborate tsarist architecture in all its splendor and opulence.

As the majority of the population lived in grinding poverty, the privileged nobles lived a sumptuous existence.

The lofty spires of a mosque.

The "onion" domes of a Russian Orthodox church.

Given the spire on the roof, this structure could be part of a monastery.

An elaborate Russian Orthodox cathedral.

One of the wide, fast-flowing rivers that abound in the Soviet Union and continually impeded the German advance.

A hastily constructed bridge of a respectable five-ton capacity.

A farmhouse in the foothills of the Caucasus. The Caucasus was the limit of the German advance in the south and almost the scene of a greater disaster than Stalingrad as Army Group South came perilously close to being trapped.

The only way to efficiently move troops, equipment, and supplies across the vast landscape was by train.

In the winter pitched battles would be fought over the possession of these dwellings.

Vehicles parked next to buildings to avoid detection by aircraft. The state of the main road was typical of smaller towns.

The result of bombing or artillery fire. The railroad tracks may have been the target.

Impressive city squares, usually named after a historical figure or a hero of the revolution, were a feature of the larger cities.

A cathedral dominates an important railroad junction.

A cosmopolitan city scene, possibly Kharkov. Four battles were fought for Kharkov before the Soviets finally recaptured it on 23 August 1943.

Despite the extensive efforts
on the part of the Communist
party, religion continued to play
a large part in the lives of the
general population.

Bomb damage and an attempt at restoration. The *Luftwaffe* did not undertake any extensive bombing campaigns against any major Soviet cities except Stalingrad.

A lush and picturesque country estate of the former landed gentry, now probably occupied by a senior member of the party.

The industrial suburbs of a major town. The Soviets performed prodigious feats of moving industrial equipment and even complete factories to the Ural Mountains, beyond the range of German bombers.

Temporary accommodation for a supply truck crew.

The direction sign seems to indicate Krasnograd; if so, this is a city in the Caucasus close to Kharkov.

The Soviet Union occupies part of Asia, whose influence is obvious here.

Most dwellings were constructed of wood and therefore were very susceptible to fire.

A roadblock and road demolition. The wet ground on the right would be difficult to traverse.

APPENDIX

Rank Comparisons

U.S. ARMY	RUSSIAN ARMY	WAFFEN-SS	GERMAN ARMY
Enlisted Men			
Private	*Krasnoarmeyets*	*SS-Schütze*	*Schütze*
Private First Class		*SS-Oberschütze*	*Oberschütze*
Corporal	*Mladshiy Serzhant*	*SS-Sturmmann*	*Gefreiter*
Senior Corporal		*SS-Rottenführer*	*Obergefreiter*
Staff Corporal		*SS-Stabsrottenführer*	*Stabsgefreiter*
Noncommissioned Officers			
Sergeant	*Serzhant*	*SS-Unterscharführer*	*Unteroffizier*
		SS-Scharführer	*Unterfeldwebel*
Staff Sergeant		*SS-Oberscharführer*	*Feldwebel*
Sergeant First Class	*Starshiy Serzhant*	*SS-Hauptcharführer*	*Oberfeldwebel*
Master Sergeant		*SS-Sturmscharführer*	*Hauptfeldwebel*
Sergeant Major	*Starshina*		*Stabsfeldwebel*
Officers			
Second Lieutenant	*Mladshiy Leytenant*	*SS-Untersturmführer*	*Leutnant*
First Lieutenant	*Leytenant*	*SS-Obersturmführer*	*Oberleutnant*
Captain	*Kapitan*	*SS-Hauptsturmführer*	*Hauptman*
Major	*Major*	*SS-Sturmbannführer*	*Major*
Lieutenant Colonel	*Podpolkovnik*	*SS-Obersturmbannführer*	*Oberstleutnant*
Colonel	*Polkovnik*	*SS-Standartenführer*	*Oberst*
Brigadier General		*SS-Brigadeführer*	*Generalmajor*
Major General	*General Major*	*SS-Gruppenführer*	*Generalleutnant*
Lieutenant General	*General Leytenant*	*SS-Obergruppenführer*	*General der Fallschirmjäger, etc.*
General	*General Armii*	*SS-Oberstgruppenführer*	*Generaloberst*
General of the Army	*Marshal Sovetskogo Souza*	*Reichsführer-SS*	*Feldmarschall*

BIBLIOGRAPHY

Adamczyk, Werner. *Feuer! An Artilleryman's Life on the Eastern Front.* Wilmington, NC: Broadfoot, 1992.

Angolia, John R., and Adolf Schlicht. *Uniforms and Traditions of the German Army, 1933–1945.* Vol. 1–3. San Jose, CA: R. J. Bender, 1992.

Bernard, Georges, and Francois de Lannoy. *Les Divisions de L'Armee de Terre allemande Heer 1939–1945.* Bayeux, France: Editions Heimdal, 1997.

Bidermann, Gottlob Herbert. *In Deadly Combat: A German Soldier's Memoir of the Eastern Front.* Lawrence, KS: University Press of Kansas, 2000.

Bock, Fedor von. *The War Diary, 1939–1945.* Atglen, PA: Schiffer, 1996.

Buchner, Alex. *The German Infantry Handbook, 1939–1945.* Atglen, PA: Schiffer, 1991.

Burdick, Charles, and Hans-Adolf Jacobsen, eds. *The Halder War Diary, 1939–1942.* Novato, CA: Presidio Press, 1988.

Carell, Paul. *Hitler's War on Russia: The Story of the German Defeat in the East.* London: Harrap, 1964.

Chamberlain, Peter, and Hilary Doyle. *Encyclopedia of German Tanks of World War.* Revised Edition. London: Arms and Armour Press, 1975.

DiNardo, R. L. *Mechanized Juggernaut or Military Anachronism?* Westport, CT: Greenwood Publishing, 1991.

Ellis, Chris, ed. *Directory of Wheeled Vehicles of the Wehrmacht.* London: Ducimus Books, 1974.

Ericson, John. *The Road to Stalingrad.* New York: Harper & Row, 1975.

Fritz, Stephen G. *Frontsoldaten.* Lexington, KY: University Press of Kentucky, 1995.

Gander, Terry, and Peter Chamberlain. *Small Arms, Artillery and Special Weapons of the Third Reich.* London: Macdonald and Jane's, 1978.

Guderian, Heinz. *Panzer Leader.* London: M. Joseph, 1970.

Hogg, Ian V. *German Artillery of World War Two.* London: Arms and Armour, 1977.

Kershaw, Robert J. *War without Garlands: Operation Barbarossa, 1941–1942.* Shepperton, England: Ian Allan, 2000.

Knappe, Siegfried, and Ted Brusaw. *Soldat: Reflections of a German Soldier, 1936–1949.* New York: Orion Books, 1992.

Lucas, James. *War on the Eastern Front, 1941–1945: The German Soldier in Russia.* London: Jane's, 1979.

Luck, Hans von. *Panzer Commander.* New York: Praeger, 1989.

Metelmann, Henry. *Through Hell for Hitler.* Havertown, PA: Casemate, 2001.

Murray, Williamson. *Strategy for Defeat: The Luftwaffe, 1933–1945.* Washington, DC: Brassey's, 1996.

Porter, David. *Order of Battle: The Red Army in WWII.* London: Amber Books, 2009.

The Research Institute for Military History. *Germany and the Second World War.* Vol. IV: *The Attack on the Soviet Union.* Oxford, England: Clarendon Press, 1998.

Seaton, Albert. *The Russo-German War: 1941–45.* Novato, CA: Presidio Press, 1990.

Smith J. R., and Anthony Kay. *German Aircraft of the Second World War.* London: Putnam, 1972.

Stahlberg, Alexander. *Bounden Duty: The Memoirs of a German Officer: 1932–45.* London: Brassey's, 1990.

Trevor-Roper, H. R. *Hitler's War Directives, 1939–1945.* London: Pan, 1966.

Tsouras, Peter G., ed. *Fighting in Hell: The German Ordeal on the Eastern Front.* London: Greenhill, 1995.

———. *Panzers on the Eastern Front: General Erhard Raus and His Panzer Divisions in Russia, 1941–1945.* London: Greenhill, 2002.

U.S. War Department. *Handbook on German Military Forces.* Baton Rouge, LA: Louisiana State University Press, 1990.

Warlimont, Walter. *Inside Hitler's Headquarters, 1939–45.* New York: Praeger, 1964.

Zaloga, Steven J., and James Grandsen. *Soviet Tanks and Combat Vehicles of World War Two.* London: Arms and Armour Press, 1984.

———. *The Eastern Front Armor Camouflage and Markings, 1941 to 1945.* London: Arms and Armour Press, 1989.

Ziemke, Earl F., and Magna E. Bauer. *Moscow to Stalingrad.* New York: Military Heritage Press, 1988.

ACKNOWLEDGMENTS

The following people deserve credit for their generous assistance in supplying period photographs taken by the combatants themselves, along with modern color images of uniforms, equipment, and weapons. In each and every case, they went above and beyond to help bring this book to life by offering their expertise and time: Pat Cassidy, Steve Cassidy, P. Whammond and Carey of Collector's Guild (www.germanmilitaria.com), Wilson History and Research Center (www.militaryheadgear.com), Jim Haley, David A. Jones, Jim Pool, Scott Pritchett, Phil Francis, and Aleks and Dmitri of Espenlaub Militaria (www.aboutww2 militaria.com and www.warrelics.eu/forum), as well as the National Archives, the Swedish Army Museum, and a few individuals who wish to remain anonymous.

FURTHER READING FROM THE STACKPOLE MILITARY HISTORY SERIES

These titles are the perfect complement to the visual chronicle in *The German Soldier in World War II*. Here you'll find riveting, gritty accounts of the soldiers who fought and died in hand-to-hand combat, stormed enemy positions, and rescued fallen comrades. There are profiles of men of the *Wehrmacht* and *Waffen-SS*, paratroopers, *Luftwaffe* aces, and Knight's Cross recipients. From the frozen Russian steppes to the scorching African desert, these are the true accounts of men who stared death in the face: Real Battles. Real Soldiers. Real Stories.

PANZER ACES I
German Tank Commanders of WWII
Franz Kurowski
978-0-8117-3173-7

PANZERGRENADIER ACES
German Mechanized Infantrymen in World War II
Franz Kurowski
978-0-8117-0656-8

INFANTRY ACES
The German Soldier in Combat in WWII
Franz Kurowski
978-0-8117-3202-4

LUFTWAFFE ACES
German Combat Pilots of WWII
Franz Kurowski
978-0-8117-3177-5

TIGERS IN THE MUD
The Combat Career of
German Panzer Commander Otto Carius
Otto Carius
978-0-8117-2911-6

THE FACE OF COURAGE
The 98 Men Who Received the Knight's Cross
and the Close-Combat Clasp in Gold
Florian Berger
978-0-8117-1055-8

WWW.STACKPOLEBOOKS.COM

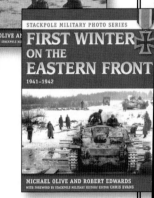